BOGDANOVICH'S PICTURE SHOWS

by
Thomas J. Harris

The Scarecrow Press, Inc.
Metuchen, N.J., & London
1990

British Library Cataloguing-in-Publication data available

Library of Congress Cataloging-in-Publication Data

Harris, Thomas J., 1966–
    Bogdanovich's picture shows / Thomas J. Harris.
      p. cm.
    Includes bibliographical references and indexes.
    ISBN 0-8108-2365-9
    1. Bogdanovich, Peter, 1939–   —Criticism and interpreta-
tion. I. Title.
PN1998.3.B64H37   1990
791.43'0233'092—dc20   90-48649

The screen is merely a sheet with lights and shadows: the complete illusion. The magic lantern projects two-dimensional images on the white screen, and therein lies the enchantment.

—Peter Bogdanovich

Contents

Acknowledgments   vii
Preface   ix
Chronology   xiii

Biographical and Career Analysis   1
Aesthetics   27
1   *Targets* (1968)   36
2   *Directed by John Ford* (1971)   68
3   *The Last Picture Show* (1971)   79
4   *What's Up, Doc?* (1972)   117
5   *Paper Moon* (1973)   138
6   *Daisy Miller* (1974)   159
7   *At Long Last Love* (1975)   183
8   *Nickelodeon* (1976)   199
9   *Saint Jack* (1979)   208
10   *They All Laughed* (1981)   228
11   *Mask* (1985)   242
12   *Illegally Yours* (1988)   278

Reviews of Books by Peter Bogdanovich   285
Filmography   291
Videography   311
References   313
Name Index   319
Title Index   324

Acknowledgments

My thanks go first, of course, to Peter Bogdanovich, for his talent, without which this book would not be possible. I am also indebted to him for various kindnesses, among them his setting aside time to answer my questions about the films and his arranging a private screening of the recut print of *They All Laughed* for me. I also greatly appreciate his genuine interest in and encouragement of my endeavor, qualities which are not always to be found in an author's subject.

I am also grateful to the following persons who have worked with Bogdanovich for graciously sharing their memories of him with me: Roger Corman, Laszlo Kovacs, Polly Platt, Cloris Leachman, Madeline Kahn, Burt Reynolds, John Ritter, Buck Henry, Alvin Sargent, Frederic Raphael, Paul Theroux, Anna Hamilton Phelan, and Kim Myers.

I thank Grace Gaetani for laboriously translating a very obscure 100-page volume on Bogdanovich from the Italian; David Stein for doing the same with two *Cahiers* and *Image et Son* interviews; J. J. Liggera for supplying the entire text (including a long interview) of the special paperback edition of *Daisy Miller*; Barry Putterman for allowing excerpts from his superb essay on Bogdanovich's films through *They All Laughed*; and Leonard Maltin for giving his always noteworthy opinions on Bogdanovich's work. Also, thanks to Heidi Friedman and Robin Carroll-Mann at Summit Public Library for their patience and help with research.

For stills: Mary Corliss & Co. at the Museum of Modern Art, and the staffs of Collectors Book Store in Hollywood and of Jerry Ohlinger's Movie Material Store in New York.

To John, Doug, and Don, thanks again for being my friends.

T. J. H.

Preface

As of this writing, the work of Peter Bogdanovich has been sadly neglected in terms of book-length criticism in English, in contrast to that of his contemporaries (Scorsese, Spielberg, Coppola, DePalma, Allen, Altman, Pollack, Nichols, Cassavetes, Penn, Kubrick, Hill, Lumet, Polanski, Peckinpah, Schaffner, Frankenheimer, Boorman, and Cimino). I suspect that one major factor which accounts for this apparent oversight is the fact that, unlike most of the above-mentioned men, Bogdanovich has not been working steadily for the past decade or so, having undertaken two voluntary hiatus periods from filmmaking (1977–78, 1980–84) as a result of personal and professional problems.

Also, in comparison with the careers of the others, Bogdanovich's is most sharply divided: a three-year period (1971–73) of astounding critical and commercial success, followed by just as quick a decline in both (1974–76), after which, as Barry Putterman comments, it now seems to have "righted itself onto a steadier, if less grandiose course." As Paul Theroux, who co-scripted *Saint Jack* with Bogdanovich, comments, the director's work would now seem to be "in a kind of middle period in which it is impossible to evaluate." There is some truth to this, to be sure, but Bogdanovich agrees with me that one book is better than no book at all.

My view is particularly relevant when one considers that many members of the critical establishment are still content, despite the considerable achievement of his comeback film, *Mask* (1985), to continue to relegate Bogdanovich to his former status (perpetuated by his chief critics, Pauline Kael and John Simon) as a plagiarist whose allegedly meager talents had been used up by the time the last film of his initial phase, *Nickelodeon* (1976), was released. To say that Bogdanovich has been misunderstood to a degree is certainly true, as I intend to prove.

Granted, Bogdanovich has made his share of mistakes (more than some, as he himself will readily admit), but his work is certainly just as interesting (if not more so) than that of several of his contemporaries—some of whom have suffered far many more critical and commercial disasters. Altman, Schaffner, and Frankenheimer come readily to mind, but especially Altman, who has had only one hit—1970's *M*A*S*H*—and who has churned out over the 19 years since then perhaps the longest string of boring, pretentious ego trips than anyone in the history of the cinema. Indeed, the title of his latest, *Beyond Therapy*, appears to many to describe Altman's current career status in Hollywood as well. Nevertheless, his work continues to be chronicled in book after book. Bogdanovich's work is also more consistent in terms of themes and ideas than that of certain other, far more impersonal, directors such as Pollack, Schaffner, Frankenheimer, and Boorman, who have also tackled a handful of genres with varying degrees of success.

Bogdanovich's persona and career evolution are certainly far more fascinating than that of almost any of the above-mentioned people (the only possible exceptions being Allen, Scorsese, Coppola, and Spielberg), as I will illustrate. However, despite all these claims—and this is where I hope this book will prove superior to many others in the same field—my intention here is not to defend Bogdanovich blindly at every turn, a feat which would entail a glossing over of his failures as artist.

Rather, what I hope to achieve is a truly objective and honest evaluation of Bogdanovich's work based on an assimilation of all positive and negative responses put forth by others over the years, weighed equally, so that, for the first time, his films can be viewed with the lack of bias which many did not receive on initial release. This is a position which, of course, only the perspective of time can permit, and now, as Bogdanovich has turned 50 in 1989, is as good a time as any to begin. For the discussions of the films themselves, I have chosen the chronological chapter-by-chapter format, the only logical one, given the direction of Bogdanovich's career in proportion to his ambitions.

Thomas J. Harris
Summit, NJ
August 1989

Chronology

1939 (July 30)—born in Kingston, New York, to recently emigrated Yugoslavian artist Borislav Bogdanovich and wife Herma Robinson; grows up in New York City

1952—sister, Anna Thea, born

1954–1957—educated at Collegiate School, New York; studies acting at Stella Adler's Theatre Studio

1955—stage debut as director of Cherry County Playhouse, Michigan

late 1950s—acts with American and New York Shakespeare Festivals

1958—Clifford Odets approves off-Broadway production of *The Big Knife*, which is favorably reviewed

early 1960s (January 1961)— makes first trip to Hollywood; collects 70-page notebook of anecdotes; begins writing on film for numerous periodicals including *Esquire*, the *New York Times*, and *Cahiers du Cinéma*; organizes retrospectives of Welles, Hawks, and Hitchcock films at Museum of Modern Art, and writes monographs on these directors

1962—marries Polly Platt, a stage designer

1964—following failure of production of *Once in a Lifetime*, moves to Hollywood (Van Nuys); begins working for Roger Corman

1966—given job as second-unit director, assistant editor, stuntman, etc., on Corman's *The Wild Angels*; revamps horror cheapie for Corman under name Derek Thomas, released as *Voyage to the Planet of Prehistoric Women*; stops writing for *Esquire*

1967—directs interview for BBC-TV's *Great Professional: Howard Hawks*

1968—Corman backs first film, *Targets*, which receives some excellent notices but is shelved after very short run in theaters

1968–1970—works on documentary *Directed by John Ford* for American Film Institute and various aborted projects; Bogdanovich's daughters, Antonia and Alexandria, born; *Fritz Lang in America* and *John Ford* published

1971—*Allan Dwan: The Last Pioneer* published; *Directed by John Ford* released at New York Film Festival, and *The Last Picture Show* nationwide, creating enormous critical attention and large box-office returns; Bogdanovich is now famous

1972—*What's Up, Doc?*, third feature, released, surpassing *Picture Show* commercially but garnering mixed reviews; Bogdanovich separates from Polly Platt and moves into Bel Air mansion with Cybill Shepherd, star of *Picture Show*; starts Hollywood column for *Esquire*, stops in 1973 after Harold Hayes quits the magazine

1973—*Paper Moon* fares about as well as *Doc* critically and commercially; Bogdanovich's divorce from Platt is finalized; book *Pieces of Time*, a collection of his *Esquire* pieces, published by Arbor House

1974—*Daisy Miller*, starring Shepherd, receives poor notices and does scant box office

1975—*At Long Last Love* critical and commercial fiasco

1976—*Nickelodeon* dies in wake of previous failure

1977–1978—Bogdanovich takes voluntary hiatus from filmmaking to rethink his priorities

1979—low-budget *Saint Jack*, produced under aegis of Corman and in association with Hugh Hefner, is released in selected cities; despite some good reviews, it does not do much to revive Bogdanovich's fortunes

1980—Bogdanovich's lover, *Playboy* playmate Dorothy Stratten, is murdered before his new film starring her, *They All Laughed*, is to be released; film undergoes distribution problems as result of collapse of motion picture division of Time-Life

1981—Bogdanovich buys back rights to *They All Laughed* and releases film nationwide to little avail; forms production company, Moon Pictures, to distribute pictures which he will produce only; withdraws from filmmaking to write memoir about his days with Stratten, published in 1984 as *The Killing of the Unicorn*

1984—lured back into directing with *Mask*

1985—*Mask* released in cut version (missing 8 minutes of footage and 15 minutes of Bruce Springsteen music the director wanted) because of which Bogdanovich attempts to sue Universal Pictures and is forced to withdraw his case;

film nevertheless becomes a box-office success ($40 million)—and is critically lauded as well—but he is forced to declare bankruptcy because of his poor investment in *They All Laughed* (which results in collapse of Moon Pictures before any new films can be distributed), and most of his salary for *Mask* goes to his creditors

1986–1987—fortunes restored to a good degree; forms Crescent Moon Productions; directs comedy *Illegally Yours* in 1987 for De Laurentiis Entertainment Group

1988—*Illegally Yours* sold to United Artists Pictures after collapse of De Laurentiis Entertainment Group; film previews in May in selected cities and is quickly withdrawn and distributed on video late in year; reviews classic movies available on video on weekly basis for *CBS This Morning*; (December 30) marries Louise Hoogstratten, sister of Dorothy Stratten, in Vancouver, B.C.

1989—*Texasville*, the sequel to *The Last Picture Show*, is filmed from August to November with members of original cast, including Cybill Shepherd, Jeff Bridges, and Timothy Bottoms; projected release date is fall of 1990.

Biographical and Career Analysis

Putting the life and career of Peter Bogdanovich into perspective, one would almost swear that his being born in 1939 was some sort of deliberate scheme on his part. For the most prolific year in the history of American cinema—the one in which two of his heroes, John Ford and Howard Hawks, released four of their archetypal films, *Stagecoach, Young Mr. Lincoln, Drums Along the Mohawk,* and *Only Angels Have Wings*—could not have been a more fitting beginning for one whose life's course has been seemingly predetermined by that same history: "I was born, and then I liked movies," Bogdanovich said in one of his earliest interviews, following the release of his first feature, *Targets,* in 1968 (Sherman and Rubin).

More than that of any other filmmaker in recent memory, Bogdanovich's entire career has been characterized by a kind of eerie fatalism, a factor which has been perpetuated by the director's own self-perceptions over the years and by his ambitions. It seems that Bogdanovich knew in what direction he was eventually headed from early youth. By the age of 10, he was already an assiduous moviegoer, thanks to the encouragement of his Yugoslavian artist father, Borislav Bogdanovich, whom the younger Bogdanovich has said influenced his life more than anyone else. His favorite films at that time were Hawks' *Red River* (1948) and Ford's *She Wore a Yellow Ribbon* (1949). Before he reached 30, Bogdanovich had befriended both of these men and helped to pioneer serious criticism of their work by writing books and monographs on them.

Bogdanovich's processes of identification at this time were extremely strong. "When I was 8," he recalled once, "I would identify myself with Douglas Fairbanks, Jr., and Errol Flynn, at 13 with Richard Widmark, William Holden, Gene Kelly, and Marlon Brando. At home, I used to act out, to the most minute details, the scenarios of *Sinbad the Sailor* [Richard Wallace, 1947], *The Adventures of Robin Hood* [Michael Curtiz–William Keighley, 1938], *Kiss of Death* [Henry Hathaway, 1947], and *Take Me Out to the Ballgame* [Busby Berkeley, 1949]" (Giacci, p. 10).

In school they nicknamed him "Bugs" because of his infatuation with Warner Brothers' popular cartoon character (in 1972, at 33, he would release his fourth feature film, titled *What's Up, Doc?*). All of this behavior would manifest itself years later when Bogdanovich became a director in his propensity for giving line readings to actors: Burt Reynolds, who has appeared in two Bogdanovich productions, says that inside Bogdanovich there lurks an imp who wants to be a leading man. In fact, Bogdanovich himself at 16 was already studying acting under the tutelage of no less estimable a coach than Stella Adler. He has in fact appeared in two of his own films as an actor—*Targets* and *Saint Jack*—as well as in a handful of those by other directors.

In 1956, at age 16, a decisive event occurred in Bogdanovich's life which would permanently determine the course of his future: he saw Welles' *Citizen Kane* (1941) for the first time. He would remark years later of the experience that it was the "first time I realized that this tremendous presence was possible behind the camera as well as in front of it" (Giacci, p. 15). Exactly 15 years later (on *Kane*'s 30th anniversary), Bogdanovich's own breakthrough film, *The Last Picture Show*, was released to overwhelmingly positive critical response, including a review by Paul D. Zimmerman hailing it as "the most impressive work by a young American director since *Citizen*

Kane." For the next decade, the French critics would court Bogdanovich as "the new Orson Welles."

Beginning in 1959, the young Bogdanovich began to direct off-Broadway theater—though he admitted that his work was not influenced, strangely enough, by that of the theater giants like Kazan, Logan, and Abbott, but rather by the motion picture directors he admired. Not surprisingly, he described his 1961 stock production of Agatha Christie's *Ten Little Indians* as "a movie. Very intricately staged, complicated, overlapping dialogue, blackouts, gunshots. It was . . . totally influenced by Welles' *Touch of Evil* [1958], of all things. I rewrote the play somewhat, stealing some dialogue from *Touch of Evil*. And there was a whole thing about a pianola which I also took from *Touch of Evil*. I didn't even know that I'd taken it from that until I thought about it years later" (Giacci, p. 21).

The same year, after having connived his way into a graduate course in film at Columbia University taught by Cecile Starr—attended, incidentally, by another future director, Brian DePalma—Bogdanovich began writing on the cinema for various magazines, including *Ivy*, *Frontier*, and the *Village Voice*. This practice—which he would continue on a fairly steady basis until age 29, after which it became more sporadic—he told Betty Jeffries Denby (June 1975) was

> mainly a way of making money or keeping my hand in until I could get a job in the field. But it wasn't anything that deeply interested me. I don't know that it was helpful to me except that I saw a lot of movies. Probably I would have seen them anyway. I was just smart enough to see them free. Also, I didn't write about movies I didn't like; I wrote about ones I liked—so, if anything, I was trying to create a climate, an atmosphere in which people would like *my* movies. Which of course I hadn't made yet. But I figured if I could get them to like Howard Hawks and John Ford—since I liked those films and knew my own movies would probably be more like those than, say, Antonioni's or Fellini's—then

people would like my films, too. I was really saying: let's stop talking about Ingmar Bergman for a minute and start talking about John Ford. But that was all very unconscious at the time.

Bogdanovich has said that "the American cinema has had the most direct influence on me, and therefore is the one I most respond to and like best." He has credited his move away from foreign films back to his natural predilection—he had begun to study the former because it was "fashionable" during the late 1950s and early 1960s—to two men: Andrew Sarris and Eugene Archer of the *New York Times*. With them (and the French critics, of course), he became one of the foremost proponents of the auteur theory, always careful to give the directors possessive credit for all works mentioned in his writings. This practice was applied not only to obvious artists like Hitchcock, Welles, and Ford with an obvious stylistic imprint, but also to lesser-known directors like Howard Hawks and Leo McCarey, who on the surface seemed to be impersonal craftsmen (both were even considered hacks by many) but who were soon revealed to have continuously exhibited a unique temperament and point of view despite the diverse genres they tackled—Hawks in particular.

By this time it was inevitable that Bogdanovich, a native New Yorker, would make his first trek west to the city with which he was so obsessed, Hollywood. After securing a letter of introduction from Robert Silvers, an editor at *Harper's* magazine, Bogdanovich headed for California in January of 1961. Although barely post adolescent (he would turn 22 that year), he managed to use the letter to schedule interviews with many of the leaders of the film industry, among them Alfred Hitchcock, Billy Wilder, Gordon Douglas, John Sturges, Dean Martin, Jerry Lewis, Jack Lemmon, Cary Grant, Laurence Harvey, Walt Disney, Richard Brooks, Mark Robson, Angie Dickinson, George Stevens, William Wyler, and Clifford Odets. Bogdanovich's collection of anecdotes about the two-week trip, culled from a 70-page journal and published first in *Esquire* in 1962, has now become legendary; it was reprinted in 1973 in his book *Pieces of Time*. He said in an introduction to the section titled "First Impressions" in *Pieces of Time* that he had journeyed to Hollywood with "the vague idea of either (*a*) being 'discovered' or (*b*) getting acquainted with some childhood heroes." The first prospect was not to happen yet, but the experience did prove to be the beginning of a long-term association with *Esquire*.

But perhaps more important, the trip provided him with his first real taste of Hollywood. Now more than ever before, Bogdanovich was determined to make the move west, and when in 1964 director Frank Tashlin urged him to do just that (at that time Hollywood was still the only center of film production), Bogdanovich needed no further encouragement. He and his new wife, Polly Platt— whom he had met while directing summer stock in 1958—left their small apartment in New York and piled into a yellow 1951 Ford convertible (borrowed from Tashlin) with a TV set and only about $150 between them (a disastrous off-Broadway revival of Kaufman and Hart's *Once in a Lifetime*, financed with their own already meager earnings, had left them virtually penniless), and somehow managed to make the two-week trek relatively unscathed. Their trip would years later be recalled in Bogdanovich's fourth feature film, *Paper Moon*.

Although Bogdanovich was later to be linked with such film-school-oriented directors as Scorsese and DePalma because of the movie-oriented nature of his first films, in actuality his evolution from critic to major director is a unique one. By contrast to the others, Bogdanovich's background was one of journalism and literature (though all of his writings were about the cinema). Also, like the pioneer filmmakers to whom he actually felt closest, Bogdanovich learned his craft solely through experience, working for 22 weeks for low-budget producer Roger

Corman in a number of capacities (scriptwriter, editor, second-unit director, extra) on his film *The Wild Angels* (1966). Another important factor had been his observing three of his heroes—Ford, Hitchcock and Hawks—in action on the sets of *Cheyenne Autumn* (1964), *The Birds* (1963), and *El Dorado* (1967). Not surprisingly, Bogdanovich's dream project (one which he finally got to realize—though not nearly with the success he had hoped for—as *Nickelodeon* in 1976) for years involved chronicling the history of the early days of filmmaking, when men from various professions sort of just stumbled into the business. Bogdanovich in fact had met Roger Corman unexpectedly one night at a movie screening—though, of course, the thought of directing had been on his mind for years.

Another "movie brat" director, Francis Ford Coppola, also served as apprentice to Corman around this time, but in contrast to him, Bogdanovich had never attended college (he had in actuality missed out on a high school diploma) or studied films seriously for credit (although he had seen many more than Coppola—some 4,500 in all; he had begun keeping a card file at age 12). Bogdanovich was also the only American *critic* making the transition to successful filmmaker (in the tradition of the French cinephiles), and as such he had very radical opinions about the state of the industry he was entering. He thought the 1960s were the worst decade in American film history, and deplored the films of his contemporaries (Kubrick, Penn, Nichols, etc.) for being overly violent, pretentious, vulgar, and flashy. The best American film of 1967 in his mind was not Penn's *Bonnie and Clyde* or Nichols' *Graduate*, but rather Hawks' old-fashioned western, *El Dorado*.

Instead of being termed, as he usually is, one of the new generation of movie directors who came to prominence in the 1970s, Bogdanovich more accurately might be described as the last of the first-generation filmmakers (despite the fact that he was virtually the same age as most of his contemporaries). Bogdanovich's first feature, the thriller *Targets*, although admittedly violent in terms of content and displaying an audacious 20-minute action climax at a drive-in, evidenced a self-effacing quality which had been decidedly lacking in American films of the recent past, influenced as they were by the New Wave, with its ostentatious techniques designed to make obvious the presence of the man behind the camera. It was in fact praised by Hawks himself (on whose work—and that of Hitchcock—it was modeled) for this quality.

The critical acceptance of *Targets*, along with the comments Bogdanovich made in interviews surrounding its release (to the effect that in his opinion the golden age of filmmaking had ended in 1962 with the release of Ford's *Man Who Shot Liberty Valance* and that he was now going to make pictures like those produced during the 1930s and 1940s), led many to believe he could very well prove to be the savior of the faltering American film industry. In 1970, when a book called *The Director's Event* by Eric Sherman and Martin Rubin, was published, an entire chapter was devoted to Bogdanovich, even though, by contrast to the other filmmakers included, he had produced only one feature to date.

By 1970 Bogdanovich had befriended and written about nearly all of the directors of Hollywood's golden era who were still living (all but Hitchcock, Preminger, Welles, and a few others had retired—though Welles had been in decline for years—and even in the case of those three, their best work was behind them). Between 1967 and 1971 Bogdanovich worked on documentaries about two of them (*The Great Professional: Howard Hawks* for BBC-TV and *Directed by John Ford* for the newly founded American Film Institute). Both contained the only filmed interviews with either director. All of these men supported Bogdanovich's ambitions, and as Barry Putterman remarks, they and several of their peers even used Bogdanovich's next film, *The Last Picture Show*, as "a club for beating out their resentment over the recent course of American filmmaking."

The release of *The Last Picture Show* in October of 1971 was an important event in the history of American cinema and a phenomenal one in the career of Bogdanovich, who achieved instant fame with it. A measure of the change in his stature because of this film can be witnessed by comparing an article published in the *New York Times* (December 14, 1970, p. 86) concerning its production (a small item in which Bogdanovich's name was mentioned only once) and a five-column interview with him conducted during the production of his next effort, *What's Up, Doc?*, in the same paper one year later (Harmetz, November 14, 1971). Bogdanovich says now that he never expected the picture to be anything near the overwhelming commercial success that it was, considering its scale and low budget ($1.3 million), and the fact that it featured no stars.

Also interesting in this regard is the fact that it was produced by BBS Productions, the radical outfit responsible for such antiestablishment films as Dennis Hopper's *Easy Rider* (1969) and Bob Rafelson's *Five Easy Pieces* (1970). And although *Picture Show* was the film which marked Bogdanovich's breakthrough into the mainstream, it paradoxically resulted from his rebellious reaction to the recent course of American filmmaking. As Barry Putterman points out, the film seemed at the time to have appeared out of nowhere: "Coming in the midst of a long cycle of films that challenged the forms and values of traditional American movies, both in reaction to imported techniques and domestic political unrest, the enormous critical and commercial success of *The Last Picture Show*, the first major American narrative film to be shot in black and white for four years, signaled the end of that cycle." Bogdanovich had proven (as he would again two years later with *Paper Moon*) that a film need not be in color to be a box-office hit. Through the years, there have been other highly creditable attempts to restore the beauties of black and white, but with the exception of Fosse's *Lenny* (1974), they have been box office failures: Scorsese's *Raging Bull* (1980), and Allen's *Manhattan* (1979), *Stardust Memories* (1980), *Zelig* (1983), and *Broadway Danny Rose* (1984). Nevertheless, one is grateful to Bogdanovich for paving the way for the artistic revival of black and white.

That *Picture Show* indicated a return to the classical, "invisible" style of the veteran directors whom Bogdanovich admired (chiefly Hawks and Ford) was certainly no surprise, considering his statements on numerous occasions that he felt no affinity with his contemporaries (Kubrick, Nichols, Cassavetes, Altman, Coppola, Friedkin), many of whom had begun to emphasize technique over content, resulting in cold, academic works. Obviously the critical establishment felt the same way, for almost without exception they embraced Bogdanovich's film as a glorious return to the values of the great American films of the past—foremost among them being an emphasis on clean storytelling and character development.

Bogdanovich also attracted the attention of many prominent industry veterans with this film (this would continue through his next four features). Among those attending the Hollywood premiere of *The Last Picture Show* at Grauman's Chinese Theatre were Robert Aldrich, George Cukor, Robert Wise, John Huston, George Stevens, and Samuel Fuller. No such comparable fanfare greeted the release of Scorsese's first major success—*Mean Streets*—two years later, but the reason for the difference is more than obvious: Scorsese's was considered by many to be an underground New York feature, whereas Bogdanovich had now firmly established himself as a member of the Hollywood establishment, which automatically implied instant widespread attention.

As everyone in the Western world who is interested in recent film history surely knows by now, Bogdanovich's next two features, the screwball comedy *What's Up, Doc?*

(1972) and the black comedy–drama *Paper Moon* (1973), were even more successful at the box office than *Picture Show* (although both received decidedly mixed reviews). Bogdanovich's next effort was an art film, an adaptation of Henry James' *Daisy Miller* (1974) which was an expected financial failure and which received even more mixed notices than the previous two features. And then, of course, came the musical *At Long Last Love* (1975) and the comedy about the early days of moviemaking, *Nickelodeon* (1976). Both of these films were resounding critical and commercial flops (although the former remains the more notorious failure), indeed so much so that Bogdanovich's career appeared over. Articles on him after *Nickelodeon*'s release bore titles like "Bogdanovich—Will *Nickelodeon* Be His Last Picture Show?" (Denby, D., January 30, 1977) and "The Rise and Fall of Peter Bogdanovich" (Roberts, May 1977)—a far cry from the "Peter Still Looks Forward to His *Citizen Kane*" which had appeared in the *New York Times* just five years earlier (Harmetz, November 14, 1971).

These and other writings have speculated on the causes behind the director's rapid fall from favor. Since I would like mine to remain the definitive work on Bogdanovich until a similar study is published, I will now respond in depth to the often-posed queries about the director's decline and how he proceeded to pick up the pieces and revive a faltering career.

Critic David Wilson wrote of Bogdanovich in 1981, "Rarely has a filmmaker been so elaborately defined by his own self-perceptions" (Wilson, p. 251). Not surprisingly, therefore, it was Bogdanovich himself who described his personality best. In a June 1987 interview for a *Kane*-like article on the last days of Orson Welles for *American Film*, the director said he realized that a character Welles had written back in 1975 for a never-completed film of his called *The Other Side of the Wind* (that of a young maverick director) was "kind of based on me: he was interesting, but not particularly attractive." This brief bit of introspection provides a good basis for illustrating how Bogdanovich was perceived during his early years (and even today) and helps explain why so many people were so eager to see him fail in his ambitions (which he eventually did).

Now, normally a filmmaker's personal behavior would be considered irrevelant in a consideration of his career evolution or his art, but in the case of Bogdanovich, the two are inextricably linked. It was around the time of the release of *Picture Show* that one could begin to detect certain changes in Bogdanovich's personality—or, more accurately, more pronounced signs of behavioral traits he had exhibited even before his sudden rise to fame.

Before this, he was perceived by those who knew him as a kind of impish young man with a great passion for cinema (and an undeniable gift for writing about it) who fancied himself an intellectual and who remained un-flinchingly opinionated (despite his age) about all matters relating to the movies—his only true love—often to the point of condescension (except in the presence of those older than he, namely the veteran directors and stars whom he idolized).

But even those who were put off by his air of superiority could not deny that they admired him for his tenacity and determination to realize his ambition of becoming a director. He was also, however irritating at times, always an entertaining presence, exuding a boyish enthusiasm which endeared him to many despite his faults. Bogdanovich always loved being the center of attention, so that under-standably when fate finally bestowed upon him the title of Moviemaker, he embraced it wholeheartedly.

Not that his sense of Hollywood history did not make him aware (at least to some degree) of the direction in which he was headed. He remarked in one interview conducted shortly after *Picture Show*'s release (Harmetz, November 14, 1971) that "when you have a success, you make any number of untold enemies, so now I've added an untold number to the ones I deliberately made," and that,

as Fritz Lang had once said, "you pay for what you get."
For the most part, however, having found himself suddenly caught in a whirlwind which was not to clear away
until four years hence, he remained blissfully ignorant of
his situation: "I tend to walk through life without being
completely conscious of certain things that are happening,
and sort of purposely ignoring things," he remarked in
1973 (McCluskey, p. 72). Also, with picture after picture,
there was simply no *time* to sit back and savor the success he
was having.

Bogdanovich says now that his biggest problem back
then was an inability to deal with success, which he says is
"insidious, because you don't realize that you *have* to deal
with it." It is remarkable that for someone so unusually
self-conscious when it came to promoting his image, he
showed absolutely no signs of introspection whatsoever
with regard to his behavior. Now that he had finally
attained the position he had been seeking for the past 15
years or so, he began to display an inordinate sense of
pride in his accomplishments, which began to alienate
many more people than he ever had before (due to his
fame)—particularly, no doubt, certain of his contemporaries, whose films he did not hesitate to put down in
interviews, which was contrary to the usual policy of
Hollywood types, who for friendship's—and career's—
sake strive to maintain a positive view of their fellow
filmmakers' work in public, whatever their true feelings
may be.

Unlike most other directors his age (including the two
other wunderkinds of the 1970s, Lucas and Spielberg),
who remained relatively camera-shy and self-effacing,
Bogdanovich voluntarily chose (to a great extent) to put
himself in the spotlight during the early 1970s, and thus
must be judged on the basis of that choice (though it is also
true that, unlike Scorsese and DePalma, for example, who
remained steadfast New Yorkers, Bogdanovich was
courted more by the press because he embodied the very

essence of the *Hollywood* director, carrying on the tradition of the great men).

From 1971 through 1976, Bogdanovich's career—an archetypal success story with, as David Denby put it, "all the clarity and decisiveness of a fable" (January 30, 1977)—became a virtual barometer for measuring the attitudes which characterized the motion picture community. In 1972 Bogdanovich officially "went Hollywood," having separated from Polly Platt, who had served as set designer on his first three pictures (and would do so once more on *Paper Moon*, despite their personal differences) and hooked up with Cybill Shepherd, the blond ingenue he had introduced to the public in *Picture Show*. He moved from his modest digs in Van Nuys to the exclusive Los Angeles suburb of Bel Air, and set up house there with Shepherd in a Spanish-style movie-star mansion (where he lives to this day).

Looking back on this period in his book *The Killing of the Unicorn*, published in 1984, Bogdanovich remarked, "I was suddenly a wealthy, famous young man. But I was still a long way from understanding myself, the woman I lived with, or the world around us." It was at about this time that Bogdanovich began to become a public personality, due to his frequent appearances (usually with Shepherd) on talk shows. He even hosted the *Tonight Show* once in 1974, a formerly unheard-of practice for a movie director—one critic described the stint as "an exercise in gigantic egoism." In this respect he joined such filmmakers as Hitchcock, Preminger, and Welles.

But unlike those men, whose reputations were firmly established and could hardly be hindered by the outrageous comments they (Preminger in particular) often made on TV about others' work, the public's and the critics' perceptions of the still-young Bogdanovich were being shaped by these less-than-becoming impressions, despite the fact that he seemed and would have liked to be considered older than he was.

Particularly annoying to many and damaging to Bogdanovich's own stature was his promotion of Shepherd, who was widely regarded as a very negligible talent and a rather silly and empty-headed personality. Her impressive appearances as icy bitches in Bogdanovich's *Picture Show* and Elaine May's 1972 *Heartbreak Kid* were considered simple self-portraits. The fact that she continually emphasized her modeling work did not help her in this regard, particularly since Bogdanovich seemed to maintain a Svengali-like hold over her every word and movement. By billing her as one of the great "finds" of recent years, therefore, Bogdanovich was unconsciously undermining the reputation he had attained as a brilliant director of actors.

It was not until the release of *Daisy Miller* and *At Long Last Love* (showcase vehicles for Shepherd), however, that Billy Wilder would utter his famous observation that "Hollywood is united in one thing—its universal hatred of Peter Bogdanovich and Cybill Shepherd." Shepherd's performance in the first was regarded mainly as hollow and amateurish—the only real fault in the film, in the eyes of many—but it was her feeble attempts at singing and dancing in the latter which aroused the consternation of the community at large and caused many to begin questioning seriously Bogdanovich's artistic judgment. As Bogdanovich put it in 1985, "Cybill and I were being kicked around by the whole country because of that film, and it was treated as though we had committed one of the most heinous crimes ever, including child-murdering and rape" (Rochlin, p. 134).

But Bogdanovich realized that even before the release of *Love* "the knives [had been] ready." He had become the victim of the old Hollywood syndrome: Everyone tells you he's happy for you while you're having success, but secretly he can't wait to see you fall flat on your face—and if you've been flaunting your fame excessively, as Bogdanovich was, then the next step after your inevitable fall is to trample on and bury you. Bogdanovich drew a particularly observant parallel between his situation and that of another Hollywood couple: "They were trying to make me replay the Marlene Dietrich/Josef von Sternberg saga. After they broke them up, they didn't let Joe work much. They sort of killed Joe for his arrogance because they thought he was hiding behind Marlene. I think some people figured we were going to play that scene." People certainly had a right to be jealous of his position, since he was the only American to make the successful transition from critic to film director.

Of course, after *Love* came out, career prospects for both Bogdanovich and Shepherd seemed dim, though admittedly the situation was worse for Shepherd, since many still considered Bogdanovich to be a top-notch director—as long as he worked *sans* his girlfriend. As is typical after such a fall from grace, many were tempted to go back and reexamine Bogdanovich's career to determine whether he ever in fact had any *real* talent and if so, what had caused him to lose sight of himself.

Part of the problem, as Barry Putterman notes, had to do with factors clearly beyond Bogdanovich's control:

> Although Bogdanovich had blazed the trail and signaled the dawn of the generation of directors whose films built on the work of previous filmmakers, tastes were shifting so rapidly in the volatile seventies that by the time of *At Long Last Love* and *Nickelodeon* Bogdanovich was already considered remotely out of touch with the spirit of the times. Whereas his films reflected the more classical traditions of the thirties, the newer directors like Lucas and Scorsese derived their inspiration from the more idiosyncratic postwar people such as Minnelli, Fuller and Michael Powell. (p. 53)

But by and large, the director himself was responsible for his decline (though in an unconscious sort of way).

Glenys Roberts, in a 1977 article in *Los Angeles* magazine
chronicling the meteoric rise and descent of Bogdanovich's
fortunes, described him this way:

> He was the man most equipped to live the life-script. The
> mimic, the would-be actor, the boy whose memory hardly
> ever failed, was trapped in his reproductive role.
> Bogdanovich was the seeing eye of a generation that had no
> chance to work out its own destiny because John Wayne and
> James Dean and Frank Sinatra, whatever name you prefer,
> had done it all for us. What he was actually trying to do was
> create a personality for himself. He was the carrier of that
> disease of impersonality we are all fighting, our heads filled
> with glib notions of perfection culled from images of screen
> heroes ten feet tall, voices amplified like the voice of God.
> (p. 128)

Bogdanovich's extreme self-consciousness in all matters
relating to his life often set him up for criticism where it
was not always due. As he himself has admitted, he was
only adding "fuel to the critical fire" by carelessly pointing
out parallels between the films he was making and those of
the veteran directors he had lionized in his writings.
Because he had said on numerous occasions that he felt "all
the good films had been made," he was, without thinking,
making himself out to be a plagiarist, a label which would
stick with him for years to come—whereas in fact the
parallels he had made reference to were highly superficial
ones.

Such statements were further aggravated by the fact that
most of Bogdanovich's features seemed to many to have
been little more than empty exercises in style (the main
exceptions being *Picture Show, Moon,* and *Daisy Miller*)—
and that in interviews the director continually emphasized
the importance of a mastery of technique over specific
thematic concerns or motifs in his work. But his position
was justified by the fact that his early films were, by and
large, genre pieces, attempts to recapture the simple

pleasures which the movies of the 1930s and 1940s had provided audiences. Unlike a director such as Sydney Pollack, who also has worked in a number of genres, Bogdanovich never attempted to add a sociological message to his works (which, in many cases with Pollack, turned out to be considerably muddled, due to his uncertainty of aesthetic purpose). That he was not striving to make statements about the complexities of contemporary America should not be held against Bogdanovich, since it is pointless to blame someone for not being something he by nature is not. Incidentally, with the exception of Scorsese, none of his contemporaries showed much of an interest in this angle either.

Rather, the question should be asked whether the pictures work on the level on which they were striving. I would maintain (and one should consult the chapters on individual films and the section on aesthetics for further elaboration on this matter) that of the three obvious genre pieces (*Targets*, *Doc*, and *Love*), only one (*Love*) does not meet this criterion, and as for the others, only *Nickelodeon* comes close to a total failure as a dramatic or comic work. But at the same time, there is undoubtedly truth in the accusation that the features of late had been losing sight of what had been the hallmarks of *Picture Show* and *Moon*: relations between people and an emphasis on storytelling values.

Part of the reason for this shift had to do with the extent of Bogdanovich's ambitions during this period—a reflection of a blind confidence in one's abilities characteristic of a young person. As Bogdanovich put it years later, "When you're young, you think you can't make mistakes. Other people do, but you don't" (Rodman, June 1987). The director made a conscious attempt to avoid the pigeonholing tactics of critics by making statements to the effect that he planned to "have a career filled with lots of different types of films." His ambitions rivaled those of one of his favorite directors—Howard Hawks—known primarily as a superbly diverse master of many genres. In fact, Bogdanovich's follow-up film to *Picture Show* was a screwball comedy called *What's Up, Doc?* which was admittedly modeled (to a degree anyway) on Hawks' definitive masterpiece of the genre, *Bringing Up Baby* (1938).

Bogdanovich remarked in a 1986 interview on PBS that he thought a large part of the reason he and certain of his contemporaries—such as Scorsese, Friedkin, and Coppola—eventually fell from favor, at least to some degree, was that everyone "reached too high"—stretched their limits. But as was not the case with his contemporaries, there seemed to be something unconsciously self-destructive about Bogdanovich's rather reckless ambitions—particularly in regard to *Love*—as though he were trying to prove his limitations as a director. Certainly neither Scorsese's *New York, New York*, being a musical biography leaning far more toward the latter quality, nor Coppola's *Finian's Rainbow*, a Broadway adaptation, could be considered as outrageous in terms of intent (an original musical composed entirely of Cole Porter songs and filmed in Lubitchian long takes) as *Love*. That Bogdanovich failed to realize his goal with the film is undeniable, but though one may scoff at the rashness of his ambitions in conceiving the enterprise, at the same time he must recall that with the exception of Hawks, none of his mentors (Hitchcock, Ford, Preminger, to name a few) proved himself capable of handling more than one or two genres with any appreciable degree of success—least of all the musical, the most specialized of all.

It is highly ironic that the most personal projects of these men (Bogdanovich's *Daisy Miller, Love*, and *Nickelodeon*; Scorsese's 1977 *New York, New York*; Coppola's 1982 *One from the Heart*, 1983 *Outsiders* and *Rumble Fish*, and 1984 *Cotton Club*) turned out to be their biggest artistic and commercial failures. The reasons for some (*Love*; *New York, New York*; *Cotton Club*) are obvious. In all three cases the directors were venturing into unfamiliar territory in attempting to tackle a musical (or in Scorsese's case, a musical biography)—though Coppola, at least, should have known better, judging from the self-admitted failure of his 1968 *Finian's Rainbow*. Only Steven Spielberg has been able to have his cake and eat it too in this regard: *E.T.* (1982), his most personal (and best) film to date, is also the top-grossing film in motion picture *history*. The same could possibly be said for Lucas and *Star Wars* (1977), but one hesitates to label films when a director's output is so severely limited; Lucas has directed only three features to date.

Related to the matter of Bogdanovich's progression toward more personal projects is another important factor which many who have known him have cited: the contribution to his work of Polly Platt, who used to serve as a sounding board for his ideas and who collaborated with Bogdanovich on his first three successful pictures (she and the director parted both personally and professionally before Bogdanovich began *Daisy Miller*, the film which inaugurated his decline). These people argue that the director's subsequent pairing with Cybill Shepherd was a very poor substitute for what Platt gave him.

First of all, it must be stated without a doubt that Platt's set designs for *Picture Show, Doc,* and *Moon* (and *Targets* also, for that matter) contributed immeasurably to the "feel" of the films, and made it much easier than it would otherwise have been for Bogdanovich's direction to evoke an authentic sense of time and place. Platt was also reponsible for coaxing Bogdanovich into taking on the *Moon* assignment by convincing him that Ryan O'Neal's daughter Tatum was a talent begging to be discovered (her prediction proved to be correct, needless to say). She has also given the impression of having had a mind of her own, unlike Shepherd, who allowed herself to be manipulated by her director-lover to a great extent.

Still, it is a bit hard to predict whether Platt would have advised Bogdanovich against undertaking *Daisy Miller* or

Nickelodeon (the latter having been a long-cherished dream of Bogdanovich's)—though there is no question she would have considered *Love* to have been a misguided enterprise from the outset. The difficulty in deciding lies in the fact that in Bogdanovich's professional life, Polly Platt and Cybill Shepherd were, it seems, mutually exclusive: both could not dominate his working thoughts at the same time. Even during the time of *Picture Show*, Bogdanovich's main interest was wavering toward Shepherd as he began to fall in love with her during production. It is no coincidence that Shepherd did not have a role in any of the films Platt designed for Bogdanovich after Bogdanovich became involved with her.

Of course, Shepherd would not have fitted in either *Doc* or *Moon*, but the point is that Bogdanovich did not begin designing vehicles for her until after he and Platt had split completely. One must also take into account that it would have been embarrassing for Platt—who was, after all, married to Bogdanovich for almost ten years—to have witnessed Shepherd's taking her place in Bogdanovich's agenda on a daily basis during filming. But reportedly—personal differences aside—she did not share Bogdanovich's opinion of Shepherd's acting skills, so that one could reasonably argue that she might have approved of *Daisy Miller* and *Nickelodeon* so long as they were made without Shepherd, which the first surely would not have been, though the second—to Bogdanovich's dismay—had to be (by order of the producers), but it failed anyway.

With regard to Shepherd herself, judging from her often grossly miscalculated antics in *Love* (her performance in *Daisy* is sporadically successful, however) and the fact that the project was designed from the outset with her in mind (Bogdanovich having become convinced of her singing skills after arranging for her to take lessons and producing an album entitled "Cybill Does It to Cole Porter"—one of the hilarious lows in recording history), it would appear that his relationship with her did in fact affect his judgment as an artist.

True, it is doubtful that *Love*, for example, would have been improved by the subsition of another actress in Shepherd's role; there were already too many factors going against the film from square one. Certainly *Nickelodeon* was a failure even without her, but the point is that certainly *Daisy* and *Love* would never have existed in Bogdanovich's canon had it not been for Shepherd's presence in his life. The concept for the latter film came to Bogdanovich after Shepherd presented him with an album of Cole Porter songs for Christmas. Many who had admired *Picture Show* on its release now began to express doubts about the merits of the commercially successful pictures that followed it: *Doc* and *Moon*. There was a widespread feeling that the director had sold out. In fact, neither film had been made by Bogdanovich in an attempt to exploit its stars (Barbra Streisand and Ryan O'Neal in the former, O'Neal and his yet-unknown daughter Tatum in the latter). *Doc* came about after Bogdanovich had been *chosen by Streisand* to direct a comedy-drama written for her (which was later totally discarded by Bogdanovich and turned into a screwball comedy), and he had become interested in O'Neal as an actor only after having forced himself to see the phenomenally popular but unavoidably icky vehicle that had made him a star, *Love Story* (1970).

As for *Moon*, the only way Bogdanovich agreed to do it was on the condition that O'Neal, who had become a friend, would be there to help him through it—the main problem being the incorrigible behavior of O'Neal's un-trained eight-year-old daughter Tatum. But the best evidence of Bogdanovich's artistic integrity was his re-fusal—despite favorable responses from the stars—to make sequels to either film, which would, he rightly argued, have been a thoroughly pointless endeavor. In fact, after *Moon*, Bogdanovich admirably decided to undertake a project which he knew from the start would have no real box-office potential: *Daisy Miller.*

There was also the complaint (and this is related to the plagiarist label placed upon Bogdanovich by the critics) that Bogdanovich had become a casualty of his love of movies—that they were too referential and therefore contained little dimension of their own. As I will illustrate in depth in the individual chapters on the films, this fault was only partly evident in two of the films—*Doc* and *Love*—and in the first half of *Nickelodeon.* In the case of the first film, the footnotes to films of the 1930s and 1940s scattered about did not seem to alienate viewers, many of whom longed for precisely the type of entertainment value they represented—and, perhaps more important, many viewers who did not recognize the references were able to accept the film as an original screwball comedy. These factors combined to make it Bogdanovich's highest-grossing ($28 million) film.

As for *Love*, the problem with that film was more related to a distancing factor which did alienate audiences. Barry Putterman describes it best: "It was as if Bogdanovich had given the public nothing but the analysis yet still in the form of thirties entertainment, thus being judged ana-chronistic and incompetent at the same time" (p. 53).

The failure of *Nickelodeon*—which forced a turning point in Bogdanovich's career—was a different story. The pic-ture was a collection of anecdotes about the behind-the-scenes aspects of picture making culled from interviews Bogdanovich had conducted with several Hollywood veter-ans over the years. Although Bogdanovich was not borrow-ing scenes from other people's films, he was occasionally stealing from his own (specifically *Doc*) this time. As Putterman says, "It looked like the work of a very tired man" (p. 53). And indeed, Bogdanovich has said he had no fun making the picture; like John Galsworthy's *Apple Tree,* a story Bogdanovich had wanted to film since his adoles-cence but decided not to when finally given the opportunity (he made *Daisy Miller* instead), *Nickelodeon* was perhaps also a project which was too long delayed.

It is also partly true that the reason the film failed at the box office had to do with the fact that it was released in the wake of the *Love* disaster; the film had received much bad press long before it opened. The picture's immediate death became a self-fulfilling prophecy for Bogdanovich's many enemies. But ironically the fact that the picture was a bust turned out to Bogdanovich's advantage, as he realized:

> I'm tired, and I want a rest. I've been going from picture to picture, and I need more time to prepare the next one, more time to figure out who I am and what I'm doing. . . . *Nickelodeon* is a kind of summation, with elements from all my pictures, as it should be, since it's a movie about the movies. For better or worse, it's the end of a chapter for me. Now I'll do something else—I don't know what, but it's like starting over again. (Denby, D., January 30, 1977)

After *Nickelodeon*'s release and subsequent demise, Bogdanovich said, "I've made nine movies, and now I think I'm ready to be a director" (Denby, D., January 30, 1977). He made a conscious decision to get back to basics, deliberately choosing for his next project (which followed a one-and-a-half-year-long hiatus) a film which would have to be on a small budget and on location in Singapore, thousands of miles from Hollywood and its bureaucracy. As with *Daisy Miller*, this film—*Saint Jack*—provided more admirable evidence of Bogdanovich's artistic integrity, since he was not particularly concerned that the picture make money, only that it recoup its budget (which it eventually did) and that he prove to himself that he could make and release a film his way without any compromises. His other previous works which had come out the same way were *Doc*, *Moon*, and *Daisy*.

The project also attracted Bogdanovich because the story had nothing to do with the cinema, so it was definitely a step in the right direction in another way, too. The film was largely experimental in nature, shunning a tight narrative structure in favor of less explicit exposition, a casually developed story, and a greater reliance than ever before on images alone to convey the meaning of certain sequences. Although the result did little to revive Bogdanovich's flagging reputation in America (hardly anyone saw it), it received generally favorable reviews, and was praised for just those qualities which had motivated Bogdanovich to make it in the first place.

Bogdanovich's next film, the romantic comedy *They All Laughed*, while boasting many of the same artistic techniques as *Saint Jack*, seemed to be a much more commercial venture—the film which would hopefully bring Bogdanovich back into the mainstream. But shortly before it was set to be released, its distributor, the fledgling Time-Life Films, went out of business, and it seemed likely that the film would remain on the shelf. Because this was Bogdanovich's most personal film to date, he believed in it more than in any of his others, and thus decided to risk his accumulated wealth by investing nearly all of it ($5 million) in the movie. Unfortunately, however, the film sold well under $1 million worth of tickets and returned less than half of that to Bogdanovich.

But more important to Bogdanovich at this time was the fact that one of the actresses featured in the picture, 20-year-old Dorothy Stratten, a former Playboy playmate who had been Bogdanovich's love interest of late and whom he had hoped to make a star with this film, had been murdered in August of 1980, shortly after shooting on *They All Laughed* was completed. The tragedy so shook the director that he decided to take a long break from filmmaking to write a book about his affair with Stratten.

The book, titled *The Killing of the Unicorn*, was published by William Morrow in 1984 (see review on page 286). It was at this time that Bogdanovich was asked by Universal producer Martin Starger to direct an original screenplay based on a true story about a deformed 15-year-old and his biker mom. The project, titled *Mask*, was Bogdanovich's biggest artistic gamble to date, being unlike anything the director had tackled previously. Bogdanovich says now that although he eventually accepted the assignment, at first he was

> not quite ready to make a film. After Dorothy was killed, I didn't really want to make any more films. And it wasn't a pose, it was a complete lack of interest. I realize now, looking back, that it was a kind of shock that it took me a long time to get past. I remember having projects that I was sort of giving away, saying, "You direct. I'll just sort of produce (Bogdanovich had set up a production company after *They All Laughed* called Moon Pictures). And when *Mask* came along, and I was asked if I wanted to make it, I didn't really. But I felt that I had to, and I jumped into it. Part of me felt that it would be good for me to just do a picture as a professional, like they used to, and I approached it that way up to a point. I really got into it after about two or three weeks.

The result surprised everyone—Bogdanovich and his cast had thought it would quickly become a cult film, nothing more—by grossing over $40 million at the box office (although, Bogdanovich rightly argues, it would have made in excess of *$100 million* had the Bruce Springsteen songs he had selected for the film been used). It also received outstanding reviews from many critics, who hailed it as Bogdanovich's best work since *Picture Show*, despite the fact that two important scenes had been deleted by the studio from the release print. *Mask* proved to be a triumphant comeback and vindication for him after his highly publicized personal difficulties, though unfortunately Bogdanovich was forced to give most of his salary to his creditors, having filed for bankruptcy—the result of the *They All Laughed* investment—in December of 1985.

Although Bogdanovich has certainly been through more

in the way of personal and professional turmoil than many, happily such events have largely turned out in his favor. Bogdanovich's manner now, at 50, shows no traces of the obnoxiousness of his younger days. He has been genuinely humbled by his misfortunes and made a better man (and artist) for them. He now willingly admits to past mistakes (formerly he had tended to blame them on others), and while retaining his boyish enthusiasm for the cinema, he has found himself capable of making films which not only capture the spirit and style of the masters of American film, but (as *Mask*, for example, amply illustrates) are revelatory of his own matured perspective on life as well.

Aesthetics

Before beginning this discussion, I think it is important to state once again that there is a certain validity in Paul Theroux's observation that Peter Bogdanovich's work is at this point in "a kind of middle period in which it is impossible to evaluate." Since the initial phase of his career as cinephile—he was the first American to be labeled as such, in the tradition of the French critic-directors such as Truffaut—ended in 1976, Bogdanovich has produced four motion pictures, and despite the promise offered by 1985's *Mask* in particular, he does appear to have a way to go before he can recapture to a significant extent the widespread critical and commercial reputation accorded him in the early 1970s. Nevertheless, as I pointed out in the Preface, his progress thus far does evidence a consistent artistic temperament and style which deserves considera-tion both on its own terms and in comparison with the oeuvre of certain of his contemporaries.

The films of Bogdanovich's initial period (*Targets, The Last Picture Show, What's Up, Doc?*, and *At Long Last Love*) could all be considered (despite the present-day settings of *Targets* and *Doc*), as Vittorio Giacci says, "acts of love and remembrance" for his cinema past. The cinema had been Bogdanovich's one overriding passion ever since his child-hood, and so it was inevitable that his first films as director would be filled with obvious (*Targets, Doc*) and uninten-tional (*Picture Show*) references to the works of the directors he most admired, among them Ford, Hawks, Hitchcock, and Keaton, as well as being themselves attempts to work within the genres established by these and other men. The ones considered to be mainly stylistic exercises (*Targets, Doc,* and *Love*) were decidedly academic in nature, taking the form of tests on the one hand for Bogdanovich to see whether he could achieve something on the level of the films' models, and on the other inquiries into the necessity for certain established conventions within the genres. These works (in addition to the others) were criticisms in another sense also, in that they were reactions to recent films Bogdanovich didn't like, films which mirrored the ugliness of contemporary society. By contrast, he sought to take audiences back to a simpler time; indeed, the publicity slogan for *Doc* was "a screwball comedy—remember them?"

It was mainly in the straight dramas (*Picture Show, Paper Moon,* and *Daisy Miller*) that Bogdanovich's personality was permitted to emerge. All three were period pieces, revealing an obsession with the past which was not a form of nostalgia but rather the most appropriate venue for a reflection of two opposing forces in Bogdanovich, the romantic and the fatalist. It also resulted from a desire to avoid dealing with contemporary issues which threaten to become dated in a very short time. Since *Saint Jack,* however, his stories have all been set in the present, partly as a reaction to the movie-oriented films of the first phase, but Bogdanovich vows that he has not forsaken the past. He is currently considering a film version of Robert Graves' *Seven Days in New Crete.*

Although his protagonists (the teenagers and their elders in *Picture Show,* Moses and Addie in *Paper Moon,* Daisy Miller) were (and still are, if we look at the case of Rocky Dennis in *Mask*) by nature incapable of escaping their rather bleak destinies or doomed to repeat their mistakes over again (though the hero of *Saint Jack* finally achieves morality at the film's conclusion), he always sympathized with them—the women in particular—highlighting their good points while never losing sight of their tragic flaws.

If Bogdanovich shares with Ford a rather innocent and boyish attitude toward relationships, unlike his mentor's, Bogdanovich's humor is never corny, just sincere. And, as he has said, even in his most serious works, there have always been comedic moments—indeed, *Paper Moon* is a black comedy. This innocence becomes much more apparent in the films with a lighter tone—*What's Up, Doc?* and *At Long Last Love* in particular—though it surfaces in the more somber atmosphere of *Daisy Miller* and eventually in the disarmingly serious one of *Mask. They All Laughed* remains the director's most mature look at love and relationships, since it deftly combines aspects of both the serious and the comic. Certainly the films since *Saint Jack* have been more revelatory than ever of Bogdanovich's personality and concerns, having been freed from associations (except for those spiritual affinities which one may ponder, particularly in the case of *They All Laughed*) with the cinema.

What one first notices upon a casual scanning of Bogdanovich's 11 features (12 if we include the documentary *Directed by John Ford*, and by all means we should) is that his is a rather courageous filmography in terms of genre and subject. Within a relatively brief time span of 20 years (actually 11, since 9 of them were spent in hiatus for one reason or another), one finds a thriller (*Targets*, 1968), a documentary (*John Ford*, 1971), four romantic screwball comedies with occasional dramatic overtones (*What's Up, Doc?*, 1972; *Nickelodeon*, 1976; *They All Laughed*, 1981; *Illegally Yours*, 1988), a musical (*At Long Last Love*, 1975), a small-town drama framed by western conventions (*The Last Picture Show*, 1971), a con man/orphan saga (*Paper Moon*, 1973), a period romance (*Daisy Miller*, 1974), a raffish "star" melodrama with flashes of black comedy (*Saint Jack*, 1979), and a tearjerker—albeit only in theory (*Mask*, 1985). All are genres established in the 1930s, whose spirit

Bogdanovich has tried to recapture, with varying degrees of success.

By contrast to such contemporaries as Sydney Pollack and Brian DePalma, who are also noted as working in several genres, Bogdanovich has assiduously avoided any sort of pretension in his treatment of them. Unlike Pollack, he does not add sugarcoated messages to his work (a factor which makes *Targets*, for example, superior to Pollack's 1975 thriller *Three Days of the Condor*, with its superficial statements about United States government and politics), nor has he ever attempted, as DePalma has, to reproduce for his own amusement certain key sequences in the work of famous directors (though *Doc*'s chase is filled with nods to Keaton, and the abundance of long takes in *Love* is patterned after Lubitsch's methods, and though he was unjustly labeled a plagiarist by certain critics early in his career). Perhaps the most of reprehensible of which—despite all the earlier pseudo-Hitchcockery—is the Odessa Steps ripoff in DePalma's, *The Untouchables* (1987).

Nor was any of the early films of Bogdanovich (despite what has been argued by some) an attempt to reproduce intact the style of one particular director, as were, for example, Woody Allen's thinly veiled homages to Bergman and Fellini: *Interiors* (1978), *Stardust Memories* (1980), *A Midsummer Night's Sex Comedy* (1982), *September* (1987), and *Another Woman* (1988). Instead, Bogdanovich simply sought to recreate the *spirit* of the films of his mentors. That his stories were not cloaked in the sort of blatantly personal autobiography which Scorsese, for example, used to mask the similarities between his *Taxi Driver* (1976) and Ford's *Searchers* (1956) made Bogdanovich's films *seem* more derivative than others', whereas in truth (with a few exceptions) the opposite was the case. It should also be pointed out in this context that Bogdanovich by inclination was distinct from all his contemporaries in that he came to film from a background of journalism (though, granted, his writings concerned the cinema) rather than from a film school.

The true—or the most significant—consistency in Bogdanovich's treatment of so many diverse genres is not to be found in a recurring character or theme *itself*, as with such directors as Altman or Scorsese (though Bogdanovich *is* fond of pairing the weak, ineffectual, bumbling male and the strong, aggressive female, particularly in comedy, and having her succeed in redeeming him), but rather in an emphasis on stylistic challenges inherent in the material and how these aspects inform the content of the particular piece, thereby allowing the director's personality and concerns to emerge from them. At its least successful (as in *At Long Last Love*), such a procedure results in an empty stylistic exercise devoid of any real directorial point of view. At its best, it allows the "feel" of a genre to be virtually recreated (as in *Targets* and *What's Up, Doc?*) or even causes the potential pitfalls of a certain one to be transcended (as in the case of *Mask*) or its conventions questioned in order to find new meaning within the genre itself (*The Last Picture Show*).

Since style is obviously such an important factor here, it should be remarked first that of all the American directors working within the traditional classical (i.e., invisible) format established by the Hollywood directors of the 1930s and 1940s (of which Scorsese is the most obvious exception), it is Bogdanovich and his contemporary Steven Spielberg who possess the most acute visual-narrative senses. Comparing Bogdanovich's work with Spielberg's, therefore, is one surefire method of assessing both the strengths and the weaknesses in the former's. Both men's quest thus far has been to provide moviegoers with the same types of simple pleasures provided by the films of their mentors, though as the 1980s drew to a close Spielberg's work was beginning to show signs of pretension to higher, more "adult" levels of entertainment. The act of

filmmaking itself interests both of them more than anything else about the films, and although there are consis-
tencies in terms of ideas in both filmographies, neither
man could be labeled an auteur in the sense that Hitchcock
or Ford or Welles could, and neither's films can be
dissected in the way that theirs can. Vittorio Giacci's
contention that the classical narrative compositions of
Bogdanovich's films are the source of the power of the
works—dealing in essence with "that heady fascination
which binds the image to the spectator"—can be used to
describe Spielberg's work also. Films like *Paper Moon, They
All Laughed*, and *Mask* are as coherent expressions of the
nature of cinema (without involving specific references to
films of the past) as are such Spielbergian efforts as *Jaws*
(1975), *Close Encounters* (1977), *Raiders of the Lost Ark* (1981),
or *E.T.* (1982).

The distinction between the two men lies partly in their
chosen models of filmmaking artistry. On the most simplis-
tic level, both men admire Hitchcock for his amazing
technical proficiency—and indeed such sequences as the
drive-in murder spree in *Targets* and the chases in
Spielberg's *Sugarland Express* (1974), *Jaws, Raiders*, and
E.T.—as well as the entirety of the 1971 telefilm *Duel*—
along with the less flashy but still gripping command of
cinematic point of view and narrative pacing throughout
The Last Picture Show, Mask, and Spielberg's *Color Purple*
(1985), are all ample testaments to his influence on their
work.

But beyond these somewhat superficial concerns lie the
fundamental differences between the two men (and between Bogdanovich and his contemporaries also), particularly in regard to their choice and treatment of subject
matter. Bogdanovich, who admires Ford and Hawks
perhaps more than any of the veteran American directors,
has consistently displayed throughout his career in his
handling of dramatic subjects (his chief forte) an honesty
and maturity reminiscent of the best work of both these

men. The calm, understated, deadly serious presentation of random violence in *Targets* was indeed praised by Hawks himself and stands in direct opposition to the rather immature (because of occasional attempts at finding humor in them) attitude toward or indulgent excesses of the same by Scorsese, for example, in such films as *Mean Streets* (1973) and *Taxi Driver* (1976). The somber, melancholy atmosphere of death and decay which permeates *Picture Show, Paper Moon, Daisy Miller*, and *Saint Jack*—all of which feature funeral scenes—is unmistakably Fordian, while the upbeat, transcendent attitude toward death which characterizes *Mask* marks a new level of maturity for Bogdanovich which becomes uniquely his own, having been fostered through harsh personal experience.

Spielberg, on the other hand, has until recently modeled his films on the work of less respected filmmakers generally considered lightweight talents. Robert Wise's 1951 *The Day the Earth Stood Still* was a major influence on the sci-fi-oriented *Close Encounters of the Third Kind* (1977), while *Raiders* found its celebration of old movie serials inspired by those of William Witney, among others. This was in keeping with his desire to provide audiences with pure, undiluted escapism. As a result, despite excellent performances from actors in such films as *Sugarland Express* and *Jaws*, the increasingly cartoonlike characters and often unbearable emotional excesses in such films as *Close Encounters, 1941* (1979), and *E.T.* seemed to indicate that his appeal did not extend beyond the child of, say, age ten. His attempt to show that he possesses depth as an artist with *The Color Purple* resulted, not surprisingly, in a prettifying of the painfully grim source novel by Alice Walker, and only his handling of the actors succeeded in making the piece rise beyond the level of the superficial— something which his most recent venture, 1987's *Empire of the Sun* (modeled ostensibly, as was *The Color Purple*, on the work of British master David Lean), failed completely to do, stubbornly remaining all style and no substance.

Another factor should be taken into account here: while Spielberg indulges in melodrama often to excess, shamelessly manipulating his audience into sympathizing with the plights of the characters in films like *E.T.* and *The Color Purple*, Bogdanovich assiduously avoids the same, leaving the audience with its dignity intact; this approach is particularly evident in *Mask*.

If Bogdanovich excels over Spielberg in his handling of characters and relationships, he nevertheless shares with him (and with most of his peers, for that matter) the distinction of being a much better *metteur en scène* than scriptwriter. Spielberg's chief flaw is logic, evidenced foremost by the innumerable, childish inconsistencies in the *Close Encounters* script, the only one Spielberg wrote entirely by himself. His fans have attempted to excuse this shortcoming by stating that it is Spielberg's "mission" which should concern us—in other words, we must allow ourselves to be manipulated by him without questioning his methods. To say the least, this is a rather unsatisfactory attempt to compensate for a lack of skill, particularly in light of the fact that Spielberg's one brilliant protégé, writer-director Robert Zemeckis, has turned out features—*Back to the Future* in particular—which offer the same lightweight entertainment values as his mentor's but which are also intelligently written and conceived, with all potential holes in the scenario neatly ironed out.

Bogdanovich's shortcoming is a tendency to silliness resulting from a too-personal attachment to his material. This quality is noticeable in the films with a comedic tone, particularly *At Long Last Love* and *They All Laughed*. Indeed, there seems to be a fascinating and somewhat alarming similarity between the careers of Bogdanovich and several of his contemporaries in the area of personal filmmaking. Just as Bogdanovich's least successful vehicles have been projects initiated by him or written primarily by him and not based on the source material of others, so too have the least satisfying films of Scorsese: *Who's That Knocking at My*

Door (1969), *New York, New York* (1977), *The Last Waltz* (1978), *The Last Temptation of Christ* (1988), and Coppola: *One from the Heart* (1982), *The Outsiders* (1983), *Rumble Fish* (1983), *The Cotton Club* (1984), *Gardens of Stone* (1987), and *Tucker* (1988). The exception for Scorsese is the autobiographical but intensely felt *Mean Streets* (1973), and for Coppola the excellent *The Conversation* (1974).

The case of Spielberg is especially interesting in this regard, and perhaps even *more* disturbing. After seemingly exhausting his childhood fantasies in his first seven features (of which *E.T.* is—and is likely to remain—his best work, because most typical), Spielberg decided to try one *impersonal* vehicle (*The Color Purple*) recommended to him by a friend (co-producer Kathleen Kennedy), only to find himself unable to shed his goody-goody sensibilities in the adaptation process.

By contrast to these men (with the exception of Scorsese), as we enter the 1990s, it is Bogdanovich who appears to have the brightest future, as he seems the most likely (despite the evidence of *Illegally Yours*) to stick with new and challenging dramatic subjects which will surely plumb new depths of mature emotion from within him, as was evidenced by *Mask*. Indeed, his next film is *Texasville*, the sequel to *Picture Show*, which is scheduled to be released in 1990. This is only fitting, since it was he who came to prominence before any of the others.

1 *Targets* (1968)

By the time Bogdanovich was given an opportunity to direct his own feature by Roger Corman in 1967, at age 28 (the offer having been prompted by the great financial success of *The Wild Angels*, on which Bogdanovich had worked: $5 million in the U.S.), he was more than ready to tackle the job. In just a little over a year's time, via his numerous capacities as second-unit director, assistant cameraman, location scout, narrator, editor, and post-dubber on *The Wild Angels* and *Voyage to the Planet of Prehistoric Women* (a low-budget horror movie recycled by Bogdanovich), he had become intimately acquainted with most of the basic skills of the trade. Indeed, the conditions under which these low-budget efforts were turned out necessitated an ability to master many skills in a limited amount of time. "It was like taking a 22-week course on how to make a film," Bogdanovich said. Years later, the director would recall this apprenticeship as essential training:

> There were practical lessons: You learned how to move fast, and down and dirty; get in and get out quick. And that was great, because that knowledge and way of working, that somewhat informal and guerrilla kind of filmmaking, should be the way everyone learns. You steal the scenes, you con locations, you do anything you can to get the picture in the can fast. ("Dialogue on Film," April 1986)

Bogdanovich's agreement with Corman included a few minor stipulations: He would have to shoot 20 minutes of footage with Boris Karloff, who owed Corman two days work on his contract from their 1963 effort, *The Terror*, and he would also have to include some 20 minutes of that film. In addition, the budget was not to exceed $130,000, and the 60-odd minutes of new footage would have to be completed within two weeks' time. Bogdanovich's initial reaction was one of "temporary insanity." However, his knowledge of film history and respect for its creators soon prevailed, and provided him with an inspiration for the film's construction.

Bogdanovich had completed his last monograph for the Museum of Modern Art four years earlier. Its subject had been Alfred Hitchcock. Bogdanovich doubtless recalled that the "master of suspense" had produced his "most cinematic picture," *Psycho* (1960), for a mere $800,000. So

Byron Orlock (Boris Karloff) as seen through the viewfinder of Bobby Thompson's gun.

it was that with Hitchcock (one of his heroes) as logical role model, Bogdanovich came to write, along with wife Polly Platt, an original thriller—*Targets*. The film follows two parallel stories which have a single point of contact at the beginning and then converge in a single finish, a sequence at a drive-in theater where a young man named Bobby Thompson (Tim O'Kelly) without warning starts sniping at the patrons. A similar case actually happened that same year in Austin, Texas—the young killer's name was Charles Whitman. The other story involves the sad decline of aging horror-film star Byron Orlock (Karloff, more or less playing himself), who after having decided to retire from the screen ends up attending the premiere of his latest flick at the same drive-in where the shootings are taking place.

Already Bogdanovich was beginning to develop the characteristics that would populate his later work. Much of *Targets* was shot directly on location in and around the San Fernando Valley, where Bogdanovich was living at this time. There is a conspicuous absence of a musical sound track—source music is employed instead, though here it is limited to the Top 40 rock selections on Bobby's car radio and thus of no real value as commentary on the motives of the film's characters; the opposite will be the case with almost all the films from *Last Picture Show* onward. The camerawork remains invisible, subordinated to the narrative. There is a great reliance on editing and point-of-view/camera placement to achieve dramatic effect in a scene, particularly those involving little dialogue and lots of action—a technique at which Hitchcock was most expert. There are several intentional tips of the hat to the American directors Bogdanovich most admires. The glory of the cinema itself is celebrated, particularly the cinema of the past. And perhaps most important, this is the director's first exploration of a popular American movie genre. Bogdanovich also takes on the small role of cinephile-writer-director Sammy Michaels, a part whose autobiographical overtones rival those in Karloff's interpretation of Byron Orlock.

Targets marks Bogdanovich's first examination of the role movies play in shaping our dreams and values. In this most unusual and stimulating effort, the director, within the context of a thriller, examines the horror film (represented by the Byron Orlock character) and its relation to present-day society (whose chief exponent is the psychotic young killer Bobby Thompson). The film is based upon a continual intermingling of make-believe and reality (and the spectator, according to a typical Hitchcock treatment, is aware of this from the very beginning), up to their ultimate convergence in the concluding 20-minute drive-in sequence. Bogdanovich's intention here is to refute the Karloff character's initial assertion that real life has become so horrifying that horror films have lost their power to scare audiences. He will accomplish this by proving that the myth-oriented world of the movies can in fact be *more* fascinating, *more* genuine, *more* humane than life itself.

Bogdanovich begins by confronting the issue of appearances, contrasting the worlds of illusion and reality in order to strip away his protagonists' masks and expose them as they really are (a theme he will not address again for 17 years, in his second socially oriented film set in present-day America, *Mask*). *Targets* opens in the screening room of movie producer Monty Landis (Marshall Smith), who, along with Sammy Michaels, is trying to persuade Byron Orlock to make a picture Sammy has written that will cast him as a real-life person rather than a bogeyman.

Our first glimpse of Orlock is very dramatic: after the concluding sequence from *The Terror* (over which the film's credits are superimposed) flickers out, there is momentary darkness. Slowly the lights come up, and we see the sullen countenance of Orlock, who is obviously displeased with the umpteenth depiction of himself as a heavy. Bogdanovich provides us with almost a minute of silence in which to come to terms with the image of Orlock. His haggard yet decidedly stern and unsettling appearance seems to be in keeping with his own unflattering assessment of himself: he is clearly an anachronism. When he states that he is planning to retire from pictures because "no one is afraid of a painted mask any longer," producer Landis cruelly throws his own words back in his face by reminding him, "If it wasn't for me, the only place you'd be playing is in the wax museums."

From this rather dreary opening we move outdoors into the bright light of day. Immediately we notice a change. The sunshine lends Orlock the appearance of an elderly and distinguished gentleman; his film personality, on the contrary, depends upon the complicity of darkness to create the make-believe terror. It is at this point that we are introduced to the young boy, Bobby Thompson. Again the introduction is immediately arresting—and even more unsettling. Orlock's face is suddenly framed within the viewfinder of a rifle. The camera's objective—which is to capture reality so as to make it live an infinite number of times as a figure on the screen—is abruptly and brutally replaced by that other objective which intrudes upon reality in order to take life away.

There is a cut to a finger squeezing a trigger. We shudder for a moment, but our fear is alleviated when the gun turns out not to be loaded. We then see the face of the would-be assassin—not the hideous figure we expected, but instead a youthful, clean-shaven boy. Already the masks of our two protagonists have been removed and their true identities (a reversal of our expectations) disclosed. The remainder of the film will continue to expand upon this paradox, continually confounding our expectations much in the manner of Hitchcock in *Psycho*, for example.

Like the typical Hitchcock thriller, *Targets* reveals that the calm, reassuring details of everyday life (the "good life") form merely a thin veneer over the darker forces of fear, destruction, madness and death. The connection between the two episodes consists of a transposition of the two personalities based on a judgment of what is "normal."

Echoes of *Psycho:* Bobby Thompson (Tim O'Kelly) carries off body of his wife, whom he has just murdered.

Orlock is condemned to a life embodying horror, whereas Bobby has all the characteristics of the "good boy." However, as we shall discover, behind Bobby's seemingly respectable demeanor lurks the horror of nothingness, whereas behind Orlock's dusky and menacing appearance there is the man. The tension of the movie lies in this rather inexorable juxtaposition of the two characters, driving them to a fate which gradually converges and becomes one.

Bogdanovich argues that the reasons for the declining career of movie star Orlock and the bizarre behavior of young Bobby Thompson without question result from the emergence of the "plastic society"—a world dominated by existential and environmetal sterility, where people are forced to survive separately within alienating and repressive structures devoid of passion, culture, or living. "God, what an ugly town this has become," observes Orlock on his way to the drive-in.

Bobby Thompson in particular is a victim of this deadening form of existence, as Bogdanovich illustrates early in the picture when Bobby returns home after stopping at a store to pick up more ammunition. It is here that the director utilizes a form of social satire reminiscent of Frank Tashlin (especially the Tashlin of *Will Success Spoil Rock Hunter?*) as he (through Polly Platt, his production designer) characterizes the Thompson family through the decor of their house. As Bobby enters the front door (the house itself is an ordinary one-story ranch, quite indistinguishable from the others on the street), an announcement is heard from an unseen TV set: "This week, on the Saturday Night Movie, James Stewart, Lee Remick, and Ben Gazzara star in Otto Preminger's compelling production of *Anatomy of a Murder*. . . . [James Stewart to Gazzara:] 'You're guilty of murder, lieutenant. . . . The unwritten law is a myth, and anyone who commits a murder under the theory that it does exist has just bought himself room and board in the state penitentiary.' . . . *Anatomy of a Murder*. Suspense worth viewing. Saturday night at 11:15 on Channel 7."

This may seem like an incidental bit of detail, but in fact Bogdanovich has inserted it for several very important reasons. First, and most obvious, it foreshadows the killing spree which Bobby will soon engage in, and reminds the viewer that he will have to pay for his deeds. But more significant, it points to an aspect of the plastic society which Bogdanovich particularly abhors: television, especially the broadcasting of classic films on television (note that the viewer is never *shown* the clip from the movie). Bogdanovich has said on this subject: "It's awful. You lose all the impact on that tiny screen, and you're having interruptions every ten or fifteen minutes, breaking the mood. How can you build a world of illusion when that illusion is always being broken by somebody selling cars?"

Otto Preminger is a director whom Bogdanovich respects very much, and *Anatomy of a Murder* is one of his finest efforts. Bogdanovich's choice of this particular film (a two-and-three-quarter-hour courtroom drama about rape) to illustrate his belief is no doubt a reference to Preminger's legendary 1966 lawsuit against Columbia Pictures, Screen Gems, and Channel 7 (WABC) in New York City for their allowing *Anatomy* to be "brutally mutilated," as Preminger put it, by no fewer than 13 commercial interruptions. Preminger unfortunately lost his case, but Bogdanovich is here defending his artistic principles by including a satiric reference to it (incidentally, Preminger himself did the same thing in the first five minutes of his otherwise abysmal 1969 comedy *Skidoo*). No one in the house is really paying attention to the announcement, a fact which echoes their attitude toward films on TV and TV in general; they will watch anything, regardless of quality or number of commercial interruptions, just to kill time. Indeed, we eventually see just how poor the family's tastes are: their regular source of amusement is *The Joey Bishop Show*, the old TV talk show for those who found Johnny Carson too erudite.

Also, the announcement is coming from a cheap local station (not coincidentally Channel 7) which is obviously planning to squeeze the film in an awkward time slot (11:15 instead of 11:00) in order to take advantage of extra commercial time. The emergence of TV is a theme which will resurface in *The Last Picture Show*. Later we will see exactly how Bogdanovich feels about films being shown in another convenience-oriented outgrowth of the sterile society, the drive-in.

In observing the details of the Thompson house, we note that Bogdanovich has made clever use of the limited budget he was allotted: the sparse furnishings are a direct reflection of the tastes of its inhabitants. The house is spotless and has no visible signs of culture—there are no bookcases, and the walls are quite bare except for one family portrait, some hunting pictures and certificates, and some antlers. There are, however, *two* television sets. The house has a blue exterior, a blue interior, blue lamps, blue bedspreads, blue dish racks, blue cloth towels, blue paper towels, and even a blue flower in the kitchen. What isn't blue is a purplish gray or off-white. According to the director, "Part of the strength of the film lies precisely in the genuineness of expression: that plastic blue is very American and really is a part of a certain USA culture." In his first collaboration with Bogdanovich (he will go on to photograph seven of his subsequent films), cinematographer Laszlo Kovacs manages to create a fairly intricate color scheme for the picture which mirrors the contrast between the two protagonists: for Orlock, dark, warm colors (brown and yellow predominating), typical of the Gothic atmosphere of horror movies; for Bobby, as we have just seen, cold colors (blue, white, gray, light green). It is difficult to believe that Bogdanovich's original intention was to shoot in black and white—it was Corman who eventually got him to change his mind.

Bogdanovich emphasizes the ordinariness of Bobby's stifling family life in order to show that such a situation often fosters an arrested development—psychological, sexual, emotional, or intellectual—which can lead to destructive actions. Signs of Bobby's immaturity include that he wears a suit and keeps his hair trim in an era when young people wear wild clothes and have long hair; that he eats Baby Ruths; that he speeds along the freeway in his flashy convertible, changing lanes without signaling; that he tinkers with his car; and that he practices shooting. He even addresses his note about the projected killing spree "To Whom It May Concern," as if he were applying for his first job.

The causes of his behavior are economically delineated in two short scenes at the Thompson home. Bobby and his wife Ilene still live with his parents; he still calls his authoritarian father sir, and his father calls him Bobby Boy (never Bob); his well-meaning mother calls him dear and says things to him such as "That's a good boy"; Robert

Senior says "damn it," Ilene says "darn"; Ilene and Bobby's mother cook together and have dinner waiting when Robert Senior comes home and says "Hello, group. Is dinner ready?"; before dinner there is prayer, and during dinner there is idle chatter.

We can see the effect that repeated exposure to such an environment has had upon Bobby's behavior. After entering the house, he wanders about, gazing intently at various objects on the walls and furniture, completely oblivious to the voices of his wife and mother, who are preparing dinner. His expression suggests the cold, vacant stare of a killer. He is obviously already close to the breaking point, a fact confirmed by his reluctant greetings to his family. He secretly relishes the fact that this is probably the last time he will have to endure the ordeal of another mundane dinner with them.

Byron Orlock awakens from a drunk, only to be frightened by his own image.

The final sign of his near collapse occurs at a shooting range, when he picks up a loaded rifle, points it at his father, and starts to squeeze the trigger. His father, who has been down at the far end examining the targets, manages to catch him in the nick of time, however. It is somewhat doubtful whether Bobby would have followed through, though, since he later waits until his father (who is still an intimidating figure to him) is out before shooting Ilene and his mother and fatally wounding a delivery boy.

It is by now clear to us that Bobby is rebelling against the sterility of his society, represented not only by his frustrating family situation but also by the supermarkets, plastics, advertising, neon lights, highways, cars, colored banners, and television which have surrounded him since he was a child. With such a sense of emotional vacuity ever present, Bobby has been left with no choice but to turn to guns (violence is a cathartic act) as his lone companions. He is tired of being merely a nonentity, and seeks to attain some sense of personal security by identifying solely with his rifle. The point is that after a while mere possession of artillery can no longer contain the impulse; Bobby must use it—and not just on cans and animals, but on the real things—though he seems unable to distinguish between animals and people, telling the clerk at the gun shop, "I'm going to kill some pigs."

There is much more in his criminal act than the killing; it is a statement of why the weapon was made, and his satisfaction above all derives from the fascination of the rifle shot itself. Bobby identifies himself with the weapon to such an extent that he in essence *becomes* the weapon. He feels no hatred, he seeks no revenge. His crime evolves into a proof to himself that he is efficient, that the mechanism of the technical device—the rifle—is trustworthy, and that it is indeed a high-precision weapon enabling him to hit the target without fail even from a very great distance. When captured his only words are, "I have hardly ever missed." His deed is all the more violent in view of his total abhorrence of violence; indeed, he avoids blood and cannot bear the sight of cadavers (recall Norman Bates' uneasiness at mopping up and disposing of Marion Crane's body in *Psycho*). After shooting the members of his family, he deposits them in the corners of the rooms and quickly departs to begin his killing spree.

From the individual crimes against his family, Bobby moves on to some against society, perpetrated on the masses taken anonymously, which he tries to eliminate nihilistically. He begins on the top of an oil-storage tank, from which he snipes at random at the occupants of cars moving along the highway below, then moves to a vantage point behind the movie screen where he shoots to death several spectators of the horror movie.

Bogdanovich depicts these happenings as the mere representation of Bobby's ultimate behavior, one of the consequences of the life-style his society has proffered him. By doing so, he emphasizes all the more the core of the tragedy which derives not from the seriousness of the crime itself but from the absence of any apparent motivation, from the absolutely gratuitous nature of the deed. Indeed, not even the slightest motivation is to be found throughout the entire story.

In response to the film's "restrictive" gun-control prologue tacked onto the film by Paramount after the Robert Kennedy and Martin Luther King assassinations ("Why in 1968, after assassinations and thousands of more murders, has our country no effective gun-control law? This motion picture tells a story that sheds a little light on a very dark and very deep topic"), Bogdanovich said:

> *Targets* did not explain, nor did it mean to explain, anything. What it did aim to show was that the most "horrific" part of such murders is their lack of motivation. We could find no reason commensurate with the size of the crime. I felt it was presumptuous to give an answer to something that psychiatrists, sociologists, and humanists don't know. I would rather

After buying more ammunition, Bobby prepares to do further damage.

the audience come out saying," Why?" because that's not so complacent an answer. (Stone, September 15, 1968)

Bogdanovich thus spares the viewer the facile psychological summation which the psychiatrist in *Psycho* provides—though Hitchcock's attitude toward that speech was decidedly mocking.

Whereas Bobby's "normalcy" is belied as the film progresses, Byron Orlock, symbol of the classical horror-movie figure, wants to return to a normal way of life—in short, to be a man again, free of his oppressive film characterization. He tells his friend Sammy Michaels that he is by now tired of eliciting a kind of fright which he knows is artificial because it is surpassed by reality. "There are too many genuinely horrible things in the world for me not to feel ridiculous with my papier-mâché horrors," he says. The grilling of Orlock on the influence of his motion picture acting as opposed to the total lack of self-interrogation on the part of Bobby is both profound and pathetic. The conversations between Sammy and Orlock give Bogdanovich an opportunity to touch upon the theme of an actor's relationship to his role. In a delicate, sensitive manner, he allows Karloff, as Orlock, to make his confession as a man, endowed with greater depth and intelligence than the screen has ever permitted the viewers to see, and embittered by the typecasting that so adversely affected his life.

The scene which best illustrates this theme (and the general tone here reminds one of John Ford, particularly the numerous Barry Fitzgerald characterizations in his films) has Sammy waking up after spending the evening with Orlock getting drunk trying to convince him to accept a role in his new film (whose title, though never mentioned, is *Targets*). It is a tender, humorous, and tragic scene. Sammy opens his eyes and in the foreground, a short distance from his face, he sees Orlock's face and instinctively reacts with fear, not because of the face itself—although it is certainly more horrible than most—but because of what that face represents by now for millions of people. And it is even more shocking that Orlock himself has the very same reaction when he unexpectedly finds himself in front of the mirror. The underscoring is ironic, but it suggests how *Frankenstein*, which won Karloff fame, still condemned him to be different, to appear forever with that mask—in short, to be what he is not.

It is here that the real tribute to Karloff lies, not in Bogdanovich's having interpolated an episode from *The Terror* in *Targets*, nor in his having remembered him in a youthful American work, Howard Hawks' *Criminal Code* (1931), which the two of them see together as Sammy explains: "I saw it at the Museum of Modern Art." Karloff, in turn, remarks, "Thanks to Hawks, I had my first really important part." The reference *is* a small homage to

Hawks, however. Sammy marvels, "He really knows how to tell a story." The scene has autobiographical overtones with relation to Bogdanovich; in 1962 he had programmed a retrospective of Hawks films at the museum. His enthusiasm at seeing the clip despite its being shown on television here is justified by the following statement of his: "[Around 1960–1964] I used television to catch up on old movies. I was furious that I had to see them that way, but I figured I'd better see them there if I couldn't see them anywhere else." This was before the advent of large 16mm rental outlets and revival houses.

Eric Sherman and Martin Rubin, in their critique of *Targets* in *The Director's Event*, have remarked further upon the significance of this scene:

> This moment marks what is probably the first full-fledged cinematic "quote" in American cinema. In this sense, the invocation of Hawks differs from, for example, the sequence from Von Stroheim's *Queen Kelly* (1928) in Wilder's *Sunset Boulevard* (1950) or from the excerpt from Minnelli's *The Bad and the Beautiful* (1952) in his *Two Weeks in Another Town* (1962), which are used more for purposes of nostalgic-historical and personal-Pirandellian reminiscence, respectively, than for indicating critical intelligence. Bogdanovich is able to integrate this reference into the context of *Targets* to the extent that it neither belies an abysmal gap between example and model (as did the sequence from *Picnic on the Grass* in Agnès Varda's *Le Bonheur*, 1965), nor becomes merely an esoteric allusion (such as the reference to *Viaggio en Italia* in Godard's *Contempt*, 1963). The *Criminal Code* reference ties into the plot of *Targets*, since the earlier film marked the first major appearance of Karloff in a motion picture. More important, the film clip (which portrays a steadily rising crescendo of pure noise during a prison riot) parallels the spasmodic bursts which emanated from the boy's car radio earlier in the film, and thus reinforces the film's central tension between the simple richness of the past and the complex

sterility of the modern world—even our ears respond differently to the two periods. The melodramatic intensity of Hawks' scene (which is frustratingly cut off by a commercial) also prepares us for the film's climax in which melodrama is affirmed and social reality sacked. Bogdanovich transcends pretensions and in-jokes, and he integrates a valid reference into an American film for the first time. A localized victory, perhaps, but an important one in a period of film history when critical self-consciousness is becoming more and more inevitable. In the scene, the young director comments, "He sure knows how to tell a story." Storytelling is a dominant trait in Bogdanovich's own visual style and selection of theme. Bogdanovich makes no attempt in *Targets* to explain the gruesome situation. Instead, he concentrates on *showing* the murders and the corpses in order to make the audience observe and feel the terror he portrays. This reliance on the simple and direct machinery of the action genre co-exists with the critical sensibility in the film. The juxtaposition of these two elements at times creates an extraordinary ambivalence (as in the climax of the film, which suspends the viewer between contradictory desires to emotionalize as well as intellectualize the moment) which indicates one of the first potentially productive marriages between the "new" criticism and the traditional style of filmmaking. (pp. 74–76)

The producers and Karloff's press agents want him to say something to terrorize the public, to publicize the film. The actor confines himself to telling his story in a closeup which Bogdanovich will use again for another important confession, that of Sam the Lion in *The Last Picture Show*. Looking directly into the camera, Orlock tells "a story to frighten the people," as the producers have requested. But instead of merely being a story about death and fate, it is, additionally, a metaphor on his situation, on the impossibility of his fleeing from the character he has been playing for so long.

Ladies and gentlemen, boys and girls, I would like to leave you with a little story for you to think over when you return home in the dark. There was, many years ago, a rich merchant from Baghdad who sent his servant to the marketplace to shop. Shortly after, the servant returned, pale and trembling: "Master, while I was at the market I was pushed by a woman in the crowd. I turned to look and saw that it was death. She made a menacing gesture to me. Oh, master, lend me your horse so I may flee far away from this city, and escape my fate. I shall ride as far as Samara and death will not be able to find me there." Thus, the merchant lent him the horse and the servant got on the saddle and galloped towards Samara. The merchant went to the marketplace and saw death among the crowd. He then asked her, "Why did you make a threatening gesture to my servant this morning when you saw him?" And death replied, "I made no threatening gesture. It was merely a motion of surprise. I was astounded to see him in Baghdad when I had an appointment with him for tonight at Samara."

The story comes from a little-known work of W. Somerset Maugham, quoted at the beginning of *Appointment in Samara* by John O'Hara. Even Bobby's action represents a no-longer-accepted separation from others, but he himself is not aware of it when, with the same repeated mechanical gesture he expresses the violence of an entire society.

Orlock and Bobby are the bases of a speech on the reportedly casual ties between the movies and reality, ties which become most manifest during the climactic drive-in sequence. Bogdanovich:

The boy shooting through the screen is like reality breaking through illusion. Originally I wanted to have a shot of the whole drive-in from above the candy stand. Slowly the camera would start moving in toward the screen. It goes all the way in, and then you see the gun poking through the screen. We couldn't do it, because it was too complicated.

Bobby munches O Henry bars and drinks soda pop while casually sniping at passersby from atop a local oil-storage tank.

> What you saw was a compromise; it was done with a cut. But the idea was the same: looking at an illusion and out of it comes this harsh reality. (Sherman and Rubin, p. 96)

At the conclusion of the film—the next topic for discussion—Bobby shoots down from the screen at the spectators, who die knowing neither who nor what has killed them. This is the clearest expression of the cinema's relationship to life. Bogdanovich's intention with the final drive-in sequence is to exculpate the cinema—despite his having shown that Orlock/Karloff's screen image as a bogeyman has obscured his real identity—by reversing the conservative opinion according to which it is the cinema which creates violence and monsters like Bobby Thompson. "As for violence," the director says, "that's a part of life. People say movies cause violence, but it's the other way around. Violence causes movies. Art imitates life, life doesn't imitate art. I didn't make up the story of the sniper. The sniper who shot those people in Central Park had pictures of Hitler and Goebbels, not movie stars" (Stone, September 15, 1968).

Let us examine this sequence in detail. As mentioned earlier, it is here that the separate worlds of make-believe and reality converge. This occurs when Bobby, disclosed to be behind the screen, is confronted by Orlock, who advances toward him in a sequence which parallels the one in *The Terror* being projected on the screen at that very moment. Bobby is confused because he sees converging on him from one point and from another the double Karloff/Orlock figures. The two images get mixed up in his mind, and they become delirium. Bobby shoots at the wrong Orlock, giving the real Orlock a chance to knock the gun out of his hand with his cane. It is interesting to note that Karloff's gesture here makes him assume the aspect of father, a motif which will be amply repeated in *The Last Picture Show*. As Bobby cowers in the corner like a small child, Orlock, aghast, remarks, "Is *this* what I was afraid of?"

Although it is evident that Orlock's discovery about what the future of society holds has deeply scarred him, we the viewing audience can at the same time see the point that Bogdanovich is making here. Despite the fact that reality has become violent and ugly, movies are still more powerful and superior to the prevailing plastic culture because *they* appeal to the imagination.

The fact that such a statement is made at a drive-in— another staple of the cultureless society—is central to understanding it. Bogdanovich abhors this typically American convention even more than television. "Film is a public event," he contends.

Unfortunately, we're moving more and more toward a kind of insular society. I hate the whole idea of seeing a movie in a drive-in. That's almost as alienating as seeing it on television. You're closed off in a car, with a horrible screen you can't see very well. Awful sound in that tinny little speaker. Sitting with two other people. It's as bad as being at home with television. It's true that you go out, but you never have to get out of your car. Horrible. (McCluskey, pp. 82–83)

But besides the damage to the aesthetic experience of watching a film, there is a strong societal implication: "Cars are so solitary and insular. The people at the drive-in are all sitting in these enclosed little cubicles where they're not aware of the killings going on outside. The main point of that sequence was *Go to a drive-in on pain of death.*" In short, the spectators at the drive-in are denying themselves the right to communicate, the right to a shared experience, and thus, Bogdanovich feels, they should be punished in

Devastation at the drive-in.

some way. After all, in a regular movie house it would be impossible for someone to hide behind the screen—or anywhere else in the auditorium, provided that it was filled to capacity. Granted, the punishment to which they are subjected is more than a little extreme, and Bogdanovich's position is clearly an immature one, resulting from an enthusiastic overestimation of the cinema. He will readjust his evaluation in subsequent works.

The final drive-in sequence, in addition to being a summary of the film's themes, is perhaps more importantly a tour de force in filming action (some 380 shots in 20 minutes), which in its own way comes just as close as the make-believe vs. reality principle to capturing the true spirit of Hitchcock. Indeed, Bogdanovich, at Corman's insistence, decided to adopt the Master's technique for shooting suspense sequences early on.

> I learned about planning *and* winging it mostly when I made *Targets* because it had to be made very quickly. Ultimately, it took twenty-five days; originally, it was supposed to take fifteen. Because it was my first picture, and because it had a very tight budget, Corman said to me, "You know about directors: Hitchcock plans everything out on paper, Hawks doesn't. Well, on this picture, please be Hitchcock. Plan it out because you'll go faster. If you know exactly what your shots are, there won't be any time wasted. When you finish one shot, you won't say, 'Let me think,' because if you add up the times you say, 'Let me think,' you'll find it's cost you days. The minute a shot is over, know where the next shot is." Every shot was planned out on paper. I wrote down in the most Germanic way—shot by shot—everything, every cut, in fact wrote much of it into the script. The whole drive-in sequence was as written, with minor changes when I was cutting the film. Not only did I know what the shots would look like, but I went to the location with the cameraman before we started shooting and said, "Now, here's the first shot. Then we move over here. Then we go here," so he knew exactly what everything was going to be so

that we could move fast. Now, the drive-in sequence, even though we planned it, was difficult to shoot because we didn't have the cars there when we were planning it. So really I was winging it while we were shooting. But I was winging it very fast, and it was all just coming to me. I'd finish one shot and, "we're over here. Okay. Cut. Now we're over here. And now we're through this window," and it was all in my head. I wasn't thinking about what I'd written down and I thought, "Well, you see that wasn't so bad." So I wondered why I'd planned it so damned much because I actually *hated* planning it. It took some of the fun out of it. (McCluskey, pp. 16–17)

Although the sequence is Hitchcockian in execution (and also, as Barry Putterman notes, reminiscent of the "anarchic spirit of Raoul Walsh's climax to *White Heat*, 1949"), it is Howard Hawks who complimented the young Bogdanovich for his audaciousness: "That stuff was good and that stuff's hard to do." Nevertheless, Bogdanovich would not attempt another comparable technical feat for five years (the chase in *What's Up, Doc?*). The extensive planning he employed in *Targets* turned out to have a permanent effect on his method of filming. To this day he shoots only a minimum of footage, having worked out the camera setups the night before. This procedure links him further to the veteran directors he admires, particularly Ford, Welles, Hawks, Preminger, and, of course, Hitchcock. He never shoots masters unless the entire scene will be played out in the master in the finished film, and will cover a scene with another angle only when he feels it isn't playing well. He is therefore opposed to triple-take filming for its own sake. "It's really a question of making the decision on the set as opposed to making it in the cutting room. Now, many directors will say, 'Let's shoot it because we *might* need it.' I don't like to do that . . . because it's footage we're never gonna use" (McCluskey, p. 34).

He also emphasizes something else he learned from Hitchcock, who always insisted that you have a point of view in the scene. That's really important to remember when you're directing, because it's going to affect everything—the framing, the size of your image, what you're showing and when. And it helps to tell a story because it puts the viewer into somebody's place. Unfortunately, most pictures don't have a point of view in scenes; they just have shots. ("Dialogue on Film," April 1986)

The Hitchcock influence is present throughout the picture. The scene where Bobby murders his family members recalls the sequence immediately following the shower murder in *Psycho*. After Bobby exits the house, the camera tracks along the carpet, where the murders have taken place. This recalls Hitchcock's surveying the corpse of Marion Crane and, briefly, the belongings in her room. Bogdanovich:

> The *Psycho* one wasn't conscious. Although the cleanliness idea was the same, it's not really done in the same way. Perkins is much more thorough than my boy. The sequence in *Psycho* is phenomenally brilliant, and I don't particularly like the scene in *Targets*. It came out of something that the Whitman boy really did in Texas. He put his wife and mother to bed after he killed them. I thought it was a chilling touch, so I used it in the film. He buried them, so to speak. The cleaning-up was just carrying that out. If I had thought of *Psycho*, the sequence might have been a little better. (Sherman and Rubin, p. 90)

Bogdanovich also indicts the viewer by forcing him to look through the viewfinder with Bobby and thereby vicariously participate in (and share the blame for) the killings of innocent people. As Renata Adler remarked in the *New York Times*, the tragedy of the whole affair is that "one does not want [Bobby] to miss" (September 7, 1968). This technique recalls *Rear Window* (1954), in which the viewer's perspective was limited to that of voyeur L. B. Jefferies (James Stewart). It is interesting to note, however, that in *Targets* Bobby does not engage in even a moment of introspection, and in the end abandons his "game" only because he is caught. On the other hand, Jefferies questions the ethics of his behavior at least once—although his ultimate reformation remains ambiguous. The one other obvious nod to the Master occurs at the moment in the drive-in sequence where Bobby tries to retrieve his dropped ammunition behind the movie screen—this is reminiscent of Bruno (Robert Walker) reaching into a drain for the dropped cigarette lighter in *Strangers on a Train* (1951). Bogdanovich:

> The *Strangers* reference wasn't conscious either. When I saw the footage, I realized what I had done, but not while I was shooting. The most fascinating thing is that it was all subconscious. Of course, *all* that drive-in sequence is *Strangers*: timing, dusk, music. I didn't know that at the time. About three months later, I saw *Strangers* again and said, "Jesus Christ! Look at this!" However, I made some references consciously. For example, there's a shot from the top of the tank as the boy runs away—I pan from the stuff he left behind over to him running. That's from *North by Northwest*, when Cary Grant runs out of the U.N.—a shot I've always loved—but I didn't want any of these shots to seem self-conscious. Hitchcock doesn't have any arty shots. They may be odd, but they're always done for an emotional, not an artistic, effect. (Sherman and Rubin, p. 91)

Also Hitchcockian is the conspicuous absence of dialogue throughout much of the film, particularly the scenes involving Bobby. As Bogdanovich puts it, "Film is a visual medium. You want to convey as much as you can visually. But words are very important, and I think there's a way to have dialogue in pictures and still have movies be a visual medium. Dialogue is very important, as long as it's not just

people talking. And sometimes people just talking is
fascinating" (McCluskey, p. 4). A good example of this is
the lengthy speech Karloff delivers midway through the
film. But despite these obvious connections, as Sherman
and Rubin point out, the comparisons are, as Bogdanovich
said, largely superficial:

> Some of the plot constructions and cutting in *Targets*,
> together with surface echoes of *North by Northwest*, *Strangers
> on a Train*, and *Psycho*, have caused critics to label the film
> "Hitchcockian" (a catch-all label which seems to be applied
> to any film involving murder and suspense these days). This
> interpretation is based mainly on the freeway murder
> scenes, which have been said to convey therapeutic audience
> identification in the manner of The Master. The parallel
> only partially holds up. In *Targets* the feeling inspired by
> glimpses through the telescopic mount and huge close-ups
> of the boy's hands and rifle seems to be mostly one of a
> detached, clinical admiration for the precise mechanics of
> lining up the sights and pulling the trigger, rather than the
> tremendous emotional-moral involvement and therapeutic
> shock which is registered by an analogous shot of Raymond
> Burr *directly* confronting the audience through James
> Stewart's field-glasses in *Rear Window*. Rather than involving
> us in an irresistible fascination with guilt and psychological
> darkness, as Hitchcock does, Bogdanovich fashions his
> moral statement by utilizing our interest in observing a job
> well done. Throughout *Targets* neither the action nor the
> images indicate that Bogdanovich is primarily interested in
> the psychological depth which films like *Vertigo* and *Psycho*
> convey. (pp. 76–77)

The two authors have also crystallized the essence of
Bogdanovich's emergent visual style and depiction of
character better than anyone else:

> Even though *Targets* is closer to Hitchcock than are *The Bride
> Wore Black* (Truffaut, 1968), *Rosemary's Baby* (Polanski,
> 1969), *Wait Until Dark* (Terence Young, 1967), and other

such pallid imitations, Bogdanovich's visual style seems much more influenced by Hawks. The flat visual surfaces of the shots in *Targets* reflect the equal geometric dispersion of the elements in one of Hawks' classical compositions, which unite foreground and background, action and setting, with equal depth into a single spacial whole. In each case, the unification of the elements of the shot into a single texture is used to express a direct, continuous tension between these elements, particularly characters and environment. The difference in the visual styles of Hawks and Bogdanovich is one of emphasis, as well as depth and experience. In Hawks, the outer environment is abstract (either a nihilistic, black void that surrounds the characters in, for example, *Only Angels Have Wings* and *To Have and Have Not*, or the chaotic patterns of the large-scale action—the airplane battles in *The Dawn Patrol* and the racing scenes in *Red Line 7000*), and the characters are concrete. In *Targets*, on the other hand, the environment is concrete (the plastic society) and the characters are abstract (a collection of types and surfaces). In other words, the dominant details in *Targets* are realized not in the characterizations but in the settings. Many of the characters slip the mind, but we remember the drive-in, the suburban homes, the projection room, the shooting range, the oil tanks. Bogdanovich is interested in his characters' behavioral patterns as an outgrowth of their society, while Hawks follows his characters' response to (and against) their surroundings, which takes the form of moral codes and desperate ethics. Accordingly, Bogdanovich's compositions lack the tension of Hawks'. In this way, Bogdanovich is able to present his social angle in cinematic rather than sociological terms. Thus, of necessity, he sacrifices some of Hawks' universality—settings (or social milieu) date more easily than characters. (pp. 77–78)

Bogdanovich's utilizing Hitchcock's traditional themes and techniques in this, his first film, deserves at least some comparison with the approaches of two other disciples of the Master—Stanley Donen and Brian DePalma (the former a temporary admirer, having made two features in

Sammy (Peter Bogdanovich) arrives on the scene as the shooting reaches a climax.

the Hitchcock vein, *Charade*, 1963, and *Arabesque*, 1966; the latter a permanent one). In his essay on Donen in *American Directors*, Jean-Pierre Coursodon terms *Charade* "perhaps the most deliberately derivative picture ever made in the Master's spirit until Brian DePalma's *Obsession* (1976) [Donen naturally leans toward the Hitchcock of *North by Northwest*, 1959, DePalma toward that of *Vertigo*, 1958], yet the work of a talented admirer" (p. 106).

Whereas Donen's film is "derivative" in the sense that it utilizes situations and tries to stage sequences in the same manner as Hitchcock, it never stoops to the level of *Obsession*, which unabashedly filches Bernard Herrmann's score from *Vertigo* (among other elements from that film) practically verbatim. Note that at the time of *Charade* Donen could have enlisted the aid of Ernest Lehman, scenarist of *North by Northwest*, but instead chose playwright

Peter Stone. It would seem that Bogdanovich has more in common with Donen, since *Targets* can stand up as an original genre piece which does not depend upon an understanding of its debt to Hitchcock (though such knowledge certainly can enhance the experience of viewing the film) for an appreciation of its contents. The various autobiographical references in the film to Karloff and Bogdanovich are, however, irritatingly alienating to the uninitiated.

This issue of references points to a motif central to an understanding of Bogdanovich's handling of genre, which will resurface in his subsequent works, specifically *What's Up, Doc?* (1972): the dichotomy between the films' primary audiences—ordinary moviegoers and film buffs—and their ability to appreciate them simultaneously. We shall see that as the choice of subject matter becomes more specialized and personal, the former faction will dwindle in size, while the latter will increase substantially to the point where, by the time of *At Long Last Love*, the film can *only* be appreciated on an academic level, if even there, and therefore loses its biggest audience. In the case of *Targets*, however, there is still sufficient distance between Bogdanovich and his material to ensure a balance between the two. He stated after the film's release that it was merely an assignment, not something he would have gone out of his way to do, although he did the best he could under the circumstances. Nevertheless, those coming to the picture cold may find it to be a very strange experience, being unable to recognize many of the in-jokes and other asides.

There are other flaws in *Targets* also. Probably the most obvious shortcoming is, despite the fact that Bogdanovich made clever use of the limited resources at his disposal, the low budget does show, and most of the film has a fairly sickly and depressing look to it, in spite of the flashiness of Kovacs' photography. This is considerably more distressing than it would normally be, since the subject matter is so disturbing already—in this respect, black and white would have worked better. Although it pokes fun at *The Terror*, the truth of the matter is that in terms of production values, *Targets* isn't terribly far ahead of Corman's cheapie. This really can't be blamed on Bogdanovich, of course, but it works against the picture nevertheless.

The performances aren't a lot better—although, considering the fact that Karloff and Bogdanovich are really playing themselves, one is not left with much room for criticism. Bogdanovich's young director is amiable enough, and the worshipful attitude he exhibits toward Karloff is occasionally touching, but one still wishes he had been daring enough to endow his Sammy with some of the pretentiousness which he in real life despised in the new generation of directors, such as Kubrick. Bogdanovich would later comment on the difficulties of a director directing himself, a feat he did not attempt again until *Saint Jack* in 1979.

Tim O'Kelly's sniper remains a cipher—a being for whom it is difficult to generate any interest, negative or positive (despite the fact that he's good enough in the part)—although we are relieved when he is apprehended at the end, mainly because the idea of someone's shooting innocent people is basically repugnant to us. The character of Jenny, Orlock's Asian secretary with whom Sammy Michaels is in love, was suggested by one of Bogdanovich's friends, director Sam Fuller. Although not a stereotype, her character doesn't prove to be very exciting, either. Bogdanovich realized the shortcomings in his cast here, and vowed that in his next feature the emphasis would be on performances. That film, of course, turned out to be *The Last Picture Show*, which received Academy Awards for Best Supporting Actor (Ben Johnson) and Supporting Actress (Cloris Leachman), among several other nominations.

Karloff remains the real center of interest in *Targets*. For perhaps the first time in his more than thirty-year-long

Bobby confuses reality with fantasy and shoots at the wrong Orlock.

career, he was allowed to play a real person, with heart and depth, and one must be grateful to Bogdanovich (as Karloff was) for giving him that opportunity. The fact that Karloff passed away on February 2, 1969, shortly after the release of *Targets*, is further evidence of the fatalism which has haunted Bogdanovich's entire career, and which is echoed in Orlock's speech and also in Bogdanovich's managing to interview (and deify) the veteran directors he admired (Ford, Hawks, Hitchcock, Welles, and Lang)—many of whom had never received serious attention before—just a short while before their deaths.

The most memorable and important aspect of *Targets* is surely Bogdanovich's direction; he also edited the picture himself. Although, as Hawks has said, the camerawork in the Karloff episodes tends to be a bit self-conscious at times (at one point there is a transitional cut from the end table in Karloff's living room to the one in the Thompson household)—Bogdanovich: "I tried very much not to cut on moves or subject matter the way Brooks did in *In Cold Blood* [1967]. . . . If I had it to do again, I'd cut the pan" (Sherman and Rubin, pp. 89–90)—on the whole the film evidences an unusual audaciousness and a firm and secure handling, particularly, as mentioned before, in the action sequence at the drive-in. But even here, as Barry Putterman suggests, there are reservations: "The film is a bit too awkward in all of its components to really come together properly." The often stiff and rigid pans and tracking shots seem a far cry from the incredibly subtle precision in *The Last Picture Show*, made just three years later and without benefit of additional practice with the camera (Bogdanovich's transitional project was a documentary, *Directed by John Ford*, in which a stationary camera photographed interviews with Ford and those who worked with him). The difference in stylistic achievement between *Targets* and *Last Picture Show* no doubt stems in part from the higher budget on the latter picture ($1.3 million vs. $125,000) and the fact that it allowed Bogdanovich to work with more sophisticated equipment (such as a Panavision camera). However, as he himself would state in 1973 shortly after the completion of *Paper Moon*, the faults in the direction were largely irrespective of such considerations: "I feel [that *Last Picture Show* and *What's Up, Doc?*] have a certain firmness and sureness about the direction that one's first picture probably can't have" (McCluskey, p. 20).

In this respect it is illuminating to compare Bogdanovich's initial period to that of Stanley Kubrick, one of his contemporaries. While the camerawork in Kubrick's first two features, *Killer's Kiss* (1955) and *The Killing* (1956—he disowns his first feature, 1953's *Fear and Desire*, and has kept it out of circulation) is self-conscious also, there is a miraculous growth of maturity between those films and the one many critics still consider to be Kubrick's masterpiece, *Paths of Glory*—made just a short time later in

1957. The elaborate tracking shots through the trenches in that film are most often cited as being exemplary. Likewise, *The Last Picture Show* (1971), with its beautifully intricate and invisible camerawork, is generally considered to be the high point for Bogdanovich.

In conclusion, *Targets*, despite its shortcomings, remains a fascinating debut picture. Unfortunately, because of its untimely appearance on American screens, it was quickly shelved by Paramount, its distributor, upon its release, and today is only very rarely shown in revival houses. It is, however, available for rental on 16mm from Films Incorporated and on Paramount videocassette. Bogdanovich: "It's very funny that there are 3,000 cassettes out there, when Paramount only made 8 prints of the picture originally."

Targets marked the beginning of many good things for Bogdanovich, not the least of which was his collaboration with expert editor Verna Fields (1918-1982), here credited as "sound effects editor." She would contribute heavily to the impact of three later Bogdanovich films, *What's Up, Doc?* (1972), *Paper Moon* (1973), and *Daisy Miller* (1974). The film was to be Bogdanovich's last link with present-day America for a while. In the meantime, he would turn to the cinema of the past and its creators for inspiration, continuing to work within established genres.

2   *Directed by John Ford* (1971)

Upon publication of his book *John Ford* for the University of California Press in 1968, and following the release of his first feature, *Targets*, Bogdanovich was asked by the newly founded American Film Institute if he would be interested in putting together a feature-length documentary on the subject of his book for what was to have been the first in a series of films on veteran American directors financed by the California Arts Commission. Regrettably, the series never came to fruition, and all of the other likely candidates died within the next 15 years.

Bogdanovich had already directed an interview with Howard Hawks for a BBC television documentary called *The Great Professional*, which aired in 1967. This time, however, he would write the narration and select the film clips as well—which entailed more responsibility since the Hawks special had been only an hour in length; this new venture would be approximately 90 minutes. The interview segments for the Ford documentary would also be shot in color, in contrast to Hawks', in which even the clips from such films as *Rio Bravo, Hatari!*, and *El Dorado* had been shown in black and white. The interviews (with Ford regulars John Wayne, Henry Fonda, and James Stewart, and with Ford himself) were shot in 1968–1969, and the final film released in 1971 at the New York Film Festival, concurrent with the wide release of Bogdanovich's first major feature, *The Last Picture Show*.

It is a testament to Bogdanovich's ingratiating manner that he was able to persuade Ford, who abhorred talking about his work, not only to comply with a book-length interview but to appear on camera to discuss some of the interesting scenes in his enormous canon of films. Even so, getting the old man (Ford was about 75 then) to open up was more than a little difficult at first, as illustrated by his answers to Bogdanovich's first few rather pedantic questions. Bogdanovich: "Mr. Ford, you made a picture called *Three Bad Men* that had a rather elaborate land rush in it. How did you shoot that?" Ford: "With a camera." Bogdanovich: "What aspect of the western most appeals to you?" Ford: "I wouldn't know." Bogdanovich: "I've noticed that your view of the West has become increasingly sad and melancholy over the years. I'm comparing, for instance, *Wagonmaster* to *The Man Who Shot Liberty Valance.* Have you been aware of this change in mood?" Ford: "I don't know what you're talking about." Bogdanovich: "Would you say that the point of *Fort Apache* was that the survival of the individual was more important than that of the Army?" Ford: "Cut!" It took a good deal of selflessness on Bogdanovich's part to include these responses—obviously he was more concerned with making sure his audience got an accurate impression of Ford than with worrying about how he as interviewer would be perceived.

Eventually, however, Ford warmed up to the project, and his subsequent reminiscences resolved themselves into a series of nonintellectual anecdotes about his experiences making films over a career spanning more than 50 years. He relates how Carl Laemmle, Jr., of Universal gave him his first directorial assignment (*Straight Shooting*, 1917), after observing him work as an assistant on another silent. "That Jack Ford yells pretty loud. He'd make a good director," is what Laemmle said, according to Ford. He recalls the time when, during the location shooting in Monument Valley (where the interview with Ford takes place, incidentally) of *She Wore a Yellow Ribbon* (1949) a tremendous thunderstorm suddenly erupted, and how he

Bogdanovich talks with John Ford (*seated*) at Monument Valley location.
(Courtesy of The Museum of Modern Art/Film Stills Archive)

insisted, against the cameraman's wishes, that they take
advantage of the situation. Ford notes that ironically the
cameraman won the Academy Award the following year
for his work on the film.

Ford also briefly describes his working methods—how
he prefers to rehearse a scene thoroughly with the camera
and then get it perfect on the first take, so the actors'
energy will be at a maximum. He unabashedly concedes
that a lot of the success in making pictures is pure luck, and
that "more often you have bad luck."

Comprising a greater part of the running time are the
interviews with the three Ford veterans: Wayne, Fonda,
and Stewart. Bogdanovich introduces each appropriately
with clips from their most memorable Ford films (or, in the
case of Stewart, who worked for Ford on only three
occasions, all of them) and then crosscuts between their

reminiscences and the illustrative excerpts. All three note the rather startling contrast between the two sides of Ford's personality: his irascibility and his essentially gentle nature, which the former masked.

Wayne and Stewart recall candidly and with bemusement their initial shock upon first finding themselves at "the bottom of Ford's list," as Stewart puts it, referring to a rather inexplicable tendency of the director to single out and embarrass a certain individual on an almost daily basis by asking him a question and then twisting his response into an insult against someone or something Ford held sacred. Richard Schickel's guess that it may have been due to Ford's alcoholism—he was known to depart regularly for a drinking binge on his boat immediately upon completion of a film—in his article on Ford in *Schickel on Film* (pp 37–59) is probably correct. This happened to Wayne on *Stagecoach* in 1939 and to Stewart on *The Man Who Shot Liberty Valance* in 1962. Fonda also describes the almost childlike naivete exhibited by Ford when he "shamed" him into playing Abraham Lincoln by using every profanity in the book. "What's all this [blankety-blank-blank] about you not wanting to play Lincoln?" was how Fonda was introduced to the great man in 1939 before production began on *Young Mr. Lincoln*—obviously Fonda, by initially refusing the part, was insulting one of Ford's boyhood heroes.

Wayne's first meeting with the director (during the shooting of the silent *Mother Machree* in 1928) had a similarly harsh feeling to it. Ford had recruited him to be a gooseherder on his picture after hearing he played football at the University of Southern California, and at one point asked Wayne to get down on his knees, at which time Ford kicked him so hard that he landed facedown in the mud. "It wasn't the sod of Old Ireland, and it really hurt," Wayne says.

Despite these incidents (which are related without a trace of bitterness on the part of any of the men—they recognize it as simply "part of Ford's nature," as Stewart says), all three display at length their respect for Ford's artistry and their affection (albeit a grudging one) for him personally and their admirable insight into the necessities for his working methods and their effect on audience response to the stories. Wayne recalls Ford's insistence that he (playing retiring captain Nathan Brittles) somewhat ashamedly don a pair of spectacles to read the inscription on the watch given to him by his men as a farewell gift in *She Wore a Yellow Ribbon* in order to cut down on the inherent sentimentality of the scene.

Fonda reveals that his balancing on the chair in *My Darling Clementine* (1946) was something suggested to him just before shooting by Ford, and became "a bit of business that everybody remembers and comments about." He also relates touchingly how, after the day's work was finished and everyone (cast and crew—the Ford "family") was gathered around a campfire for supper, Ford would send a lone man off into the woods to blow taps, and that at the sound "people would cry—it was that moving."

Stewart says that Ford "dares you to do things right," and that this instilled in him a great desire to please him—so much so that when Ford bestowed a rare compliment upon him for improvising a yawn during a scene in *Two Rode Together* (1961), it "meant a great deal to me." And Wayne (who, Stewart remarks, was like a son to Ford, because of their long and fruitful association) recalls fondly how the director "keeps you on your toes when you're not the most important actor in a scene, but then handles you like a baby when your turn comes up." All three agree that Ford liked a sparsity of words, preferring to convey as much as possible visually, and that he would often tear whole pages from the script if he found it unsatisfactory.

These interviews take up approximately half of the documentary's running time. The remainder constitutes Bogdanovich the scholar's evaluation of Ford's oeuvre (interspersed with illustrative clips as before)—which, as

Bogdanovich (*far right*), John Wayne (*far left*), and cinematographer Laszlo Kovacs (*center*) prepare to shoot Wayne's interview. (Courtesy of The Museum of Modern Art/Film Stills Archive)

narrator Orson Welles points out, is not comprised of "135 individual films, but rather is a body of work that can stand with the singular achievement of a great artist or poet." Bogdanovich stresses recurring motifs—mainly that of the individual silhouetted against the background of history, glorious in defeat—and notes Ford's recurrent use of composer Alfred Newman's Ann Rutledge theme from *Young Mr. Lincoln* in a similar scene from *The Man Who Shot Liberty Valance* in order to illustrate how Ford uses music to convey the underlying emotions of his characters.

Bogdanovich also observes that Ford's visual style was characterized in the 1930s and 1940s by a certain "duality, varying between a conscious pictorialism and a more natural simplicity," and that the two were memorably combined in 1948's *Fort Apache*. He says that although *The Informer* (1935), one of Ford's most famous films, is a work of "considerable artistry," it "nevertheless belongs to a tradition of studio atmosphere." Bogdanovich argues that Ford's most personal and important works (those made after World War II) were shot on real locations like Monument Valley—films like *Rio Grande* (1950).

The final 30 minutes consists of a montage of clips from approximately 20 Ford films, from *The Iron Horse* (1924) through *Cheyenne Autumn* (1964), which are arranged chronologically according to their historical setting (covering an almost 200-year time span, from 1775 through 1950), in order to show how Ford's work is a reflection of his country's growth. But finally, Bogdanovich argues that it is "not the concentration on Americana, but rather his singular poetic vision" which distinguishes Ford's films from those of all other American directors. Indeed, as he shows us by having his camera scan the den of Ford's home at the outset, Ford is America's most honored filmmaker, with six Oscars and four New York Film Critics Awards, among his many other honors from around the world.

The core of the criticism that has been leveled against the documentary probably has most to do with this final lengthy segment, consisting entirely of clips without commentary. John Baxter, author of a brief survey of Bogdanovich's work in *The International Directory of Films and Filmmakers*, describes the whole enterprise as being characterized by "uncertain scholarship." He is most likely referring to the imbalance between criticism/interpretation and anecdotes giving glimpses of the director's personality—the latter seem to comprise the bulk of the effort.

As is typical of Bogdanovich, he had already anticipated such a statement when he wrote in his study of Ford that "neither this book nor my TV documentary can even begin to do justice to what Ford has accomplished in terms of film history and art." Surely, to unearth and detail properly the innumerable complexities of Ford's work would take several lengthy volumes (and quite a number have already been published), or a six-hour film. Ford's canon is surely the largest of any American director—approximately 140 features in all—though unfortunately, as Bogdanovich points out in his book, the majority of his silent films have been irretrievably lost, so we are left with his sound pictures, about 60 in all, many of which are unanimously considered cinema masterpieces.

Bogdanovich has described himself on numerous occasions as more of a "popularizer" than a critic. "I was never much good at theorizing or at analyzing in depth the hidden symbolism or sociological significance of the pictues I liked. The best I've ever been able to do—and not at all as well as I'd hoped—has been to try to pass on my passions and enthusiasms with some semblance of intelligence," he wrote in *Pieces of Time*. His approach—and one which, incidentally, is the only valid one for critiquing the work of any important filmmaker—consists of linking the director's personality with his films, in order to illustrate their perfect compatibility.

Despite his avowed stance, however, Bogdanovich in this film—as well as in his book on Ford and monographs on other major American directors—reveals himself to have a certain undeniable critical acumen. But because he uses only a handful of examples to back up his points, as compared to the great number at his disposal, his statements about Ford's visual style and his themes are left dangling somewhat, and therefore seem vaguely unsatisfactory—even somewhat pompous. Although he states in his book, for example, that *The Searchers* (1956) is Ford's best work, he says nothing about it in the documentary, except to use its famous beginning and end moments to lend a framework to his film (the door of the farmhouse opens and closes on Ford's world)—a rather inventive if perhaps specious device.

Although Bogdanovich wisely devotes a good portion of the film to illustrative clips from Ford's many great works, allowing them to speak for themselves, and his selection of excerpts is well chosen—encompassing 27 films in all—many would quibble with his devaluing the importance of such Ford "prestige" pictures as *Stagecoach, Grapes of Wrath* (1940), and *How Green Was My Valley* (1941—there is not even a clip from this film in the concluding segment) in favor of the director's later work, which no one can argue is not more personal, but most feel is decidedly more labored.

But if one chooses to quibble about such matters, two important factors must be kept in mind. First, there are the limitations of space in a 90-minute film; inevitably, one *must* be choosy, and therefore end up omitting things which would have been included if more time and a larger budget had been allotted. It must also be noted that in fashioning a work which, after all, was intended for consumption not just by film buffs but by the less well informed but nevertheless interested public, Bogdanovich was forced to limit himself to those points which were readily apparent in short clips, not dependent upon some prior intimate knowledge of other unseen works on the part of the spectator.

Because of the overwhelming ratio of anecdotal information to critical insight (about 2 to 1), Bogdanovich might have been better off avoiding making statements about Ford's visual style, for example, since they seem somewhat out of place here. The recollections by the three stars—and by Ford, whose only taped interview this was—are invaluable, however, and reveal the true position of Bogdanovich with regard to the cinema of Ford—more a popularizer than a critic in the strict sense of the word, as he says. Incidentally, a discerning viewer might take note of the fact that in Stewart's segments, there is no evidence of retakes or splicing, as there is in those involving the other two stars and Ford—important evidence of Stewart's sharpness and sureness as a storyteller, in contrast to the somewhat patronizing image of him as an uncontrollable stutterer which many impersonators have perpetuated.

Perhaps the most impressive quality of *Directed by John Ford* is that even though it is a documentary in the strict sense of the word, it displays an unusual warmth throughout. Bogdanovich as interviewer is usually visible in the frame, and one can sense his boyish enthusiasm for the tradition which the men he is questioning represent. It is also a surprisingly personal work for Bogdanovich, allowing him to illustrate for the viewer his favorite moments in the career of Ford—and thereby allow him to see where some of the inspiration for the best moments in Bogdanovich's own subsequent films came from. Vittorio Giacci has described the enterprise best:

> It is much more than a documentary. It is the prototype of one method of making film criticism which is, in itself, film, such as happens with the best of literary criticism, which similarly can become poetry. It is the moment for the work of the critic to be synthesized with the work of the director into an experience which contains them to their mutual enrichment and is the testimony of love for a great

filmmaker toward the end of his life [Ford died on August 31, 1973] tendered by a young author aspiring to collect the master's teachings before turning out his own most beautiful film, *The Last Picture Show*. (p. 70)

Unfortunately, despite the quality of the work, it remains something of an obscurity—though it is available for rental on 16mm and pops up occasionally on PBS stations thoughout the country.

3   *The Last Picture Show* (1971)

As I pointed out earlier in this study, Bogdanovich's films through *Nickelodeon* were forged from his remembrances of his moviegoing past. Despite the present-day setting of *Targets*, the reader will recall that the director's statement about the degeneration of society was implicitly tied to the corresponding disappearance of the traditional movie-going experience. Like Hawks throughout his career, Bogdanovich during this initial phase had no desire to make statements about the times in which he was living—"It's hard to find a present-day topic that doesn't date immediately," he said. He simply desired to entertain us in the manner of the veteran directors he admired, with films which he hoped would evidence the same spirit. For that reason I see no cause to judge *The Last Picture Show*—the best of the lot, and certainly a seminal work—as a treatise on the decline of American society in the 1950s per se, but rather only with regard to how that decline relates to the American cinema and its history.

What James Harvey has said about Hawks applies to a great degree to his disciple Bogdanovich also (and not just to the latter's pre–*Saint Jack* pictures either, though the impulse was more obvious there): "He is involved in just those aspects of the conventional movie experience that seem most magical. In a way, his whole career is an exploration of that magic—*as* magic, and not something to be explained away." Harvey quotes Godard: "One sees in Hawks an increasingly precise taste for analysis, a love for this artificial grandeur connected to movements of the eyes, to a way of walking, in short a greater awareness than anyone else of what the cinema can glory in . . . through a rigorous knowledge of its limits, fixing its basic laws" (Sherman and Rubin, p. 90).

If, as Vittorio Giacci argues, Bogdanovich's early films are primarily concerned with that "heady fascination which binds the spectator to the image," then *The Last Picture Show* can surely be considered his most profound exploration of that connection. "Rarely has a filmmaker been so elaborately defined by his own self-perceptions," writes David Wilson, referring to the unusual degree of directorial self-consciousness which Bogdanovich showed in his writings. The director's initial attraction to Larry McMurtry's novel about the death of a small Texas community in the early 1950s provided only further evidence of this. "It was the title," he told Paul McCluskey. "Doesn't it sound like the kind of title I should make a movie out of?" (p. 64).

With this film Bogdanovich continued to explore the ties between the cinema and life which he had forged in *Targets*. However, for this and the five pictures to follow he was to turn his attention to the past, the literal past in every case except *What's Up, Doc?*, which technically took place in contemporary San Francisco but which in actuality had nothing to do with present-day reality, only with the movie past—Bogdanovich's movie past.

In *Targets*, set in contemporary (1968) Los Angeles, Bogdanovich chronicled the unsavory results of the decline of American society—in particular the dominance of the two most hideous staples of the insular society: the drive-in theater and television. With *The Last Picture Show* (set in 1951 Texas), he turns back the clock to recapitulate the historical moment of transition from a rustic farm society to an industrial one (represented by the closing of the town's picture show, the Royal), with the resulting demise of the earlier culture in the process of a general vulgarization caused by the banal models of the burgeoning consumer society—television being foremost among them. Roger Ebert, in his review of the film in his *Movie Home Companion,* has captured better than anyone else what that transition meant to millions of Americans who had grown up with the local movie house:

> There was something about going to the movies in the 1950s that will never be the same again. It was the decade of the last gasp of the great American movie-going habit, and before my eyes in the middle 1950s the Saturday kiddie matinee died a lingering death at the Princess Theater on Main Street in Urbana. For five or six years of my life (the years between when I was old enough to go alone, and when TV came to town), Saturday afternoon at the Princess was a descent into a dark magical cave that smelled of Jujubes, melted Dreamsicles, and Crisco in the popcorn machine.

Sam the Lion (Ben Johnson) with Sonny (Timothy Bottoms) and Billy (Sam Bottoms) in the café.

The Princess was jammed to the walls with kids every Saturday afternoon, as it had been for years, but then TV came to town and within a year the Princess was no longer an institution. It survived into the early 1960s and then closed, to be reborn a few years later as the Cinema. The metallic taste of that word, cinema, explains what happened when you put it alongside the name "Princess."

Bogdanovich believes that the 1950s marked the demise of the golden age of moviemaking in America. With *The Last Picture Show* (as well as his next few films) he sought to restore the beauty of the cinema, so that his movie might be considered an act of love and remembrance for a long-forgotten tradition. Like *Paper Moon* and *Daisy Miller* which followed it, *Picture Show* is a period drama, a scrupulous recapturing of a time and place characterized by a critical examination of America's cinematic past (though this last factor is certainly much more true in the case of *Picture Show*).

The Last Picture Show is the means for recognizing a certain period. Bogdanovich: "The main thing that interested me (at first) was the period of the early fifties, because I had lived through it at an impressionable age. The reconstruction of the period through television, songs, movies, interested me a lot" (McCluskey, pp. 64–65). In order to develop the feeling of Anarene (the name of the fictional Texas town where the story takes place), Bogdanovich and company

> went down there and found out what the people were like. It's what the Germans call *Stimmung*, what the French call *milieu*—it's a kind of atmosphere. You get a feeling for it, and then you try to convey it. . . . I was very Germanic about researching the period elements [one must single out production designer Polly Platt's obsessive attention to detail]. The actors were good—I had them spend a good two weeks with the people down there before we started to shoot so they picked up many things from their contact.

The director offers a particularly astute explanation of what makes a good period film—one which will be of concern in the chapters on *Paper Moon, Daisy Miller, At Long Last Love, Nickelodeon,* and even *Saint Jack,* despite its contemporary setting:

> I think it's important that the story exist within a certain period and therefore the evocation of that period is simply part of the story. . . . It's a question of steeping yourself in the period and then letting it seep out on the screen. . . . If the period is imposed on the story, then you're not going to make a very good movie. Anybody can get the right clothes and the right cars and so on; it's a question of the characters: they must exist in that period because they *have* to. Then the period becomes another character in the story. (Denby, B. J., p. 78)

Despite the amazing stamp of authenticity which Bogdanovich and his production team managed to give to the film, there is an important point to remember here, one which the critics up until now (Ebert included) have failed to grasp: Bogdanovich did *not* intend his film to be confused with a film of the 1950s.

Giacci: "Bogdanovich's film reexperiences the past of forms which a certain period assumed, bringing them out in the open with their many qualities intact—qualities which speak of the past and present at the same time" (p. 40). That the picture has of necessity to be viewed from the perspective of the 1970s (it was not intended to be taken as a film *of* but rather *about* the 1950s) is unavoidable, considering that, obviously, it was not made in the 1950s but rather in 1970, and by a director who was then only 31 years of age.

The fact that Bogdanovich anticipated a retrospective reaction from audiences (the majority of whom had presumably grown up, as he had, in the 1950s) was evident from his explanation of why he chose to run a clip from

Mrs. Farrow (Ellen Burstyn) discusses the future with her daughter Jacy (Cybill Shepherd).

Vincente Minnelli's *Father of the Bride* in his film: "I wanted it to be a movie of 1950, with recognizable actors. . . . I opted for Minnelli's because Elizabeth Taylor was very well known by the public, so that when they saw her they would say, 'Look how young she was!' and immediately get a feeling for that period." (Giacci, p. 41) The effect, therefore, is not the same as if *Father of the Bride* were the main feature, since it is evident that a *re-creation* of a period is being attempted here. *The Last Picture Show* could not, as Ebert asserts, be labeled "the best film of 1951."

But the execution of the plan went deeper than that. Robert Surtees' black-and-white photography does not resemble any of his earlier (or subsequent) work, which is lush and glossy almost without exception. Perhaps this accounts for his receiving more Academy Award nominations and statuettes than any other cinematographer—the voters have always favored the slickest-looking properties. When Blake Lucas complains that the look of Surtees' compositions in *Picture Show* suffers in comparison to his work on Minnelli's *Bad and the Beautiful* (1952), he misses the point entirely: that Surtees' images are drab and depressing here is deliberate and totally in keeping with Bogdanovich's mournful retrospective gaze. The film consistently refutes the theory that the "good old days" were as wonderful as some would remember them.

Thus, *Picture Show* was obviously not intended to resemble a typical Hollywood prestige picture like Stevens' *Place in the Sun* (1951), for example. The fact that many made this mistake was more a reaction to the fact that this was the first black-and-white feature to emerge in four years, that Bogdanovich's simple classical style was in direct contrast to the flashiness of the films of his contemporaries, and finally that the film was set in the past.

Bogdanovich has said that the subject of *The Last Picture Show* is "despair—the fact that there was no more cinema and that there was television." The film proved to be a much more dispiriting work than *Targets*. Whereas in his first picture Bogdanovich showed (by having Karloff succeed in disarming the young sniper at the drive-in) that the power of the movies could triumph over a depressing reality, given the chance, here the last image is a slow fade-out on the town's movie house, closed forever (the film begins with a similar image, the only difference being that then the theater is still in operation). So perfectly does this framing device convey the fact that the fate of the dying community is sealed that one critic remarked that the picture more rightly should begin with the final image (much in the manner of a film noir).

Giacci, in his book on Bogdanovich's films through *Daisy Miller*, best summed up the gist of *Picture Show* and the perspective of its director: "Bogdanovich is not a moralizer and his representation is not another *Peyton Place*, but rather the sorrowful recording of a vast panorama of

individual and collective feelings, of disillusions and inani-
ties. . . . *The Last Picture Show* is the story of a city in the
American Southwest where people young and old are
consumed by an aimless existence, by the boredom of an
insufferable present, and by resignation to an impossible
future." (p. 48) Bogdanovich has often been accused of
having adopted a nostalgic outlook in his early films.
Instead of a wistful yearning for bygone days, what exists
in *Picture Show*, and continues through *Paper Moon* before
finding its most eloquent expression in *Daisy Miller*, is a
deep sadness, a "classical sadness which is an awareness of
destruction, that objective destruction which time visits
upon society" (Giacci). Perhaps a large part of the reason
that certain critics ascribed to Bogdanovich a penchant for
nostalgia has to do with the fact that his characters often
indulged in nostalgic memories in an attempt to escape
from their oppressive environment. Most often cited in this
regard is the monologue which Sam the Lion delivers to
Sonny and Billy at the water tank:

> You wouldn't believe how this country's changed. First time
> I seen it there wasn't a mesquite tree on it—or a prickly pear
> neither. I used to own this land, you know. First time I ever
> watered a horse at this tank was—more than fifty years ago.
> Reason I always drag you out here, probably—I guess I'm
> just as sentimental as the next fella when it comes to old
> times.

Despite the fact that this scene is beautifully photographed,
directed (in one long take, like Karloff's speech in *Targets*),
and played (it was largely responsible for winning Ben
Johnson the Oscar for Best Supporting Actor), the general
feeling it generates is hardly a heartwarming one.
Bogdanovich, while respectful of the tradition Sam represents, nevertheless wants to show that such nostalgia is
merely the ulterior symbol of the crumbling of a life; and
indeed, Sam dies just a few scenes later.

That the character Sam the Lion is played by Ben Johnson is perhaps the most significant indication that Bogdanovich intended the central subject of the film—the death of a small community—to be inextricably tied to the corresponding decline of the American cinema. As Barry Putterman notes,

> Bogdanovich set the yearnings of the naive, uncertain young generation searching for values and ideals in the mythic, historic mold of the western film genre, thus organizing the material self-consciously along defined aesthetic and ideological lines. The traditionalist conservative structure of the John Ford western, with each generation handing down rituals and values for the new generation to use as its social and moral guide, becomes framed as the necessary resolution for the confused teenagers and the death of the town, i.e., the death of the land becomes the death of the dreams and hopes of the older generation who have nothing to offer the youngsters . . . this motif was extended by having Ben Johnson, long identified with Ford, play the positive, paternal moral figure who dies, as the land dies, before he can complete his task of molding the new generation. (pp. 50–51)

That Ben Johnson is also the star of Ford's *Wagonmaster* (1950), a film about a community struggling toward the new promised land, is particularly significant in this context. Just as Sam the Lion, once a towering figure in the community, now sadly reduced to a "decrepit old bag of bones," as he describes himself, represents the last link to the Old West, *The Last Picture Show* may be considered a sort of *Wagonmaster* on the dark side, since it too is a meditative film, but on the theme of death. The community spirit depicted in Ford's film is shown in Bogdanovich's to have been replaced by individual selfishness. The happy days spent in singing about the daily hope in one's own future have given way to individual isolation and the moral collapse of the group. Thus *The Last Picture*

Show could be termed a critical discourse on the western, embodied in the figure of Sam.

The Last Picture Show confronts and overthrows the two basic themes of Hollywood movies: the respectability of middle-class morality and the myth of the frontier, both exemplified cinematographically by the two films being shown at the Royal: *Father of the Bride* and Howard Hawks' *Red River* (1948). Bogdanovich's film includes these two different types—the sentimental comedy and the western—to illustrate the decline of the power of what they represent: the reassuring, paternal image of the hero and the dimension of the stable family unit with its middle-class values.

Both selected films share the theme of the father/child relationship as the emblem of a society on the rise, strong in its own homogeneity and certain that its personal ethical values shall continue. *The Last Picture Show* takes note of the end of those values. The most succinct evidence of irremediably broken family relationships occurs during the Christmas dance at the American Legion hall when Sonny and his estranged father have a short, painfully banal exchange.

More specifically, the comedic flavor of *Father of the Bride* contrasts with the failed relationships of *The Last Picture Show*. That Sonny wishes his current mate, Charlene Duggs, were more like the idealized Elizabeth Taylor in Minnelli's film is obvious from his concentrating on her image while necking with Charlene (the local girls idolize Taylor also). Sonny asks Sam, "Is being married always so miserable?" Jacy tells her mother, "You're rich and miserable. I don't want to be like you." The happy father/daughter relationship between Spencer Tracy and Taylor also contrasts with the bitter drawings of conjugal life (Lois's and Ruth's).

As for *Red River*, Bogdanovich wanted the picture show to close with a great western, instead of the crummy one

(*The Kid from Texas*, a Universal potboiler starring Audie Murphy) featured in the novel. He had two choices— *Wagonmaster* and *Red River*—and finally chose the latter because the action took place in Texas. He also changed the name of the town in *Picture Show* from Thalia to Anarene to correspond to Abilene, the city in Hawks' film. The connection between the two films (Bogdanovich's and Hawks') is obvious, as Barry Putterman notes: "The movie theater closes down with the land, and the last picture show of the title is *Red River*, a film very much about the expansion of the land and a generation coming of age with positive values." The sequence which Bogdanovich selected—in which John Wayne urges Montgomery Clift to "take 'em [the cattle] to Missouri, Matt"—crystallizes a moment of positive tension, the outset of a goal to be aspired to (the expansion of the West), and thereby contrasts with the reality of the present day in his own film, so devoid of purpose or ideals.

The foremost exponent of the anesthetization of the town of Anarene—and of American culture in general, Bogdanovich implies—is television. To this end Bogdanovich pointed out an interesting parallel between his film and Welles' *Magnificent Ambersons* (1942)—both are at least partly concerned with the demise of a society due to the emergence of some aspect of industrialization (in the Welles film, the automobile). Unfortunately, this led many critics to believe he was thereby trying to render homage to *Ambersons* (more on that subject presently). The reader will recall that in *Targets*, television was seen to have been at least partly the cause of the characters' limited intellectual growth and also represented the unfortunate fate which befell motion pictures when they were sold to TV stations. Similarly in *Picture Show* the coming of television is viewed as a negative thing. Putterman writes that "Bogdanovich implies that it is the classical Hollywood films of the studio era [films like *Red River* and *Wagonmaster*, whose poster is displayed in the Royal's marquee] which exert the moral force of the western for the generations of the twentieth century."

The director provides us with several insightful glimpses into the absurdity of the convention which, having replaced the cinema (which, Bogdanovich argues, is oriented primarily toward the outside, since one must leave his home to go to the movies, and since it is a community activity) would produce the insular society of *Targets*. The most notable one occurs in the very last scene—the most crucial of any in the film, from an emotional standpoint—wherein Sonny and Ruth are attempting a reconciliation after their long separation. In the background during this long and painful scene, we hear a ridiculous commercial jingle for Grandma's Lye Soap.

In chronicling his saga of the demise of the town of Anarene, Bogdanovich inverts one of the traditional motifs of the western, that of the village. Here, instead of the bustling atmosphere of a community on the rise, we are offered a vision of the country town as prison, for the young as well as the old. Bogdanovich:

> It's all over for them [the young people of Anarene] after high school. That's the story. Life ends at sweet sixteen. I remember we were down there looking at locations, and there was this group of teenagers in a car, and all they were doing was driving around. We kept passing them. I thought it was marvelous. That's why we did that scene where Sonny drives up to the top of the hill, just drives up there and gets out and looks back at the town while he eats a candy bar. There's no place to go. The city-limits sign is sort of the Great Wall of China—this incredible barrier that you don't ever really get past. It takes a great deal of will power and energy to drive past that sign. (McCluskey, p. 71)

Everything in Anarene is a dead end without purpose, except for that of relieving at any cost overwhelming boredom—a goal which Bogdanovich shows again and

again to be an impossible one. In contrast to the elders in
the story, the young people cannot seek refuge in memories of their past, since they have no past. Instead, they turn
to the most obvious alternative: sex. "What I was really
interested in," Bogdanovich said, "was showing sex as
being funny. For the teenagers in the story, sex is the focus
of their attention. Particularly in a small town where there
isn't much else to do except think about sex or go to the
movies or play some pool or just drive around."

To this end Bogdanovich fashions many exquisitely
observed moments: Sonny's (Timothy Bottoms) girlfriend
(Sharon Taggart), parked with him after a movie, remov-
ing her blouse "as routinely as for a medical exam"
(Kauffmann); the pathetic, furtive attempt at lovemaking
by Sonny and Ruth (Cloris Leachman), the coach's wife,

Genevieve (Eileen Brennan) with Sonny: "You can't sneeze in this town
without somebody offering you a handkerchief."

the emotional resonance of which is accentuated by the creaking springs on the ancient bed; the idiotic Lester Marlow (Randy Quaid) fumbling with the bra strap of the prettiest girl in town, Jacy Farrow (Cybill Shepherd), who comments, "I'm glad it wasn't on fire; I'da burned to death before you got one button undone."

Although these episodes are partly comic, the predominant tone is tragic. Yet at the same time the romanticism of Bogdanovich often shines through. The relationships he depicts may be ultimately doomed, but he cannot resist celebrating the glory of the moment. To this end, one recalls scenes such as that where Sonny enters Ruth's house from the side door, and the camera dollies forward and reaches the open window just as he presents her with a gift and the two embrace; or when Jacy seduces Sonny with a passionate kiss in a car near the lake. Such moments will recur in *Daisy Miller* and in *Mask* and, in a somewhat lighter context, in the musical *At Long Last Love* and the romantic comedy *They All Laughed*. McMurtry, in adapting his novel with Bogdanovich, noticed this quality in him early on:

> My task, for a while, was to keep the balloon of Bogdanovichian romanticism from lifting us clear off the earth. . . . The novel was a mixture of modes and motives. A certain amount of affection struggled in it, and a certain amount of genuine hatred. Affection lost, and the predominant tone of the novel is rather harshly satiric. Bogdanovich, coming to the material without the corruption of having lived it, was gentler to anyone than I had been. (p. 121)

Perhaps the most important change Bogdanovich made in this respect involved Sam's monologue, which in the novel was nothing more than a remembrance of urinating off a porch. On the whole, however, the film remained painstakingly faithful to the author's original text. Bogdanovich will display similar respect for the texts of *Daisy Miller* and *Saint*

Jack, although *Paper Moon* will be altered considerably, as we shall see.

As was the case with Karloff in *Targets*, the protagonists of *The Last Picture Show* suffer from feelings of loss and regret. Even the youngsters, who have their whole lives ahead of them, seem to be acutely aware of the bleak destiny which awaits them. Bogdanovich's chronicle of small-town life is seen largely from the point of view of 18-year-old Sonny Crawford. Sonny can be considered the first incarnation of the passive, dreamy male character which will become a staple in most of the director's later films. Sonny serves as the audience's link to the key events of the story, and in the scene where the old man tells Duane, Sonny's best friend, and Sonny that Sam has died, it is Sonny's reaction which Bogdanovich focuses on.

The choice of Timothy Bottoms for the role was crucial, according to Bogdanovich: "Tim had these extraordinary eyes which looked as if they carried the sorrow of the ages in them. It looked as though he was feeling sorry for the world. His eyes had an epic sorrow." Regrettably, one of the scenes which ended up on the cutting room floor (due to the producers' fear that the picture was getting too long) was perhaps the most eloquent expression of that "epic sorrow." It was a scene where Sonny and some other boys are driving to a picnic in Wichita Falls. Here is how it is described in the script:

> Sonny is abstracted, not paying attention, as he sits by the back window, looking sadly out the cracked window. Past his reflection, the gray wastes of West Texas can be seen. The car passes a tank dam. Tears come into his eyes as he looks out at the barren landscape, and the other boys' wild revelry goes on behind him.

The other male characters are either less sympathetically or more tragically treated. Even Sam, once the stronghold of the town, has declined both symbolically and physically (he is afflicted with a hacking cough and sundry ailments), and as a result is forced to stand helpless as he watches the signs of moral and tangible decay envelop the once-thriving community. In addition to his speech at the lake, another Johnson triumph of effortless acting (one could say he *was* the part) occurs in the scene where he confronts the boys after seeing the damage done to the idiot child Billy (Sam Bottoms) by the hideously overweight prostitute (Helena Humann) to whom they have taken him as a joke. "I've been around that kinda trashy behavior all my life, and I'm gettin' tired of puttin' up with it," is his response, and one could not ask for more conviction in the delivery than Johnson provides here.

Besides Sam, there is Duane (Jeff Bridges), who adopts—very unconvincingly—the facade of the macho

Lester Marlow (Randy Quaid) asks out Jacy behind her boyfriend's back. (Courtesy of Movie Star News)

hero he has seen on the screen. Duane is unable to accept the fact that Sonny, who is appreciably less of an athletic type than he, could succeed in making love to "his girl" (Jacy), and feels compelled to test his friend's honesty, mocking him when he discovers the truth: "I knew Jacy's never let you screw her. You're not man enough." His decision to enlist in the army during the Korean War does not arise from any deep-seated political convictions on his part, but rather is simply a reaction to a lack of sexual satisfaction in the town. "Not a goddamn thing to stay for," he says.

Jeff Bridges does a wonderful job of suggesting Duane's intellectual density and emotional immaturity—always acting on gut instinct—particularly in the scene where he hurls pool balls against a wall after discovering that Jacy, having used him in order to lose her virginity, has jilted him for rich kid Bobby Sheen. His casual attitude toward his destiny ("See you in a year or two if I don't get shot," he tells Sonny before leaving for Korea) is especially unnerving.

The other male characters are minor, but nevertheless penetratingly observed. There is Andy Fanner (Charlie Seybert), an old man who bitterly betrays his hatred at having been excluded from the modest benefits of Sam's will (significantly, Sam has left his estate to Sonny). There is dumpy Coach Popper (Bill Thurman), who turns to sport to compensate for his failure as a man and a lover, using it as an alibi for his inability to get close to his wife, and who looks down on all activities which are not physical. "If you take my wife to the doctor's I'll get you out of civics class," he promises Sonny as though he were offering him a prize. And there is the retarded child Billy, whose special importance to Sonny is stressed when the latter repeatedly adjusts his cap. It is Sonny who is the first witness to Billy's death, and the fact that the actors are brothers in real life only increases the emotional value of their brief scenes together.

In a pattern which he will continue in subsequent films, Bogdanovich reserves most of his compassion for his female characters, who (in true Howard Hawks tradition) are aggressive and resilient, though not invulnerable. Especially admirable is the character of Ruth Popper, the coach's long-suffering wife, played by Cloris Leachman. In contrast to the other adults in the town, she does not seek refuge in reminiscences of her past, but rather takes positive steps to satisfy her lonely existence by beginning a relationship with Sonny, though she soon realizes this, too, is doomed when he neglects her in favor of the much younger Jacy.

Ruth's final reconciliation scene with Sonny remains the highlight of the picture. It is a scene which, incredibly, the producers originally wanted Bogdanovich to cut; fortunately, he resisted, claiming, "I made the picture only so I could have that scene in it." McMurtry agrees that "without it the film, for all its style, would have had no bottom, no fullness, no real dimension." Its tremendous impact on the viewer is the result of a delicate blend of acting and directing expertise (the latter all the more praiseworthy when one considers that the scene is almost wordless). It has been described before, but never better than by McMurtry himself:

> A boy comes back to an aging woman, herself hopelessly married. He has left her for a pretty face, the pretty face dropped him; his friend is sent to Korea; another friend is killed; alone, he comes back to the woman he hurt. She hates him, she explodes, but then, nonetheless, knowing she is foolish, knowing in a matter of months or years he will leave her again for another pretty face, or she will grow too old, or something will happen to destroy them, she finds the fact that she can feel more important than anything that has happened or can happen—in brief, that feeling outweighs the inevitability and pain of its own extinction—and she takes him back. It leaves us, not just with a movie about defeat, but with a movie about living-in-spite-of-or-in-the-

teeth-of-defeat, a superb thing for any work of art to try to be about. The woman is not smart or optimistic, she is just brave in relation to her life, as are several of the people in the film. (pp. 122–123)

It stays with us as a splendid, desperate sequence in which we sense all the anguish and the fear of loneliness previously hinted at in the film, and we see it as emblematic of a society where people no longer in control of their own destiny yield to it. Cloris Leachman (who received a Best Supporting Actress Academy Award for her performance) is nothing short of extraordinary, especially in the haunting moment when we see her after a long absence as she answers the door—pale and haggard, a faded beauty queen.

The other prominent female character is Lois Farrow (Ellen Burstyn), a beautiful but miserable 40, who married for money early in life and has been carrying on affairs ever since. She is typical of the matriarchs who destroy their own men and then turn their efforts to getting the best setup for their daughters, in order to make them as unhappy as they are themselves. She suggests to Jacy that she attend a good school where she will meet an eligible, wealthy man. No one has ever managed to convey the half-comic-half-tragic feeling of resignation to an impossible future better than Ellen Burstyn does here; a wondrous moment has her informing her daughter that "forty is kind of an itchy age" and then offering her an orange. Burstyn's big scene is her soliloquy toward the end, the disturbing nature of which is emphasized by the barrenness of the town square where her car is parked and by her large, dark eyes. McMurtry again sums it up quite well: "The scene quivers with the intricacy of her feeling for the dead man [Sam, her childhood lover], the boy [Sonny], herself, and the drift of her life."

The pivotal female character is Lois's daughter Jacy, the icy bitch played by Cybill Shepherd (who would not be so perfectly cast again until Martin Scorsese's *Taxi Driver* five years later). During the course of the film she manages to twist all the male characters—with the exception of Sam—around her little finger. Blake Lucas is correct in observing that although Jacy is a character whom Bogdanovich "clearly hates," he nevertheless "treats her with an awareness that his hatred is part of a fascination he feels for her." As Paul Zimmerman comments, he "artfully draws from her a performance that embodies every crummy virtue in town—duplicity, hard ambition, role obedience to every local shibboleth."

Pauline Kael's description of Shepherd as an "object" is particularly appropriate in this context—not in any negative sense, though the opposite would be the case with *Daisy Miller* to a certain degree and especially with *At Long Last Love*. Perhaps her finest moment has her lying supine on a motel bed, eyes closed, waiting for Duane to penetrate her, telling him, "I don't like to be tickled." Although Jacy and Duane are a couple for much of the film, it is her brief relationship with Sonny which is more important. He has been secretly infatuated with her for a long time, and thus her double-crossing him by marrying him only to stir up gossip in the town and scheming to have her parents get them an annulment before they can consummate the marriage represents his ultimate disappointment—his realization that she is "part of the harsh and unfeeling world that defeats all of the hopes for a rebirth of the land and of positive values" (Putterman).

With regard to character motivations, one should take note of Bogdanovich's use of source music as counterpoint to many key scenes. Hank Williams' "Why Don't You Love Me (Like You Used to Do)?" is first heard on the radio in Sonny's 1941 Chevrolet truck at the start and becomes the theme song of the film; Tony Bennett's rendition of "Cold, Cold Heart" cunningly plays against an image of Jacy sitting on her bed reading a movie magazine. Eddie Fisher singing "Wish You Were Here" is brilliantly employed by the director as an ironic contrast to the scene of Jacy and Duane's aborted lovemaking in the motel to indicate the emotional distance between them (specifically Duane's perception of Jacy), which is the probable cause of his impotence. Lefty Frizzell's "Give Me More, More, More of Your Kisses" is heard in the poolroom as Duane furiously hurls the pool balls against the wall after realizing that Jacy has tricked him.

Although some of the women may have subordinate roles (such as Genevieve—Eileen Brennan—the waitress at the café who is always giving practical advice to Sonny), and although Bogdanovich, in his presentation of the Duane/Sonny relationship, develops the common Hawksian theme of male friendships, an important distinction must be made here between the two directors. The misogyny of Hawks is only faintly present here—in Duane's considering

Sam reminisces about his life. (Courtesy of The Museum of Modern Art/Film Stills Archive)

it his right to spend his last night before departing for Korea with his best friend and the assumption (encouraged by the *Red River* clip) that their relationship is strong enough to transcend their mutual involvement with a shallow girl (Jacy).

Blake Lucas is incorrect when he says that Bogdanovich deliberately intended the clip from the Hawks film to explain the nature of their relationship; the director has stated on more than one occasion that his choosing the Hawks film over the Ford one had nothing to do with either film's director. That he did finally choose the Hawks one is, however, one of those happenstances usually associated with a coherent artistic vision, whether conscious or otherwise. Bogdanovich's own style remains closest to Hawks', as we have seen.

In contrast to the typical Hawks western or adventure, it is the women who dominate the scene in Bogdanovich's film—and the men who spend most of their time not indulging in sports (Duane and Sonny are consistently ridiculed for being poor athletes, in fact) but in thinking about girls. Duane remarks just before he leaves for Korea that he still hasn't gotten over Jacy, and Sam's speech at the water tank is mainly a reminiscence of the times he used to bring a young lady out there to go swimming and horseback riding. We discover later that the girl was Lois.

This is in keeping with Bogdanovich's romantic outlook, which is in direct contrast to the macho image Hawks presented in his films and embodied in real life. Despite Bogdanovich's big-shot facade and idolization of such movie stars as John Wayne (to the point of purchasing pairs of his old cowboy boots and jeans and wearing them on the sets of some of his early films), he has always remained a gentle sort at heart. Although this quality emerges in his early films, it will not come to full fruition until 1981's *They All Laughed*.

Bogdanovich is particularly tactful about the sexual theme of *The Last Picture Show*. He deliberately destroys that spurious aura which Hollywood created around it, when with modest coyness the camera would slip out of the bedroom and focus on a light being turned out or a door being closed or the shades being lowered, so as to suggest what must have happened. Bogdanovich suddenly flashes on the light again to show us the less rosy reality of couples clumsily entangled in bedcovers or clothing, of beds creaking, failed embraces—all producing grotesque situations that are half-comic and half-tragic. An illustration of this is the scene in a motel where Duane and Jacy have their first rendezvous. Her disappointment at the unsuccessful encounter doesn't prevent Jacy from feigning an "ecstasy" she feels impelled to display to her friends waiting outside.

But while he exposes the reality of such encounters, at the same time he still manages to remain discreet—he does not film a sexual encounter, because it is against his principles, especially his aesthetic principles (in fact, he has stated in print his intense distaste for such films as *Last Tango in Paris* and *Deep Throat*), but more subtly shows us the bitter consequences that might ensue. Many persons—including screen legend Marlene Dietrich—have remarked that the film evidences an overemphasis on sex. In fact, there is only about 7 seconds of nudity (shots of Cybill Shepherd's breasts) total, and the fact that the young people (and their elders) frequently have sex on their minds is, as mentioned earlier, an inherent result of their stifling environment—the theme is never explored gratuitously.

Tied in with Bogdanovich's treatment of the subject of sex is his ability to avoid at all times and with the deftest of touches all traces of sentimentality inherent in the subject matter (a technique which will be employed to a greater degree in *Mask*). This is not to say that his characters are not sentimental—they certainly are, as shown by their constant indulgence in old memories—but rather that due to the director's admirable restraint, our emotions are never shamelessly manipulated, and as a result we are left

with our dignity. Again, the distinction between Bogdanovich's own melancholic outlook and the nostalgic one of his
protagonists must be stressed.

Most memorable in this regard are the funeral for Sam,
starkly photographed and penetratingly directed, with an
emphasis on close-ups of the principal characters (Sonny
and Ruth in particular) typical of the style of the rest of the
film (funeral or cemetery sequences will recur in *Paper
Moon*, *Daisy Miller*, *Saint Jack*, and *Mask*); the moment when
Sonny, weeping, drags the dead Billy across the dusty
street to the steps of the café; and the exquisite final
encounter between Ruth and Sonny.

Now that the second period of Bogdanovich's career is in
full swing, now that his style—having undergone a sea
change with *Saint Jack* and *They All Laughed* to emerge
revitalized in the brilliant narrative execution of *Mask*—has

Sonny presents Ruth Popper (Cloris Leachman) with an anniversary
present.

become more relaxed and thereby more revelatory of his own personality than ever (in order for this to happen, he had to shun his ties with the cinema's past), and now that he is finally dealing with the contemporary world and its concerns, *The Last Picture Show* (still considered by many to be his definitive work) may be evaluated in a way not possible ten years ago. While I agree with Blake Lucas that the film, viewed in retrospect, is not the flawless master-piece it was taken to be at the time of its release, it can now be seen to have been more indicative of the unique outlook of its creator than was apparent in 1971.

In the course of this analysis I have touched upon the romantic and pessimistic aspects of Bogdanovich's person-ality. Now that we have seen (in parts of *What's Up, Doc?* and *Nickelodeon* but most thoroughly in *At Long Last Love*) that his tone is capable of degenerating into the realm of the embarrassingly silly, it seems a good time to ask just how much of the maturity of *The Last Picture Show* is owed to its director. Is the general tone of the film merely the result of its source, which the director, in respecting the text, could not help but reproduce (one must keep in mind that *What's Up, Doc?*, *At Long Last Love*, and *Nickelodeon* are all *original* screenplays, more or less)? Bogdanovich him-self, referring to his success in capturing the look of the period, has said, "I have to give great credit to the book: much of it was there in the book" (McCluskey, p. 65).

Nevertheless, both Larry McMurtry and Paul Theroux (who co-wrote the script for *Saint Jack* with Bogdanovich) agree that there is something inherently melancholic about Bogdanovich. McMurtry: "The quality in Peter which ultimately made *Picture Show* the triumph that it is was his elegiac sense. He is moved, as I am, by the ending of things, by the waning of periods, generations, human couples, a town. I might have deduced this from his feeling for Ford or Hawks, the most elegiac of our directors." Alert viewers will note that the theme featured at the Christmas party is Ford's favorite, "Red River Valley." Theroux: "There is something melancholy about Peter—something of old Europe rather than the USA—perhaps a true understanding of loss or tragedy."

Since a similar tone pervades *Paper Moon, Daisy Miller*, and *Saint Jack*—three subsequent literary adaptations which have little or nothing to do with the cinema—it must be concluded that it was the stylistic challenges which confronted Bogdanovich in his attempts to recapture the spirit of old genre forms in the three films in question (*Doc, Love*, and *Nickelodeon*), as well as the lighter nature of the material in those cases, which prevented such mature observation from emerging. Interestingly, however, *They All Laughed* is also an original screenplay and a stylistic exercise (albeit one significantly devoid of all self-consciousness) *and* is sustained in a lighter vein, and yet is much more sophisticated than any of its three predecessors—especially *At Long Last Love*, to which it is particularly instructive to compare it.

Another, still more important, issue which prevented the unique outlook of Bogdanovich in the early non-genre pictures (*Picture Show* and *Paper Moon* in particular)—as well as the genre ones (*What's Up, Doc?* especially)—from seeming as obvious as it now appears and which was entirely the fabrication of the critics, was that of homage—or, as Bogdanovich put it, "the tree which hid the forest." Was he in these films making conscious nods to the veteran directors whom he had deified in his writings in the 1960s? The director himself has said:

> The only time I've ever done a conscious homage was when it was put quite literally on the screen. In *Targets*, I had a clip from a Howard Hawks movie and I as the director (I was acting in it) said, "That's a good movie," and Boris Karloff, who was also in the movie, said, "Yes, Howard Hawks is a good director." *That* was an homage to Howard Hawks. Then in *The Last Picture Show* there was a clip from *Red River*—again, Howard Hawks—and Sonny and Duane came

out of the movie and one of them said, "That was a good movie," and the other said, "Yes, I saw it before." That's a tip of the hat. But they say some long shot is my homage to John Ford. It's not true; it's just the way I thought the scene should be. The fact that John Ford did beautiful long shots is certainly true—but so did Griffith. Neither of them hold the patent. (Denby, B. J., p. 76)

This process of picking out alleged references to other directors' films in Bogdanovich's works quickly became, as David Denby put it, "something of a show-off game for critics"—no doubt fueled by the director's having gleefully pointed out references to other motion pictures and other directors (Hitchcock and Hawks in particular) in *Targets*. Bogdanovich had excused himself for doing that by claiming that a director is entitled to a few intentional tips of the hat in his first feature, and he was certainly justified in feeling that way.

However, the critics at large failed to grasp this simple theory and assumed that now that Bogdanovich, the critic turned filmmaker who had deified the great American directors of the past, had completed his first major feature, the borrowings would be more rampant than ever. As a result, such normally respectable critics as John Simon and Stanley Kauffmann felt compelled to make idiotic claims that Bogdanovich in *Picture Show* was making bows to George Stevens, of all people.

Not only is Stevens not even one of Bogdanovich's favorite directors, but the alleged references which these men enumerate are so insubstantial as to seem ludicrous— as though *Giant* (1956) were the only American film to feature a long shot of a lonely house (supposedly aped by Bogdanovich in the brief moment when Sonny is glimpsed from a distance filling a butane tank at a country farmhouse), or that the brief burial of Sam the Lion on a hill in Bogdanovich's film was intended to rival the much more intricate and involved funeral sequence in *Shane* (1953).

Such statements merely leave one with no choice but to side with Bogdanovich's assertion that "those certain critics who are always beating through the underbrush trying to scare out the little homages are wasting their time. . . . They end up not seeing the movie."

But by the same token, there *is* some value in comparing the style and approach of Bogdanovich in *Picture Show* to that of the two directors to whom he is closest in spirit: Ford and Hawks—particularly the latter, as we shall see. The only legitimate reason for such a comparison, however, is to illustrate how Bogdanovich's own unique personality emerges from the contrast, not to rate his success in reproducing their style intact—something which could never be done and which Bogdanovich, as one of their most devoted admirers, would not dare attempt. As he himself has said numerous times, "Whenever I go into making a movie I have this terribly depressed feeling that it's all been done better, so why am I bothering?" (McCluskey p. 39).

This is not to say, however, that although *Picture Show*, like *Paper Moon* and *Daisy Miller*, is less obviously an exercise in style than the genre pictures *Targets, What's Up, Doc?* and *At Long Last Love* (though thematically *Picture Show* works within the tradition of the western) it did not represent a stylistic challenge for Bogdanovich. As I mentioned in the section on aesthetics, the actual physical process of making a picture seemed during this first phase of Bogdanovich's career to be of more interest to him than any specific subject matter.

The point here is that in choosing a style to suit the material (a "classical" one), Bogdanovich inevitably ended up adopting a technique similar to that of, say, Ford or Hawks, since they had perfected that technique many times over. This does not mean that Bogdanovich was trying to *be* either one of these men, but rather that working with their tools he hoped to create his own vision—a lesser one, perhaps, but his own nevertheless.

Jacy seduces Sonny after being dumped by Bobby Sheen.

"That he should have occasionally created films which *deserve* comparison [with those of Ford or Hawks—*The Last Picture Show* being one of them]," John Baxter (1984) writes, "argues for his skill and resilience."

Martin Rubin remarked in his analysis of *Targets* that Bogdanovich's "flat" visual style was similar to Hawks' in that both exhibited equal geometric dispersion of the elements within the shot in order to express a tension between those elements—particularly characters and environment. Rubin said that the two men's styles differed, however, in terms of emphasis—that in Hawks, the characters were concrete and the environment abstract, whereas in Bogdanovich's film it was vice versa: "Bogdanovich is interested in his characters' behavioral patterns as an outgrowth of their society, while Hawks follows his characters' response to (and against) their surroundings." Beginning with *Picture Show* and continuing through *Paper Moon* and *Daisy Miller*, Bogdanovich's style alters, falling between the two extremes. Since these are period dramas, the characters *and* environment are concrete. As we have seen, the characters in *Last Picture Show* are both products of and reactors to their environment. Most notable here is Sonny's aborted attempt to drive away from Anarene following Billy's death.

Hawks throughout his career was always more interested in character than plot. Bogdanovich's films—with the exceptions of *Paper Moon* and *Daisy Miller*—also revolve around a series of parallel subplots as opposed to having a straightforward narrative development, and place much concern on character. The director has said that what he was after in the case of *Picture Show* in particular was

> a solidarity in the performances, which I felt *Targets* lacked. Boris Karloff was good, and the boy—Tim O'Kelly—was good, but everybody else was iffy; they could have been better. So what I really wanted to do on the second picture was to concentrate on the actors, to get some performances. I came to feel that this was probably the most essential thing you can do in pictures, to have really good performances—not necessarily really good actors but really good performances. (Denby, B. J., p. 81)

Such later films as *Saint Jack, They All Laughed,* and *Mask* (which may be Bogdanovich's best film to date in terms of performances) share this emphasis on acting and characterization over traditional plot development. The difference is that in these three films Bogdanovich is dealing with real people, not types. Granted, the same could be said for *Last Picture Show* (and *Paper Moon* also) to a great extent, but the fact that Bogdanovich is now dealing with contemporary stories which have nothing to do with the cinema marks a subtle difference between *Picture Show* and *Mask,* for example.

Even in a nongenre film like this, what interested Bogdanovich just about as much as getting good perform- ances from his cast was the stylistic challenge of recreating a period and that of telling a story in a simple, unselfcon- scious manner. To his credit, Bogdanovich never cuts for the sake of cutting or to make an obvious point—even in the intricately staged confrontation scene between Sonny and Duane around the latter's Chevy—and his technique never even approaches the flashy (and alienating) camera movements of Scorsese in *his* otherwise outstanding first major release, *Mean Streets* (1973). On the other hand, however, there is a certain (though far from obvious) feeling of calculation about the work—which no doubt results in part from the director's planning out many of the

Duane (Jeff Bridges) smashes a bottle into Sonny's eye after discovering he's been having an affair with his girl, Jacy.

key sequences on paper before shooting them, as he had done with *Targets*. As Pauline Kael has said, one is aware of the scene's having been set up, though only a discerning eye could sense this here—it will become more obvious in the case of the subsequent, genre-oriented pictures.

Since Bogdanovich continues to plan out sequences to this day, and since this technique is not felt in the least in his latest drama—*Mask*—one must conclude that in this and other early films he was trying to recreate or breathe life into a period. Bogdanovich has admitted that his films since *Saint Jack* are better because they are not "packaged"—they have a contemporary setting and are freer and looser in style, allowing the atmosphere to emanate naturally from the narrative rather than forcing it upon the viewer.

This is not a serious problem in the case of *The Last Picture Show*—with its "blatantly emotional connections," as Barry Putterman describes them—but it will become more pronounced as Bogdanovich's approach becomes more icy and detached in such films as *Paper Moon* and *Daisy Miller*, culminating in the musical *At Long Last Love*, a stylistic experiment totally devoid of any sense of reality.

It seems fair to speculate at this point (as I did with *Targets*) to what degree—despite the fact that Bogdanovich was not rendering conscious homages to his favorite directors in the style he adopted for the film—*The Last Picture Show* might seem confusing to audiences not familiar with America's—or, more accurately, Bogdanovich's—movie past. As Blake Lucas points out, "For those who are familiar with and attached to the classical cinema, the film provides a somewhat different experience." Lucas, however, is hung up on the "homage" issue; he even believes that Bogdanovich intentionally copied from *The Magnificent Ambersons* the tracking shot which initiates the Christmas dance sequence.

I agree with Stanley Kauffmann that Bogdanovich is "addressing better material"—less obviously oriented toward the cinema—here, as compared with *Targets*. However, that statement relates more to Bogdanovich's source than to his treatment of it. As mentioned earlier, Bogdanovich made many important changes in the novel which have direct correlations to the history of the American cinema and certain specific films and names. A noninitiate will certainly not grasp the significance of Ben Johnson's presence in the film nor, perhaps, the contrast between the situations in the clips from *Red River* and *Father of the Bride* and that of *Picture Show*. Nevertheless, Bogdanovich's references in no way prevent the film from being termed an original work. Certainly he would consider it to be a failure if they did.

This is due to the fact that, unlike in the original screenplay *Targets*—whose protagonist, Orlock, was virtually indistinguishable from the real-life persona of horror-film star Boris Karloff—the characters and situations in *Last Picture Show* in themselves have nothing to do with movies; they are the creations of McMurtry first and of Bogdanovich second. Even though the average moviegoer might not share Bogdanovich's knowledge of the cinema, he can admire his expert interpretation of the characters and their stories.

With regard to the film's being an original work revelatory of the personality of its director, Stanley Kauffmann had this incredibly naive comment: "Bogdanovich has real abilities and has progressed happily in most ways—except the central matter: self, being, style. I still don't know much more about him from his work than that he loves films and can make them. But who is he? That's a question which all really good directors answer about themselves, sooner rather than later." For someone so gung ho about pointing out supposed allusions in Bogdanovich's second feature to the films of the directors whom he had deified in his writings, Kauffmann shows an incredible lack of awareness as to the progression of these men's careers—a progression which could reasonably have been seen at the time to indicate the direction of Bogdanovich's own career.

All of Bogdanovich's favorite American directors— Ford, Hawks, Hitchcock, Welles—began their careers by making brilliantly energetic (and, with the exception of Welles, impersonal) features and ended them with longer, slower, and far more personal works of art. Compare Ford's *Informer* (1935) to *The Man Who Shot Liberty Valance* (1962) or *Cheyenne Autumn* (1964), or Hawks' *Scarface* (1932) to *Rio Bravo* (1959), Hitchcock's *39 Steps* (1935) to *Marnie* (1964), or Welles' *Citizen Kane* (1941) to *Chimes at Midnight* (1966)—or, to pick another important example, Kazan's *A Tree Grows in Brooklyn* (1945) to his *America, America* (1963)—though Bogdanovich is not one of Kazan's admirers.

Certainly Kauffmann's remark was typical of the unusually high expectations most critics held for Bogdanovich based on the success of *Picture Show*. At that point in Bogdanovich's life (he was only 31, remember) watching films and making them *were* his main interests. He did not grow up in an unusual environment—like Martin Scorsese in the ghettos of Little Italy, for example—but rather on the relatively peaceful Upper West Side of Manhattan. He would return ten years after *Last Picture Show*, however, to produce an ode to the Big Apple, *They All Laughed*. He went to the movies regularly and was provided with a certain cultural background by his parents. In fact, what may have helped achieve the authentic atmosphere of *Picture Show*, Bogdanovich said, is the fact that he was depicting an environment foreign to him: "There was a kind of tension between me and the material that I think was very valuable." Although it is hard to tell now, it would not be unreasonable to guess that Bogdanovich's work will become more introspective as the years pass.

If *The Last Picture Show* has a significant flaw, it is that we are not given so much of an opportunity to get to know the principal characters as we would like, and that their stories

Ruth lashes out at Sonny after he deserts her for Jacy.

are resolved too abruptly. Larry McMurtry has explained the reasons for this and also how the film could have been improved:

> By the time [the film] had been in production a week, what had seemed, in script, like a tidy two-hour movie had somehow stretched itself into a potentially awkward three-hour movie. The difference was not in the script, but in the playing, and, since the producer didn't *want* a three-hour movie, about a third of the script at once became dead weight. Something like 30 percent of the script had to be altered once production started, because the scenes were playing longer than anyone expected them to. I think now that generally Bogdanovich needed more time. His penchant for the narrative film is so pronounced that I think it is remarkable that he did so well with a book that is narrative only secondarily. There are those who would argue that he was lucky to keep people interested in Archer City for even two hours; still, I would have liked to see him try to do it for three. I think rapidity of pace is usually a vice in art and would have liked a kind of American *Apu*, a *cinéma fleuve* that would have allowed for the slow filling-in of a progression. Finances apart, the short movie is another result of zombie-state conditioning; no one enters a theater with the comfortable assumption that no matter who the people in the movie are, or how lovable or hatable they may be, one will only have to be involved with them for 119 minutes or less. I would have liked, perversely, to see Bogdanovich cross that assumption and make his audiences and his producer accept and even enjoy having these small-towners from the 50s in their lives for 180 minutes. In that length of time one might have come to love them or hate them, rather than merely to marvel at the way they love and hate one another. Narrative is not, finally, memorable; one forgets stories and even outcomes and remembers moments, just as in life one forgets years, even decades, and remembers—moments. There were scenes cut from the script (by common accord, because there was no money to shoot them with) which would have lived with audiences as

long as all but one or two of the scenes which were shot. (pp. 121–122)

Blake Lucas and Stanley Kauffmann have summed up the effect which such shortening had on the final film. Kauffmann:

> The script is framed just as neatly as the film is with the two shots of the picture show. In order to define the end of a period in the hero's life, things are *made* to happen. Heavy hands are making the calendar turn over. There's personal observation, possibly autobiography, in the script, and I suspect that Larry McMurtry's justification might be, "But that's the way it really happened." If so, it only proves again that life is no artist. (p. 361)

Lucas:

> All the characters change in the course of the story, but there is no clear progression which would make it possible to define the story in terms of a beginning and end. As a result of being comparatively naturalistic, the narrative rambles along. . . . Not wishing for the story to be boring, Bogdanovich goes from one essential scene to another, trying to have it both ways, consistently credible and consistently dramatic. As a consequence, the film betrays its weakness in the last few reels. Attempting to resolve the principal threads of the narrative in a realistic manner, but without permitting the film to drag out, Bogdanovich cannot avoid causing an impression of three successive climaxes, each of them given equal weight. (pp. 1315–1316)

As we shall see, *Mask* presents a similar structure, since it too is based on a true story—though much more so.

Despite its flaws, however, some 18 years after its release, *The Last Picture Show*, Bogdanovich's breakthrough film, has lost very little of its cinematic value. Although it is remembered fondly by many, its popularity has been overshadowed by the director's other commercial successes, *What's Up, Doc?*, *Paper Moon*, and 1985's *Mask*. It is to be hoped that this seminal work regains its former footing with the public who embraced it so wholeheartedly back in 1971. And with the imminent release of the videocassette version of the film, as well as the theatrical release of its sequel, *Texasville*, that may just happen.

4   *What's Up, Doc?* (1972)

Of all the films of Bogdanovich's initial period, the screwball comedy *What's Up, Doc?* is the only one to which considerations of cinematic borrowings are truly pertinent—and indeed the film has often been slighted on the grounds of being too referential. The question raised by reviewers at the time of the film's release was whether Bogdanovich had succeeded in reviving as well as updating a bygone genre. His intentions were reflected in the picture's advertising slogan: "A screwball comedy—remember them?" This was going to be just like films of the 1930s and early 1940s.

Unfortunately, however, as is typical of Bogdanovich, he succeeded in defeating his own purposes by stating on more than one occasion that his film was inspired by Howard Hawks' classic 1938 farce *Bringing Up Baby*, which starred Katharine Hepburn and Cary Grant. Critics immediately assumed, therefore, that his players, Barbra Streisand and Ryan O'Neal, were merely imitating the two greats, and that the film in general was an attempt to replicate Hawks' comic style and technique and nothing more. This was not the case, but it *was* evident that, as Rex Reed observed, Bogdanovich's humor was "rooted in reruns of the best film clips and comic ideas of the past thirty years" (from Capra, Keaton, Hawks, McCarey, and others) and that "almost everything that happens in *Doc* is a takeoff on some other scene in some other movie" (right down to the title itself, Bugs Bunny's catchword). *Doc* remains the only Bogdanovich film which can really be termed an homage. Its sources are too obvious to ignore. But if one is to critique the film intelligently, he must not object to the borrowings in themselves, but rather assess the way in which Bogdanovich employs them in order to achieve his aesthetic purpose—also noting the Bogdanovichian qualities of the film in the process.

The question brought up by *Doc*, given its origins, is whether Bogdanovich has succeeded in creating the *appearance* of an original farce which can be appreciated by those unfamiliar with his cinematic past. As he says, "There are only certain ways you can apply paint to canvas. It's *how* you put the colors together that matters. Every director who's talented, who's an artist, who brings himself to his movies is, in essence, making something new. It's new because it's *him* at work, not because he used some new cut or shot or plot gimmick." Ironically, despite what I said earlier, one of the the best ways to assess Bogdanovich's success in this area is to compare his film to *Bringing Up Baby*, the archetypal model for the screwball comedy in the eyes of many. My argument is that in most, if not all, ways Bogdanovich has surpassed Hawks.

I probably should point out now—though it will become increasingly evident as this discussion wears on—that I am not a fan of *Baby*. With few exceptions, I do not find it to be funny, for reasons I will elaborate upon—though it is definitely a well-made film. I realize that I am in the minority in voicing this opinion, but I agree with Judith Crist that *Baby* seems "less hilarious at each revival," while Bogdanovich's film continues to provide "a barrel of carefree laughs" whenever it is screened. Indeed, *Baby* was a resounding flop in its day, and only in recent years has it attained classic status, thanks to the auteurist revival—spearheaded by Bogdanovich—which brought about serious consideration of Hawks' work for the first time. In fact it was the release of *Doc* in 1972 (along with Bogdanovich's statement) which had a lot to do with this. Bogdanovich said in 1973 that he was waiting till the year 2006 for the definitive word on his film—the time length corresponding to the 34 years between the release of Hawks' film and *Doc*, which received mixed notices initially—but, unlike *Baby*, reaped a fortune at the box office.

I should begin by pointing out that Bogdanovich borrowed from Hawks' film his overlapping dialogue, the premise, and two basic character types. Both films concern a professor trying to obtain a grant for further study who is diverted from his pursuits by a wacky woman who gets him into all sorts of predicaments. This in itself might lead one to believe initially that *Doc* might be a mere replication of *Baby*; certainly, despite what Bogdanovich told David Wilson, what he has is more than just "a girl chasing a guy." But the similarities (except for one admittedly filched joke:

Howard (Ryan O'Neal) meets Judy (Barbra Streisand) in a drugstore.

the accidental tearing of the man's jacket by the woman) happily end there, proving to be merely superficial.

Whereas Hawks' film concerns itself almost unflinchingly with the predicament of the two protagonists (in their attempts to recover Hepburn's pet leopard), Bogdanovich structures his film around a series of subplots which are linked by the presence of four overnight bags of identical design, though the Streisand and O'Neal characters—Judy and Howard—figure prominently throughout, and Judy is the catalyst who brings havoc and chaos to everyone. Paradoxically, although Bogdanovich's film is necessarily more complicated, allowing for the introduction of and concentration upon a handful of other characters in addition to the main ones (most notably that of Howard's fiancée, Eunice—her counterpart in *Baby* was virtually ignored), it succeeds in remaining more consistently interesting and pleasurable.

The main problem with *Baby* is its excessively frenetic pacing and its generally rambling narrative. There is not a single truly relaxed moment throughout its 102 minutes, a factor which seems appropriate enough at first (after all, a screwball comedy is supposed to be fast moving), but becomes increasingly irritating as the film wears on, and finally succeeds in tiring out the viewer and negating most of the comedy—and our interest in the Grant/Hepburn relationship. There is very little relief provided from the central situation, which could really be stretched only so far anyway (and Hawks went overboard), given the fact that two people chasing an animal in itself is not the most amusing premise in the world—at least not to me. Also, Hawks creates little if any genuine human warmth between his two stars, which is very surprising considering that they are on screen together over 80 percent of the time, giving us scant excuse to care about them.

It is surprising to me that critics have knocked Bogdanovich's film for displaying these very same weaknesses—when in fact he in general has astutely avoided

Judy rips Howard's coat, a gag taken from *Bringing Up Baby*.

them. Jay Cocks wrote of *Doc* that it seemed to have been made by a man "who has seen a lot of movies, knows all the mechanics, and has absolutely no sense of humor." Why then can Bogdanovich's film be labeled "engaging" and Hawks' merely "chaotic"? The reason lies in the fact that Bogdanovich is a romantic, whereas Hawks was an unabashed macho man. His world was one dominated by tough men and—when they were featured at all—equally tough women; however, it was the men's vocations which primarily interested him. The reason a film like *His Girl Friday* (1940) is more successful than *Baby* is precisely because it is set in such a world. Although Hawks was always a master of timing and camera placement (and this shows in *Baby*), he seemed out of his element with a story which demanded a gentler, more intimate approach. Critics have accused *Doc* of being cold and solely an exercise in style over substance, whereas the charge should really be leveled at *Baby*—and even in terms of visual style, Bogdanovich's film is much more exciting. Let me now supply illustrations to back up my claims.

Baby seems totally asexual (whatever attraction exists between Hepburn and Grant is downplayed to such a degree as to make it seem nonexistent) and thereby devoid of charm. Sadly, the same may also be said of Hawks' *Man's Favorite Sport?* (1964), despite a very sexy title tune by Johnny Mercer and Henry Mancini, an invigorating cred- its montage, and the presences of Paula Prentiss and Maria Perschy, both of whom are more conventionally sexy than Hepburn. *Doc*, on the other hand, consistently focuses on the triangle of Eunice-Howard-Judy (the Eunice—fian- cée—character was significantly neglected in *Baby*). From the outset, the extroverted Judy is shown to be more than willing to compete with the prim and repressed Eunice for Howard's affections. She senses that Howard has been trapped by Eunice in a stuffy existence which is apparently suffocating the looser, more "hip" personality that is buried beneath the surface—she even adopts her own, more appropriate name for him, Steve. It was a very smart idea of Bogdanovich's to cast O'Neal in this role, since it was admittedly at conflict with his "cool" off-screen per- sona.

Judy continues to impose herself upon Howard to the point where, at the banquet sequence, she (due to an extremely clever bit of wordplay on the part of writers Henry, Benton, and Newman) literally assumes the iden- tity of Eunice and is willingly (because of her ingratiating manner) accepted as such by everyone—not the least of whom is Frederick Larrabee (Austin Pendleton), the founder of the organization whose grant Howard is seeking. Perhaps the most delicious bit of dialogue occurs when Howard first spots Judy sitting at the table in Eunice's place, and stammers, "You—you," only to be saved from an embarrassing situation when Judy inter- rupts with "Eu-nice, dear, Eu-nice. We must get that stammering corrected." The same situation is repeated with Howard's name when Howard continues with "How—how." But the crucial moment for Howard occurs when the real Eunice (Madeline Kahn) comes bursting into the reception room—"Who is that dangerously unbalanced woman?" Larrabee asks—and Howard states that he has never seen her before. Bogdanovich cuts to a reaction shot of a pleased Judy to signal that her spell is beginning to overtake her prey.

An important moment (and one without counterpart in Hawks' film, devoid as it is of any real feeling) in the Judy/Howard relationship, and the scene which most adequately displays the difference in personality between Bogdanovich and Hawks, occurs in a later, superbly constructed scene in which Howard, asked to leave the

Howard discovers that Judy has replaced his fiancée, Eunice, at the banquet. Austin Pendleton and Kenneth Mars are in the background. (Courtesy of Movie Star News)

hotel after demolishing his room, steps into a waiting elevator which, to his dismay, has already been pressed to go up. He finds himself stranded on the roof, and decides to take a breather. Placing his leather case down on an object covered with a dropcloth, he hears a muffled dissonant piano chord. He lifts off the cover to find a piano—and Judy perched seductively on top. She bizarrely begins to imitate Bogart, and beckons him to play "As Time Goes By," whose lyrics she cunningly uses to get him to say "I love you," thereby expressing his subconscious impulse—an impulse which becomes physical when, after Judy produces a letter from Larrabee stating that he has won the grant, he instinctively grabs her and kisses her on the mouth, an opportunity which Judy takes full advantage of, pulling him to the floor. Before long, he has temporarily forgotten the name of his fiancée. Bogdanovich emphasizes the commonness, the singularity of their shared personalities, their developing relationship, by first having an unbroken dolly shot circle around Streisand as she lifts herself off the piano top and moves around to position herself on the bench where O'Neal is sitting. The rest of the scene is an unbroken two-shot of them talking, sharing their dilemmas with each other. What is wonderful about this scene is the sense we get that the two were fated to come together: note all the strange coincidences which brought Howard to the roof at this moment—surely Judy could not have controlled everything. There is not a single moment in *Baby* which even approaches this one in terms of an overt display of emotion; there is no kissing there, just a lot of chasing about.

Some critics noted a discrepancy between the personality traits which Hepburn and Streisand brought to their characters and their subsequent abilities to sustain romantic interest. Paul D. Zimmerman of *Newsweek* summed this up best: "There is something gay about Hepburn chasing Grant because we know she can have anyone she wants. Streisand tracking O'Neal smells of desperation." Granted,

Streisand is not a conventional beauty, as Hepburn more or less is, but the interesting fact is that Streisand transcends this seeming handicap by *making herself* attractive (so much so that she captivates nearly all of the men at the banquet)—and her comic timing is no less perfect than Hepburn's. By contrast, Hepburn's attractiveness is taken for granted by Hawks—and we never see other men pursuing her as Zimmerman would argue—and therefore made to seem far less interesting. Hepburn's pursuit of Grant is also diverted by the search for her pet leopard, whereas Bogdanovich keeps his two stars firmly at the center of attention throughout. And Hawks' final scene centers more upon the suspense surrounding a joke (the impending collapse of Grant's dinosaur as the result of Hepburn's ascending it) than on the clinching of a romantic pairing. The sole intent of Bogdanovich's climax, wherein O'Neal discovers that Streisand has boarded the plane taking him back to Iowa and is planning to enroll at his university so they can be close—and, we assume, eventually wed, is just such a pairing.

With regard to the male protagonist in each film, there is no real equivalent in Hawks for the lady's loosening up of the hero; by the end of *Baby*, Grant seems no less befuddled and insecure than he was at the outset, whereas O'Neal has shed his glasses and square ways—he looks infinitely more relaxed and happy with Judy than he had been with Eunice—while still retaining his scholarly bent. With regard to the performers, although Grant has been lauded for his comedic skill in this and similar roles, he seems to me largely uncomfortable playing a type whom we (and he) know is by nature his total antithesis—he appeared even more so when he more or less repeated this characterization in another, even more intolerable Hawks screwball farce, *Monkey Business* (1952).

What is most brilliant about *Hitchcock's* manipulation of Grant's persona in *North by Northwest* (1959)—Grant's finest role, in my opinion—is that the director allows Grant to

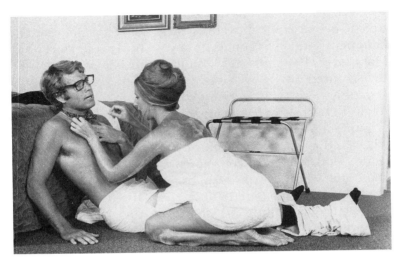

Judy attempts to help Howard after he falls down.

start off as intellectually and sexually in control (the image with which he is ineluctably associated), and then be forced to grapple with many uncertainties when the rug is pulled out from under him through a series of bizarre circumstances. Now, certainly Bogdanovich saw in O'Neal (who comedically comes very close to Grant) the same opportunity which Hawks had in Grant—to elicit laughs by subverting the actor's conventional image (though, in contrast to Grant and *Baby*, in truth O'Neal did not really have an established screen persona before *Doc*—it was more a personal tactic on the part of Bogdanovich, who knew that in real life O'Neal was a "hip, swinging guy"). However, since Hawks did not really take advantage of the opportunity to play the conversion theme to the hilt, he succeeded in unintentionally robbing much interest from

Grant's character—and by extension from the Grant/ Hepburn relationship as well.

Content aside, a discussion of *Doc* must of necessity concentrate primarily on style, since Bogdanovich's main goal with the film was to measure himself against the established masters of film comedy. *Doc* has been termed by many a pastiche, and I would agree that the word is appropriate. However, for the most part, the film succeeds in avoiding too-obvious references through clever and tight structuring of the plot. Although the type of humor is largely familiar, it is the handling which makes it seem fresh. Basically *Doc*, like Bogdanovich's earlier stylistic exercise—*Targets*—develops two parallel plot lines (one involving the central characters, Judy, Howard, Eunice, etc., and the other a band of assorted scheming thieves and government agents) which eventually converge due to the mix-up of identical traveling bags belonging to all the aforementioned parties. Basically the film resolves itself into a series of sequences of varying lengths: a long series of run-ins in the San Francisco Hilton, culminating in the destruction of an entire floor; a gathering at the home of Larrabee which culminates in a wild free-for-all when the crooks intrude; an elaborate car chase down the streets of the city; and a courtroom sequence wherein all concerned parties are thrown together to the consternation of an unbalanced judge (Liam Dunn).

Because the film was designed to include as many of the elements of classic screwball comedy as possible, critics have accused it of being overly calculated and mechanical in the unraveling of plot. In fact, *Doc* is the only film of Bogdanovich for which he planned the least before shooting, making up many of the gags on the set. That the pace seems more studied than that of the traditional screwball comedy is due only to the pastiche nature of the construction. Bogdanovich carefully controls the building of each sequence, allowing for periodic breathers (the scenes with the crooks switching suitcases from room to room) so that the audience does 'not become overly exhausted. It is true, however, that the scenes which do not involve the protagonists are in themselves not nearly so successful comedically, and that one tires quickly of trying to keep track of which suitcase is where. In order to judge Bogdanovich's success in matching the comic styles of his predecessors, one must first note the distinction between verbal and visual comedy. In terms of staying power, the latter by far outweighs the former. Verbal humor exists solely on the surface, and is easily forgotten (Bogdanovich has said that it is very hard for him to recall any funny things from Bob Hope movies). It therefore does not lend itself to regurgitation by others, having been coined by its creator and become forever identified with him, so that any borrowing is immediately termed sacrilege and seems pointless (as so many of the antics in Woody Allen's early films—particularly 1975's *Love and Death*, an unnecessary regurgitation of most of Hope's *Monsieur Beaucaire*—do).

By contrast, visual humor—which, when it is attempted nowadays, presupposes that, as Bogdanovich has said, everything was already done in the silent days—involves more than a simple rehashing, since it is linked to the basic power of the medium, that of the moving image. The operative word in this case is *re-creation*. Provided that the timing is right, an audience will accept the restaging of a gag without questioning its origins. Good visual humor is timeless, whereas even the best jokes sometimes pale in comparison in terms of staying power.

The case of *Doc* would seem to bear out these contentions. With regard to the verbal aspect, although the dialogue adheres admirably to the patterns set by the classic screwball comedies (it is witty, fast paced, and overlapping), the film threatens to date because of several blatant references to older films which are scattered throughout. Buck Henry, who considerably rewrote—and improved upon—the original draft of the script by Robert

Chaos in Howard's hotel room: Ryan O'Neal, Barbra Streisand (*at window*), and Madeline Kahn as Eunice.

Benton and David Newman, based on Bogdanovich's story conception, says that that draft contained "dozens" of movie references which he immediately threw out, claiming they were "a little too cute"; he also says he was not aware that the ripped-coat gag was stolen from *Baby*, or he would have deleted that also, simply out of "writer's ego."

Chief among these is Judy's final line to Howard: "Listen, love means never having to say you're sorry," and his response, "That's the dumbest thing I ever heard"—a reference to the ridiculous famous last line of *Love Story* (1970), the film which had made O'Neal a star. Howard's line (penned by Henry) became Bogdanovich's revenge for having to sit through the film in order to discover O'Neal, whom he had never seen previously. It was also an act of triumphant liberation for O'Neal, needless to say. Henry admits that today, 17 years after *Doc*'s release, the reference is already "hideously dated"—no doubt it will be even more so as the years pass, since *Love Story* certainly does not look like a film which will stand the test of time.

Two others which stand out are Judy's greeting Howard on the hotel roof (before she gets him to launch into "As Time Goes By") with "Of all the gin joints in all the towns in all the world, he walks into mine. Play it, Sam." These two lines were of course, spoken by Bogart and Bergman in *Casablanca* (1942). Although the appearance of such dialogue is in itself totally gratuitous, in all likelihood people will continue to recognize "As Time Goes By," simply because *Casablanca* will undoubtedly remain a classic motion picture. The only other reference of this nature (and the most clever) is the courtroom judge's playing with iron balls, which reminds us (again) of Bogart, this time in his famous interpretation of Captain Queeg in *The Caine*

"As Time Goes By": Judy seduces Howard.

Mutiny (1954). Despite the fact that the gag's origin must be recalled in order for it to work, it is admirable in that it is a comic inversion of something taken very seriously in the original film (Queeg's nervous habit was but another sign of his mental instability). One could say the same thing about the *Love Story* line, except that in the case of that film, the original line was inherently fatuous. As for *Casablanca*'s famous lines' reappearance, the result is too bizarre to come off as more than just private amusement on the part of Bogdanovich. But it is to the director's credit that he never quite stoops to the level of Mel Brooks in his juvenile Hitchcock spoof *High Anxiety* (1977), for example, in which the references more often than not do not work at all in context, but depend on simple recognition alone, as though Brooks is just checking to see whether the viewer has seen the same films he has—indeed, that is what characterizes the substance of his film. So it appears that verbally *Doc*'s occasional referential quality will most likely cause the film to suffer in the long run, if it hasn't already.

The verbal highlight of the picture is undoubtedly the climactic courtroom scene, a set piece which is perhaps the best evidence of Vincent Canby's assertion that *Doc* is "completely contemporary in a back-handed way" because "the things it doesn't notice [blacks, Vietnam] give it an intentional lack of relevance." In this brief but side-splittingly hilarious scene (I hesitate to repeat any of the banter here, for fear of taking away from the freshness of each viewing), Bogdanovich and company truly recreate the spirit of the best comedy directors without any obvious borrowing—and, please note, without the use of profanity, something which has become a staple in alleged comedies in recent years, only providing further evidence of the lack of talent on the part of their writers. The most important inspiration here is undoubtedly Capra and his famous courtroom sequences in *Mr. Deeds Goes to Town* (1936) and *You Can't Take It with You* (1938)—particularly the former. The deliciously maniacal Liam Dunn (a former casting director whom Henry had discovered two years previously and picked to appear in another Henry-written feature, *Catch-22*) is surely the most memorable element of the scene; his threatening manner is what lends true contemporaneity to the proceedings, the 1930s models now seeming somewhat tame and a bit faded by comparison. It is also curious to note that the scene works so well that the star of the film, Streisand, is not missed for its duration (necessarily absent, she appears briefly at the end, however, to relay the surprise element and ensure the collapse of the judge's desk, the perfect metaphor for Bogdanovich's assault on the conventions of 1930s farce).

As I mentioned before, however, it is its visual gags for which *Doc* will be remembered, if at all. Bogdanovich's visual-narrative sense is as finely tuned for comedy as it was for the poignant drama of *Picture Show* and the suspense of *Targets*. Perhaps his most admirable achievement in this area is his refusal to cheat his audience by using process shots: there is not a single one in the entire film. The use of real locations throughout (the whole picture was shot in San Francisco) lends immeasurable believability to the goings-on. One need only note such touches as Streisand (actually her double, of course) photographed from street level hanging off the ledge of the San Francisco Bristol Hotel and then from atop the high window ledge climbing back into the room; Streisand and O'Neal shown in full shot as he runs alongside the delivery cart which she has stolen and then jumps onto it (inspired by Buster Keaton's theory that a comedian should always allow his feet to be seen); and all the cars flying off the pier and into San Francisco Bay at the end of the chase (with one actor clinging to a banner as he is standing up in the speeding car and then flying off the ledge).

There are sequences such as the destruction of Howard's hotel room which build effortlessly, but none so brilliant as the final ten-minute chase through the streets of San Francisco, a feat which surpasses anything Capra or Hawks

Keatonesque comedy: O'Neal and Streisand and delivery cart.

or McCarey ever attempted in the field of visual comedy (and incredibly, Bogdanovich planned not a single shot of it and, as the best evidence of his justified confidence in his abilities, refused a second unit). Bogdanovich has said, "It was me desperately trying to achieve something on a level with Buster Keaton" (McCluskey, p. 76) and Giacci has noted certain parallels between scenes in Bogdanovich's chase and those in Keaton's work, notably the Chinese dragon race featured in *The Cameraman* (1928), the cans rolling down the street in *Seven Chances* (1925), and the truck which is dismembered in one minute in *The Three Ages* (1923). The one gag which has no precedent (the pane of glass being broken in an unexpected manner) was conceived by Henry.

Now, because we are dealing with visual comedy here, the crucial question is, Do the gags *work*? The answer is an unequivocal yes: Bogdanovich's skill in staging each phase of the elaborate sequence is astounding, particularly considering his relative inexperience with the medium at the time (*Doc* was only his third feature film) and the fact that he had never before attempted anything of this magnitude (not even the drive-in sequence in *Targets* can match it). It has been asserted by some that the famous chase in Peter Yates' *Bullitt* (1969) inspired Bogdanovich, but that is highly unlikely, since Bogdanovich was down on contemporary films during this period, and therefore it is highly unlikely that he even saw Yates' film (critics draw the comparison mainly because of the superficial coincidence of both chases having been filmed in San Francisco, and also because good chase sequences have become a rarity in contemporary films). The sequence in *Bullitt*, however, is a bit more daring than Bogdanovich's in one respect: it shows action viewed from *inside* the cars (but the fact that Yates used a second unit makes all questions of comparison immediately lose their validity). Equally important to the success of the chase in *Doc* is the fact that audiences continue to respond to the sight gags without thought of their origins. This is perhaps the best proof that ultimately Bogdanovich makes films not just for himself but for audiences as well.

I have still not discussed the main flaws of *Doc*, shortcomings which are solely the result of its pastiche nature. The piece never really achieves a unified comic style through which one can identify its director's personality—this despite the romantic overtones I alluded to earlier. One senses this in the performances also, despite the fact that all are uniformly excellent, although Kenneth Mars' characterization—a parody of Bogdanovich's least favorite film critic, John Simon—is totally out of place and does not seem funny at all if one does not recognize the reference; certainly it will not help the film to stand the test of time. This can be attributed directly to the stock nature of all of the characters. Also, the actors seem at times to be on the verge of looking overrehearsed. It is the actors themselves and their lines which overcome this feeling for the most part, however). This is related to Paul D. Zimmerman's observation that

> there is something careful and all too obviously artful about even the chaotic moments. In the screwball films of the 1930s, the wildness sprang from the anarchic impulses of the comedians and the directors, as though destruction were the only satisfying response to the foolishness they had to bear in the world. Bogdanovich's impulse is one of nostalgic attachment and respectful imitation. (p. 48)

Now granted, Bogdanovich's reference point, as Giacci has noted, is not 1920s and 1930s comedy in itself but more specifically, comic *films*, and his act in *Doc* is one of a loving look at his past, though his decision not to set the film in the

Liam Dunn as the frustrated Judge Maxwell.

1930s—as he would do later in the musical *At Long Last Love*—was a wise one; this time he would not seem, as Pauline Kael said in her review of *Love,* "genuinely pulled back." This is echoed visually by the director's decision to begin and end the film with the image of an old-style photo album being opened and closed. The use of Cole Porter's "You're the Top"—sung by Streisand unwillingly, according to Bogdanovich, hence the rather belted-out rendition—over the credits, however, seems inexplicable—though in the final chorus it has unexpected relevance when O'Neal sings to Streisand, "You're the *nose* on the great Durante," and she is temporarily offended. Bogdanovich says he chose the song because he had enjoyed Ethel Merman's rendition of it on an airplane headset. It seems to emerge strangely from nowhere. But getting back to the main issue, it is precisely this decision to delve into his movie past which prevents *Doc* from becoming a true updating of the screwball comedies of the bygone eras, despite the fact that it is fun and funny (we share Bogdanovich's enthusiasm because of his skill in directing the whole show—also amusing is his use of Muzak in the background of all the chaos, particularly "Red River Valley"—John Ford's trademark theme song).

Another point of note: the film has been attacked by some for seeming cold and lacking atmosphere. While this is indeed a valid criticism for such other Bogdanovich works as *Paper Moon,* it is of little relevance in the discussion of any comedy, not just this one. A measure of the truth of this statement lies in production designer Polly Platt's decision to make her sets cartoonlike in keeping with the crazy nature of the piece.

I should conclude by noting the historical importance of *Doc* over the years since its release. Just as its compact 90-minute format proved far more palatable than the overblown excesses of such previous attempts at resuscitating slapstick as Stanley Kramer's *It's a Mad, Mad, Mad, Mad World* (1963) and Blake Edwards' *Great Race* (1965), so it remains, 17 years after its release, virtually the only film in recent memory which is worthy of the term *screwball farce* and of comparison with the great achievements of the golden age of moviemaking. It is still too early to tell whether it will stand the test of time, but if it does not, it will be only because of its too-referential nature (a factor which also prevents it from being considered one of Bogdano-vich's absolute best works, despite its many excellences), and if it does, it will be solely the result of Bogdanovich's directorial prowess—his ability to make the derivative seem original.

5   *Paper Moon* (1973)

Paper Moon, perhaps the best-remembered feature of Bogdanovich's early period, was ironically the one property in which he initially expressed almost no interest at all. As was the case with *What's Up, Doc?*, the project had been initiated by a studio (Paramount in this case) before Bogdanovich even heard of it (though in this case there was more than just a bare thread of an idea to work from), and screenwriter Alvin Sargent had already been assigned to write an adaptation of Joe David Brown's recently published novel, *Addie Pray*, a story about two con artists set in Depression-era Georgia. At the time, Bogdanovich had been planning to do a western with James Stewart, John Wayne, and Henry Fonda which was postponed (it was never made), and the offer to direct the picture "came up out of nowhere really. But I thought it would be better than sitting around for nine months waiting."

According to Polly Platt, what got Bogdanovich interested in the idea was her suggestion that Tatum O'Neal, the 8-year-old daughter of Ryan O'Neal—who in the interim had befriended them—play the central character, a precocious little girl named Addie Loggins. Bogdanovich agreed to take on the film only on the condition that Ryan O'Neal be signed to play the other protagonist, Moses Pray, a 30-year-old man whom Addie insists is her father because of a past relationship he had had with her mother.

Even with this initial obstacle overcome, however, Bogdanovich found that he was not terribly pleased with Brown's novel, and his feelings were shared by Alvin

Sargent. Bogdanovich said that he "fought the story from the beginning, because the characters didn't seem believable. But I became rather interested in doing that kind of travel movie with a story that is really rather picaresque." Sargent agrees that he himself "lost interest very quickly" in the book's rambling series of folksy anecdotes about the adventures of Addie and "Long Boy" (whose name was changed to Moses—perhaps to correspond to the central character in Ford's 1935 *Steamboat Round the Bend*, whose title is displayed on a movie marquee in one scene). "I decided to reconstruct it as a story centered around time clock destinations," says Sargent. Working closely with Bogdanovich, he threw out the entire second half of the book, including most of the major protagonists.

The result was mainly a series of lengthy episodes which followed the journey of Addie and Moses across the Depression-scarred Kansas landscape. At Polly Platt's suggestion, the location was switched from Georgia, partly "so we wouldn't have those phony Southern accents, which I hate," but also for a more personal reason. She recalled the perilous journey from New York to Hollywood which she and Bogdanovich had made back in 1964. Traveling in a yellow 1952 Ford convertible which Harold Hayes, Bogdanovich's then-editor at *Esquire*, had lent them, with only about $150 in cash, it had taken three days to cross the plains of Kansas, and they nearly baked to death because the top wouldn't go up.

"I didn't want to do the Depression with the food lines and all those stupid signs, and I thought, How can I make it clear that life is tough and that it's O.K. that Ryan steals?" Platt says. "And I remembered Kansas and how small and insignificant I felt in that car with Peter—a lot of sky, little horizon—and I thought that was all that was necessary to convey their neediness—the fact that they were stuck together in this car traveling this great distance, uncertain about where their next meal was coming from."

In contrast to Bogdanovich's three previous features, *Paper Moon* has a more traditionally straightforward narrative structure. This time he concentrates on two protagonists who are stuck together for the duration of the film, instead of on parallel subplots with two or more unrelated characters moving toward a climax where they finally converge (*Targets, What's Up, Doc?*) or interacting with each other throughout (*Last Picture Show*). The story begins as Moses Pray stops to pay his respects at the funeral of a former girlfriend—only to be pressured by neighbors into transporting the deceased woman's nine-year-old daughter Addie to her aunt's home in Saint Joseph, Missouri. Moses, a petty swindler, immediately decides to turn this unexpected burden into an advantage. He extorts $200 from the brother of the man who caused the car accident which took the life of Addie's mother.

Instead of giving the money to Addie, however, Moses uses part of it to buy himself a car and a railway ticket to Saint Joseph for Addie. But his plan to get rid of the child backfires as Addie creates a scene in a luncheonette by shouting that Moses owes her $200, and that she feels Moses may be her father because of a certain resemblance between them, which Moses vehemently denies. Thoroughly exasperated, he has no other recourse than to take Addie along with him until he can raise the $200 she insists belongs to her.

From this point, the film becomes the story of their trip. Moses doesn't pass up any opportunity to ply his petty criminal activities. From an obituary printed in a newspaper, he finds out a widow's name, prints it in gold letters on the cover of a cheap Bible; he then introduces himself to her and offers her the book as though it were a gift from her late husband. Apparently no widow can resist this gift, posthumously received. Business begins to look up.

Addie is a quick learner. In fact, after observing Moses in action for a while, she quickly proves herself to be even more adept at the confidence racket than he, jacking up or

Addie and Moses (Tatum and Ryan O'Neal), posing as Bible salesmen, con another widow.

bringing down the price of the books according to the lifestyle of the victim of the scam (her appraisal is based on the furnishings of the widows' houses and on their way of dressing), and she even helps Moses invent a routine enabling her to swindle $20 bills from harassed cashiers at general stores.

Moreover, Addie has an innate sense of economics. She always keeps track of how much money there is in the box with their savings, unlike Moses, who liberally spends whatever is "earned." Through a series of minor adventures of this nature, we get to see more and more clearly how well the child has adapted and how superior she is to Moses who definitely is more vulnerable. It is Addie who (along with Trixie's dispirited maid Imogene, played by P. J. Johnson) succeeds in implementing a complicated plan for getting rid of Trixie Delight (Madeline Kahn), a prosperous amusement park dancer of easy virtue who has wedged her way into a relationship with Moses and on whom he is squandering their rapidly diminishing funds.

It is Addie, too, who plays a large part in helping Moses carry out an elaborate scheme to sell a bootlegger (John Hillerman) crates of his own whiskey for $625. Moses and Addie are subsequently arrested by Sheriff Hardin (John Hillerman), the bootlegger's brother, who threatens Moses with a long prison term unless he turns over the money. Once more taking the initiative, Addie (who has hidden the cash in her cloche) instigates a daring getaway, during which Moses eludes the sheriff following a hectic car chase.

After swapping his roadster for a dilapidated pickup truck, Moses drives a despondent Addie across the state line into Missouri. Upon their arrival in Saint Joseph, however, Addie's despair turns to delight when Moses asks her to assist him in his next venture. But as Moses sets off to meet a big-time operator to discuss future dealings, he is seized by the sheriff who, though unable to arrest him, takes all his money and severely beats him.

Later that same day, a defeated Moses drops Addie off at her aunt's home, where she is accorded a warm welcome. Stopping to repair his stalled truck a short distance away, Moses suddenly sees a tiny figure running toward him. But when he desperately tries to persuade Addie to return to her relatives ("I don't want you riding with me no more!"), the little girl firmly retorts, "You still owe me $200!" Without another word, Addie (still clinging to the belief that her undemonstrative companion is actually her father) and Moses climb into the truck and drive off into the sunset on a dusty and seemingly endless road.

Paper Moon marked a return by Bogdanovich to the past of America—and, by extension, of American cinema also. The reader will recall that what had first attracted him to McMurtry's novel had been the title. It should therefore come as no surprise that the first move he made in adapting the novel *Addie Pray* was to change its title to make it correspond to the cinema. By choosing *Paper Moon*, Bogdanovich, whether consciously or not, succeeded in eliminating the barrier between cinema and life forged in his last three films (his next film, *Daisy Miller*, as we shall see, had nothing whatsoever to do with the cinema). Here, instead of having the characters viewed in relation to specific films and genres (the demise of which was marked by the title, *The Last Picture Show*), they in fact became themselves the creators of a brand new fiction which was a direct reversal of traditional themes.

The title *Paper Moon* represents the essence of cinema or the moviegoing experience. Orson Welles told Bogdanovich it sounded so good by itself that he should just release the title and forget about making the film! Vittorio Giacci describes its meaning as

> "the illusion of a moon made of paper, a synthetic and brilliant reality like the light of a film which can be real only if we are willing to believe for a moment, even though we are aware of its being make-believe.
>
> As the words of the song go, "It's only a paper moon, sailing over a cardboard sea, but it wouldn't be make-believe if you believed in me." And in the relationship between image and imagination we can become everything, even the symbol of Addie's frustration over not getting her picture taken with her "dad" on the paper moon in the amusement park because he is with Trixie instead. Or Moses' melancholy moment when he finds the picture Addie had taken of herself—alone. Paper and celluloid: two illusory things, but also two instruments for communicating, for feeling alive amid the death of a world reconstructed by a short-lived remembrance. (p. 61)

Paper Moon emerged as Bogdanovich's most original film to date precisely because instead of simply trying to bring back a past film tradition intact (as in *What's Up, Doc?*), he took a common motif from the cinema of the past (that of the wanderer or tramp) and completely inverted it,

A typical argument on a desolate Kansas road.

investing it with new meaning. Granted, he had done this
with the motif of the village in *Last Picture Show*, but the
similarities end there. Here there are no implied references to earlier pictures, despite the presence of a handful
of movie marquees throughout. Bogdanovich was therefore understandably infuriated by the remarks of such
critics as Vincent Canby, who stated that the film was
inspired by *Little Miss Marker*, a 1934 Shirley Temple
vehicle, and another which suggested he was trying to copy
Frank Capra.

Instead of *re-creating* the Shirley Temple myth here,
what Bogdanovich was doing was providing a *caricature* of
it. His position was encapsulated in the character of the
perspicacious Addie, who poses as an ingenuous child but
who in secret smokes and sprays herself with perfume like
an adult and who understands perfectly well what possibili-

ties are open to her in her privileged status as a minor. Bogdanovich has said that this particular portrayal is very truthful. "I think one of the mistakes made with children in movies is that they're too sweet—something I tried to correct here. Children are not sweet—they're savages who are slowly being tamed to live in society. I think adorable children are either not real, or if they *are* real, you want to hit them" (Rubin, p. 15).

Contrary to what Blake Lucas has said, it was not in *Last Picture Show* but instead here that the true pessimism of Bogdanovich emerged (it had surfaced in *Targets*, but this time the result was more mature for being disassociated— at least in an obvious way—from the cinema). The film remains his darkest to date (but far less eloquently tragic than *Daisy Miller*, as we shall see), concentrating on the antithesis of the motif of the happy-go-lucky adventurer and on the theme of the disintegration of youth.

Gone was the temporarily optimistic romanticism of the pairings in *Last Picture Show*. Bogdanovich was determined that the relationship between Addie and Moses be depicted in the harshest way possible, so that although they obviously enjoy their success as a team of swindlers, ultimately each is dissatisfied with the other's shortcomings: Addie always seems like a burden to Moses, and likewise she remains irritated by his inability to admit that he may be her father. The director said he was "afraid that the characters would be sentimental, but I think the picture has a hardness to it—it's kind of a love story, but Moze and Addie never kiss, never say 'I love you,' never even touch really."

Significantly, Bogdanovich eliminated all of Moses' frequent referrals to Addie as "Sugar" which were present in Brown's novel and in Sargent's first-draft screenplay. Also important in this regard was the fact that Ryan O'Neal "found a lot of his character in a kind of laugh he did in rehearsal, kind of a cackle, and in the way he walked." The director also stressed the effect which the black-and-white cinematography had on the audience's perception of O'Neal's character. "I was worried about Ryan. Here is this very good-looking, blond Irishman who we've always seen in color, and I felt he had to be deglamourized as much as possible. I knew that in black and white he would immediately look different from anything film audiences had seen him as" (McCluskey, p. 61).

Fundamentally the film could be described as the story of two people struggling individualistically for survival, who inevitably exploit each other until they reach the point of not being able to manage without the other. In its own way, it is thus a story of love, of the obsessive search for one's father (although the degree of Addie's fixation on Franklin Roosevelt was cut down from Sargent's first draft), but not a search for the father/daughter relationship. It is instead the quest for togetherness as opposed to

The twenty-dollar-bill con game.

solitude; it is rebellion as a spontaneous impulse of the soul; it is the rejection of the domestic amenities (Addie's fleeing her aunt's home at the end) for the carefree pursuit of freedom.

But however valiant that quest for freedom might be, Bogdanovich views it as ultimately futile. Here is his interpretation of the last scene: "I thought it was sad, like the end of *At Long Last Love*. I thought they were driving off to a life of absolute disaster" (Sarris, 1975). In the adventure of Addie and Moses, a sense of death certainly prevails; the film opens with a funeral, and the scam Moses practices depends on death.

In the agreeable machinations of the two, in their petty intrigues, there lies a desperate struggle for existence in a rural America wearily trying to recover from the tragedy of the Great Depression. And everything is seen from the point of view of the disinherited, of their day-by-day struggle which will not allow them to rise above their restricted existence, in a world where delinquency is akin to law and where duty coexists with violence in a way that is as vague as it is threatening.

One need only allude to the exchanging of the car for the truck on the farm. This was not regulated by laws of trading but by the more practical ones of eventual need, and the decision was arrived at by fighting with the most handsome of the large rural family, in keeping with a primordial code. This enlightens us on the conditions in the backwoods of the region, inhabited by large patriarchal families—a decadent reminder of the mythical epic of the frontier—reduced to a life of hunger and suspicious violence.

There is also the dry and measured firmness in Bogdanovich's enunciation of the brutality of the law exacting revenge for a wrong done to protected criminals. There is a terrifying moment as Ryan O'Neal flees from the jail only to discover the sheriff and his men parked in front with their arms crossed, waiting to pounce on him.

Ironically, this is the one film from Bogdanovich's early days to which people almost unanimously ascribe a nostalgic bent; in reality, however, it is without question (at least as far his intentions were concerned) his bleakest vision of the past.

The fact that *Paper Moon*, as I mentioned earlier, proved to be more popular with audiences than either *Last Picture Show* or *What's Up, Doc?* is very surprising, considering that, as Barry Putterman observes, "while *What's Up, Doc?* looked back to *The Last Picture Show* [in that it displayed blatantly emotional connections], *Paper Moon* represented the first, hesitant steps toward the more distanced, ironic approach to the characters that Bogdanovich would take in his later films."

If Bogdanovich's next film (*Daisy Miller*) looks better today than when it was released because the ironic distancing, berated as an incorrect approach to the story at the time, can now be seen to have been entirely appropriate, *Paper Moon* conversely suffers for this same reason—particularly when compared to the films of Bogdanovich's second period. The film displays the main inadequacies of this approach (without carrying them to the extremes of *At Long Last Love*, however), characterized as it was by the "chilly calculation with which human interaction was manufactured" (Lucas, "Picture Show," p. 1317).

Particularly relevant here is Bogdanovich's radical restructuring of Sargent's first draft screenplay into a series of elongated episodes. Perhaps this reflects his uneasiness with the normal, straightforward narrative format. In particular, Addie and Imogene's plan to get rid of Trixie is given close to 20 minutes of screen time, providing for an elaborate hotel-corridor scene such as we were treated to in *What's Up, Doc?* However, as Roger Ebert notes, "this time the scene is played not as farce but for pathos and for the understanding of the child's earnestness."

Bogdanovich was not terribly concerned, one will recall, with making statements about society, whether past or

Trixie Delight (Madeline Kahn) confides in Addie.

present, during this phase of his career. He significantly cut from Sargent's script a scene wherein Moses takes Addie to see FDR against Moses' wishes. The fact that they do exist at all in the finished product may be attributed to the original sources. Recall that with the exception of *Targets*, all of Bogdanovich's original screenplays during this period were genre films whose subject matter was removed from reality to a large degree. Also, that the characterizations are more developed in *Paper Moon* than in any of his three previous pictures may be attributed entirely to the straightforward narrative structure of the film and the simple fact that there are fewer characters on which to concentrate in this case. Bogdanovich will not find himself in a similar situation again until *Mask*.

What is annoying about the film is that, although it should have come across as Bogdanovich's richest film to date, it remains curiously unsatisfying—but not to any great degree. This can be attributed entirely to the distanced tone which the director adopted, coupled with his choice of cinematography (black and white) and cinematographer (Kovacs). I am not objecting to the use of black and white in itself (certainly not after Surtees' astounding work on *Last Picture Show*), but rather the result of its employment in this particular case. Bogdanovich has explained what motivated him to shoot the film in black-and-white:

> For a long time, I felt I would shoot it in color. Three things really made me decide to do the picture in black and white. First, color photographs of the locations looked too pretty, while black and white photographs taken *today* immediately looked like the Depression. Second, the story is inherently sentimental—a child and a grownup together, no matter how it's handled, has implicit sentimentality that can be dangerous—and I felt I had to undercut the sentimentality as much as possible to convince myself that the story was real, or at least a metaphor for something real. I think black and white was the right way to make the story and characters seem more real. And there was a third reason: I also wanted the movie to be very stark. (McCluskey, p. 61)

First, with regard to the second reason, it seems from the evidence onscreen that Bogdanovich tried so hard to avoid sentimentalizing his characters (a potentially fatal flaw he overcame beautifully in *Last Picture Show* and would again later in *Mask*) by approaching them with a sense of disenchanted irony that he somehow succeeded in stifling almost all feeling for them (except for what the excellent acting of his principals managed to elicit in spite of this, particularly that of Tatum O'Neal, for whose performance Bogdanovich deserves much credit, since the eight-year-old was hardly disciplined at this stage).

Many have said that *Paper Moon* is his coldest film (*At Long Last Love* being spared this dishonor only because of the color and its pseudoromantic feel). I would amend that judgment by stating that it is also (along with *At Long Last Love*) his most artificial. One finds oneself continually frustrated in trying to respond to the antics of Addie, or the outrageous character of Trixie Delight—who finds she must relieve herself quite frequently, much to the consternation of the child. Particularly baffling is the director's explanation that he "deliberately didn't play some scenes for comedy—the Bible-selling scenes, for instance—although they could have been done that way. But that would have been dead wrong" (McCluskey, p. 89).

Even though Bogdanovich did not intend their adventures to be played for laughs, there was simply no other way they *could* be interpreted, given the nature of the material and the winning performances of the O'Neals

Addie studies a photo of herself without Moses. Note eponymous paper moon in background.

(their best work to date)—this obviously was not a documentary of the Depression, despite the stark cinematography. Apparently what he was aiming for was a kind of sustained feeling of melancholy, such as that which pervaded *The Last Picture Show*. And certainly with the Depression as backdrop to his story, he was not incorrect in thinking that such a tone might be appropriate here.

The problem is that even though he and Sargent made radical changes in the very funny original novel—so much so that Bogdanovich could rightly comment that "it's not *Addie Pray* any more"—they still retained the basic characters (Addie and Moses) and, by association, their occupation: swindling by means of clever ruses. This accounts for the conflict between the audience (which finds itself wanting but nevertheless unable to connect fully with the protagonists and enjoy their escapades) and the director (who wishes the characters to be viewed as mildly amusing but mainly tragic).

One of the scenes which retains all of its potential impact in spite of this distancing factor is the conversation between Trixie and Addie in the meadow, when the latter refuses to continue the trip because of Trixie's invasive presence. Here we have the most penetrating observation in the film: The lesson in being womanly which Trixie promises to give Addie is fruitless, while her request for reconciliation is working. Addie doesn't want makeup advice, but she does show herself sensitive to the sincere confession of a human condition.

From the initial little girl's whim, therefore, there might thus be the possibility of a more sincere friendship and the grotesque person of Trixie (another excellent Madeline Kahn characterization—she received an Oscar nomination for her role here), forced into a "role" for sheer survival, gradually reveals a basic humanity. There is already evidence of that understanding and that affection for women which will be seen again in *Daisy Miller* and *At Long*

Last Love and which will find its full expression in *They All Laughed*.

Getting back to the ending, what is most confounding about it is that one finds it difficult to view it completely *either* way, since he has been confined to observing the characters from the distanced, objective perspective of the director. Furthermore, the song "Keep Your Sunny Side Up" does not play against the scene (as was intended), but rather augments the already amused outlook of the viewer toward the characters. The other musical selections and excerpts from radio shows scattered throughout the film are similarly disappointing in terms of their effectiveness—there is none of the razor-sharp commentary on characters' motives present in *Last Picture Show*.

We understand that such radio personalities as Jack Benny and Fibber McGee and Molly served as an escape for victims of the Depression, but the point doesn't really hit home the way it should, and the sketches seem thrown away. Even the title song hints at a cutesy approach to the characters, which was the opposite of what Bogdanovich intended—though thematically it is appropriate.

I do not generally agree with John Simon's appraisals of Bogdanovich's early films, but I do think he was on to something when he labeled *Paper Moon* a "fake antique" (though his tone is too harsh). I also think Stanley Kauffmann's "I've never seen a film that looked so unlike what it was about" is apropos. Much of the reason for this can be attributed to Kovacs' cinematography and to the use of Polly Platt's production design. Bogdanovich once made the following observation about black and white:

> There is something more *and less* real about it. Less real in the sense that it's less realistic—after all, life is in color. But in a way it *seems* more real—maybe because we grew up with all those black and white news photographs. Maybe because it's tougher, harsher, therefore more "real," less glamorous,

less pretty—things tend to look "pretty" in color. (Denby, B. J., p. 78)

The key word is "photographs," and it points up an important distinction between Surtees' work on *Last Picture Show* and Kovacs' work here. In the first case, the drab, gritty look of the film combined with Bogdanovich's penetrating direction succeeded in bringing a period of history to life. Here, on the contrary, the effect is one of looking at a painting (or photograph) of the period, rather than of reliving it. Much of this has to do with the director's distanced perspective, but Kovacs, after all, shot the film. His work here seems artificial. John Simon's remark that the final shot of the winding road "looks like that cartoon road along which the Roadrunner eludes his eternal antagonist, the Coyote" is particularly significant—the

Addie and Trixie's maid, Imogene (P. J. Johnson). (Courtesy of Movie Star News)

reader will recall that that was precisely the look which Kovacs (along with Polly Platt) was aiming for on *What's Up, Doc?*, with its glossy cinematography. *Paper Moon* occasionally gives the impression of being a black-and-white *Doc*.

It is also interesting to compare Kovacs' work on *Paper Moon* to Gordon Willis's use of black and white in Woody Allen's *Manhattan* (1979) and *Broadway Danny Rose* (1984), which also seem out of place. Interestingly, Allen's four forays into period comedy/drama to date—*Love and Death* (1975), *Midsummer Night's Sex Comedy* (1982), *Purple Rose of Cairo* (1985), and *Radio Days* (1987)—were all shot in *color* (which was Bogdanovich's original choice for *Paper Moon*). Kovacs' photography here has been compared by some to Gregg Toland's on Ford's *Grapes of Wrath* (1940), but I do not think the comparison is a just one.

Paper Moon has often been termed Bogdanovich's homage to John Ford, because of the abundance of long shots in the picture and because it reminds one vaguely of such Ford films as *Grapes of Wrath* and *Tobacco Road* (1941) with a similar setting. In reality, it is here that his style comes closest to Martin Rubin's definition of Hawks' style. In contrast to *Last Picture Show*, the environment here is abstract—that "nihilistic, black void" similar to the ones which surrounded the characters in Hawks' *Only Angels Have Wings* (1939) and *To Have and Have Not* (1944). And like *Last Picture Show*, the characters are concrete, so that we follow their response to and against their surroundings (exemplified by Addie and Moses' schemes to cheat the Depression by swindling people).

The problem with the environment's being abstract is that the effect of Polly Platt's painstaking efforts on the production design is considerably dissipated. Whereas in *Last Picture Show* the environment was so concrete that the period became another character in the story, here it is merely a backdrop, and as a result we do not get nearly so much of a feeling for the setting as we should (other than the fact that it was a barren wasteland, of course). The

Stealing whiskey.

period (along with the accompanying black and white) almost seems imposed on the story, since the film generates very little atmosphere—particularly when compared to such later films as *Saint Jack* and *They All Laughed.* I remarked in the chapter on *Last Picture Show* that that film seemed "packaged." That flaw is much more apparent in this case, but still in its early stages—*At Long Last Love* is two years away.

With reference to Bogdanovich's visual style, an alert observer should note the deliberate paucity of close-ups and de-emphasis on cutting here—especially in the scenes in the car, which are done almost entirely in unbroken two-shots—in contrast to the predominance of the same in *Last Picture Show.* Bogdanovich has noted on more than one occasion that the angle of a shot has a subconscious emotional effect on the viewer. The reason *Last Picture*

Show is, in Larry McMurtry's words, "remarkable for the sheer *feeling* which it releases" is precisely due to the subjective tone created by the director's remarkably facile and dextrous editing throughout.

One need only contrast certain similar scenes in the two films—such as the quarrel between Bottoms and Bridges around the car in *Picture Show* with Ryan O'Neal's brief fight with Randy Quaid here—to note that there is a world of difference between them in terms of viewer response. The first is exciting and disorienting; the second is only mildly diverting at best. And that description pretty much covers this viewer's response to most of the film. It becomes increasingly wearying as it moves along, particularly as the settings become darker. This may have something to do with the fact that Bogdanovich did not enjoy making the film—interestingly, the same was true of *Nickelodeon*, which

Addie contemplates leaving Moses and going to live with her aunt.

also suffered from a feeling of directorial enervation, though to a much greater extent. It proved to be the film's fatal flaw.

Typical of Bogdanovich's feelings about the stylistic aspects of *Paper Moon* was this statement of his: "The idea of doing a comedy chase in *What's Up, Doc?* was exciting because it was something I hadn't done and it was a different kind of action. . . . But when it came time for the chase in *Paper Moon*, I was bored with it—I already knew I could do a chase, so the challenge was gone." What is ironic is that in *Paper Moon* Bogdanovich's technique seems more effortless than in his three previous pictures, which is probably why he remarked at the time that it was his favorite film to date, but the resulting work is not so interesting as any one of them—but still superior to his next three efforts.

6   *Daisy Miller* (1974)

After three enormous commercial successes, Bogdanovich decided he could make a film "for myself"—one that would probably not spark much of an interest with the public, but which appealed to him personally as an interesting subject. Having established an enviable position for himself by joining with Francis Ford Coppola and William Friedkin in an association known as the Directors Company, whose films would be distributed by Paramount (*Paper Moon* had been the first of these), Bogdanovich now had carte blanche—provided, however, that he stay within a budget of $3 million. The director told Martin Rubin how he finally came to settle on Henry James' novella *Daisy Miller* as the choice for his next film:

> I was going to do *The Apple Tree*, a story written by John Galsworthy in 1916. Actually, the story is similar to *Daisy Miller* in many ways: it's a love story about missed opportunities, it's about class differences, it's about an unwillingness to commit oneself emotionally to something that is alien or different. . . . I had been planning to do this story since I was about sixteen. For years I tried to get the rights, but they eluded me. . . . Finally, when I went to Warner Brothers to make *What's Up, Doc?*, it turned out that Warner now owned the rights, and I was free to make it. So I hired Gavin Lambert to write the screenplay, and it was quite a good script, but I just didn't want to make it. Like many beloved projects, you want to do it for so long that by the time you do get to do it you just don't want to anymore. It's almost as

though you'd made it already and so there's no longer any
challenge left.

Then I was developing yet another story based on an
incident that happened to an Italian friend of mine when he
stayed at the Plaza Hotel in New York: he came out around
two in the morning, it was so hot, and found an absolutely
stunning girl lying on the fountain, asleep. In the story, she
turns out to be this girl from Texas, a real Amazon, who hits
him every time he makes a pass at her. Then it went into a
cross-country trip—what I really wanted to do was make
Lolita, but it was not possible. I thought it would be funny
with, say, Cybill Shepherd and Marcello Mastroianni. We
tried to develop it, but it didn't work out, probably because
it was just one good incident that wouldn't develop into a
script.

So I didn't have a picture. Around about here, somehow
or other, I read *Daisy Miller* again, not having read it for
many years. And it seemed exactly the right thing to do, like
a sign from heaven, because there was the whole idea of an
Italian versus American background which I had become
interested in after going to Rome in 1969. And it also had
the same basic idea as *The Apple Tree*, the same-theme of
missed opportunities, yet done better, much more elegantly
and less sentimentally. And a great part for Cybill Shepherd, with whom I had wanted to make another picture ever
since *The Last Picture Show*. (Rubin, pp. 7–9)

Since Bogdanovich stated at the time of its release (15
years ago at this writing) that he "hoped the movie of *Daisy
Miller* could stand on its own, and not be forever stapled to
the book," it seems only fair (though many will doubtless
refer to this approach as sacrilege) to discuss it—on the
whole—only so far as it reflects the temperament and
concerns of its creator, Bogdanovich. There have been
numerous writings—including the original reviews—noting at length its "faithfulness" (or lack of same) to James,
but practically none (with the notable exceptions of essays
by Barry Putterman and Vittorio Giacci) which attempt to
critique it strictly as a Bogdanovich film and not as just

another filmed adaptation of a minor (though there are those who would argue this point) but important work by a great novelist.

Granted, in contrast to Bogdanovich's adaptation of *Last Picture Show*, for example, the nature of the transformation in this case may not at first glance seem to permit such a radical interpretation. *Daisy Miller* was Bogdanovich's first film to contain no explicit allusions to the cinema (indeed, it was set in a period before the invention of motion pictures). They had been the distinguishing feature of Bogdanovich's style and approach thus far, compensating for his lack of genuine social commitment. This time out, however, the uniquely Bogdanovichian characteristics which formerly thrived on his reservoir of knowledge about the movies managed to find newer, more personal sources of inspiration. This does not mean that with *Daisy*

Barry Brown as Frederick Winterbourne.

Miller he became a statement-oriented filmmaker, only that his general outlook seemed more mature for not having any obvious precedents.

Barry Putterman observes that despite the fact that the film "owed much of its structure to James" (to whose sequence of events Bogdanovich, after several initial radical changes, decided to remain faithful), it managed to "emerge as the clearest distillation of Bogdanovich's concerns." In addition, Giacci has remarked that it was Bogdanovich's "most successful film [to date] in terms of form, in the sense of a total identity between story and style" (p. 90)—a feat the director would not surpass until 1985's *Mask*.

For Bogdanovich, *Daisy Miller* was basically "a love story about missed opportunities . . . class differences . . . [and] an unwillingness to commit oneself emotionally to something that is alien or different." Bogdanovich views the relationship between Daisy (actually Annie P.) Miller (Shepherd), a young American girl who is spending her summer vacation abroad, and Frederick Winterbourne (Barry Brown), an American transplanted in Europe for quite some time, as doomed from the outset and thus the film in general, as Giacci puts it, ultimately becomes "a long death vigil for the girl" (Daisy dies at the conclusion)— though technically, as Bogdanovich has said, "it only takes Daisy a reel to die, whereas it takes Winterbourne a long time." Bogdanovich embodied this idea in the character of Daisy's little cousin, Randolph (James McMurtry), a character he toughened from James' original conception. As the director explained it, there is

> an element of foreboding about Randolph, as if he somehow knows what's going to happen. Children do have, I think, a sixth sense, because they're closer to their feelings than adults. In a subtle way, I wanted Randolph to feel what was happening between Daisy and Winterbourne, which is why I added that abstracted little moment where he's up in the

tree and goes "Bang" with the fake rifle after Winterbourne. Then, later, we see Randolph fooling around with a noose. Children are obsessed with death anyway—they're more ghoulish than grownups. (p. 15)

The tragic overtones of the story immediately recall *Last Picture Show*. This time, however, the characters and situations took on a completely original dimension. Barry Putterman has described the change accurately:

> Whereas in past films the gentle dreamers either found their mates to be part of the hard reality of the defeating environment (*Picture Show*) or the triumphant topography of a higher level of humanity (*Doc* and *Moon*), here Bogdanovich was showing us characters who combined aspects of dreamers and realists. The socially untutored but emotionally incisive Daisy and the socially mature but emotionally naive Winterbourne are shown in all their foolishness but as essentially good people whose mis-matched failings made them tragically vulnerable to the surrounding society. (p. 52)

Daisy Miller remains Bogdanovich's most important study of the interrelationship between love and death, his two main obsessions. The film's tone is both romantic and fatalistic at the same time, the former characteristic being chiefly embodied in the figure of Daisy, the latter in both, but particularly in Winterbourne. The general feeling is also decidedly more melancholy than ever before; Bog-danovich's two protagonists are not even permitted a momentary clinch this time (though they do spend a good amount of time together in the first part of the film).

Now that we know from *Picture Show, At Long Last Love*, and *They All Laughed* (but most importantly from the last film) that Bogdanovich's main sympathies have always been with the women in his films, it is possible to view *Daisy Miller*, his first work to feature a single woman as its cynosure, as the most significant early manifestation of this

Mr. Giovanelli and Daisy (Cybill Shepherd) in the castle at Chillon.

motif (in fact, he joked at the time that his detractors would probably take this film to be his homage to George Cukor). But because *Daisy Miller*, unlike the two later efforts, was not nearly so much of a stylistic exercise, Bogdanovich was permitted more leeway to deal on an exclusive basis with the theme of innocence, prevalent but somewhat overshadowed in his earlier works and tied in with his romantic temperament.

Bogdanovich molds his heroine, Daisy (dressed throughout in virginal whites, blues, and golds), to represent the traditional concept of the immaculate female. Whether she is in terms of the story itself actually "pure" is of no consequence to him, as he simply admires the ideal of female perfection. In fact, he uses this concept as a means for indicting the hypocritical Winterbourne, who spends the duration of the film wondering whether Daisy is, in fact, innocent, and thereby worthy of his attention, and ends up with only an uncertain verification by her intimate companion, the Italian Giovanelli (Duilio Del Prete), after her death. As the director has said,

> It is not important whether Daisy [was], in fact, innocent. The fact that maybe she is, which is what Giovanelli tells Winterbourne, is an interesting point, but I don't think it matters. It's as though if she weren't innocent, then Winterbourne's reactions would be correct and justified. . . . If you're making a movie about a girl who's a flirt—who, as Giovanelli says at the end, "did what she liked"—then it isn't a question of whether she is innocent or not. We're saying, "Why shouldn't she do what she likes?" (Rubin, p. 25)

But Daisy has additional significance for Bogdanovich which extends beyond the confines of the story. He has described her as "a symbol of the vitality and life [characteristic of] the New World" (Winterbourne, on the other hand, remains trapped between the Old and New World cultures, forever incapable of establishing a firm allegiance with either). For Bogdanovich, she became the means for affirming the image of original innocence and cultural stability on the part of America (qualities which were called into question by the established American expatriates who felt most comfortable in their new European environment). This attitude had a great deal to do with the fact that Bogdanovich himself was a first-generation American, and therefore "tended to embrace America in a way that subsequent generations didn't." Thus the film's theme becomes innocence in its dual aspect—individual and collective, real and metaphorical—as related to a woman as well as to the place she is from.

Bogdanovich contrasts the image of Daisy with those of the two representatives of the American community of expatriates in Europe who disapprove of her behavior, the dark and mysterious Mrs. Walker (Eileen Brennan), and

Conference between Mrs. Costello (Mildred Natwick) and Winterbourne in thermal baths at Vevey.

the elderly, repressed spinster Mrs. Costello (Mildred Natwick). The director has stressed, however, that his identifying the essential purity and optimism of his home-land with Daisy only and the decadent and unwholesome (even evil) refinement of the Continent with the latter two characters was not intended to be taken as any kind of overt microcosm in either case.

> I decided not to tell [the story] in terms of other people's reactions [to Daisy's behavior] on the street. It seemed to me that Mrs. Walker [and Mrs. Costello were] the [ones who were] reacting badly, and if you generalized it, then it would become a social story, which I don't think is terribly interesting. If everybody is stopping to look at her, it becomes a story about how this just isn't done in this society. I don't think it's about society condemning her, it's about one or two people condemning her. I think that's always an easy way out, to say, "Well, society . . ." Society is made up of a bunch of people, and it's the one or two you know that screw you, not the whole world. (Rubin, p. 24)

This approach is reminiscent of and consistent with the indirect social commitment which had characterized Bog-danovich's treatments of his two previous films derived from novels dealing with America's past: *Picture Show* and *Paper Moon*. However, it is all the more obvious this time around for not being compensated for by an identification of the story's past with that of the cinema. Paradoxically, this does not make *Daisy Miller* a less weighty film than the other two, but instead allows for a more satisfying explora-tion of Bogdanovich's themes (and, by extension, style, as we shall see shortly) while still permitting the director to confine himself primarily to the task of telling a story simply and clearly.

If Daisy represents an ideal of beauty and goodness for Bogdanovich, then Winterbourne is the direct antithesis of that ideal: by contrast to Daisy's image, a dark, shady, somewhat sinister mien characterizes him. Bogdanovich has remarked that he "tried to hate him but couldn't, although he stands for everything I loathe. He's a coward, he's a judge, he's meanspirited" (Rubin, p. 14). This view is particularly interesting when one considers that Bogdanovich had originally considered playing the role himself; he finally decided against it because it would have seemed like an ironic commentary on his public persona (he was living with Cybill Shepherd at the time).

Bogdanovich's comments remind one of Welles' description of the disreputable cop Hank Quinlan whom he played in his thriller *Touch of Evil* (1958): "He stands for everything I hate." But despite the fact that Barry Brown, instead of Bogdanovich, plays Winterbourne, certain aspects of Bogdanovich's personality do shine through nevertheless, particularly in Winterbourne's moony gazes at Daisy and his affected haughty reserve with regard to her behavior.

It is only Winterbourne's actions which Bogdanovich views as reprehensible, since it is *his* lack of initiative which finally prevents him from reaping the happiness he might have had with Daisy. Daisy's "unconventional" behavior is viewed as a natural response to an already too-repressed European culture (represented by Mrs. Walker and Mrs. Costello). By contrast to the aggressive women in Bogdanovich's other films, Daisy is viewed mainly as an object, someone to be worshiped from afar.

Although Bogdanovich does indicate at several important moments (most notably in Mrs. Walker's parlor when Daisy reacts to Winterbourne's reproving statements with "I prefer weak tea") that she knows more than either Winterbourne or the audience thinks she does, she is basically the toy of the men in the film (specifically Giovanelli, who beats Winterbourne at his own game by initiating a relationship with her). It should be noted, however, that, in contrast to the character Jacy in *Picture Show* (also played by Shepherd), the conquest of Daisy is viewed as a positive thing by Bogdanovich. The latter,

Puppet show at Pincio.

despite her aloofness, is basically sweet and good-natured, whereas Jacy had no heart.

This idea of object worship ties in both with the distanced approach to the characters which Bogdanovich once again applies (as he had in *Paper Moon*), but with far greater success this time around, and also with the theme of voyeurism evident in Winterbourne's behavior throughout. Just as Bogdanovich (and by implication, the audience) views Daisy and Winterbourne from a somewhat remote perspective, judging the actions of the latter while vindicating the former at every turn, so the viewer also (because of the director's identification with the male protagonist) confines himself to observing Daisy from a distance along with Winterbourne. This motif of voyeurism will reappear in *They All Laughed* and *Illegally Yours*—and in *Saint Jack* also, but in a different type of context—

and in all three cases Bogdanovich stresses that merely looking is no substitute for the real thing, though he does not view the John Ritter and Rob Lowe characters in the first two films harshly, due to the fact that they are in a comic as opposed to a tragic context.

J. J. Liggera, in an article on the film, has described the effect which Bogdanovich's approach finally has upon both the viewer's perception of Winterbourne and of himself:

> We [have seen Winterbourne] so subtly and quickly [as effete in a moment at the Pincio earlier on wherein Winterbourne proved himself incapable of responding either to Daisy or to a more mature woman who caught his eye] that we [have remained] dependent upon his view of things to the end, failing to withdraw from him until too late. The secret of James' novel is brought home: the viewer doesn't really care about the frivolous Daisy until he himself learns, also too late, what a suspicious prig he has been and how he has betrayed his best instincts for love, as well as his culture, for acquired standards, acquired from the rather cowardly Winterbourne. (Liggera, p. 20)

Bogdanovich's point is that Winterbourne can only become sentimentally close to Daisy after her death (when, of course, it is too late), due to his inability to break out of his own moral boundaries for fear of participating in life. Because of this impotence, he remains for the duration of the film (even after Daisy's death, when her innocence or lack thereof is never clearly revealed) incapable of distinguishing what Daisy really is from what she seems to be, and thus doesn't succeed in resolving the misunderstanding about unconfessed feelings. The director's rather cool, objective stance serves the delineation of this particular character—a man who suffers from an inability to become emotional—especially well.

Barry Putterman has explained how the technique Bogdanovich adopted in *Daisy* complemented his aims in terms of the story and characters:

Giovanelli (Duilio Del Prete) steals Daisy away from a jealous Winter-bourne.

[Whereas none of Bogdanovich's previous films] seemed to have much dimension beyond finding the proper style to suit the material, *Daisy Miller*, done in Wellesian deep focus with overlapping dialogue, on the other hand, found its style enhancing the tensions in the material and helping to put a layer of modern commentary upon the nineteenth-century story, which neither condescended to nor disengaged the viewer from the film. (p. 52)

Certainly the most obvious—and often cited—influence on the style of the film is Welles—in fact, according to Bogdanovich, he was originally going to direct the picture, with Bogdanovich and Shepherd as costars, but eventually decided the project was better suited to his protégé's sensibilities. Nevertheless, Welles made several important suggestions to Bogdanovich about his approach to the story (including the idea to begin the film by introducing the boy, Randolph, first). And Frederic Raphael, who adapted the novella to the screen with Bogdanovich, notes that the latter spoke constantly of Welles for the duration of their time together.

The elaborate downward pan which opens the film recalls three similar moments in *Citizen Kane* (1941): the first and second-to-last shots scanning the length of the chain-link fence, and the upward climb to the theater wings where one of two stagehands holds his nose to express his distaste for Susan Alexander's singing. To note this similarity is not nitpicking; one can be certain that Bogdanovich got the idea for this shot—whether consciously or not—from *Kane*, since it is one of his most-loved films (he had seen it over 15 times before 1974, when he made *Daisy*).

The other Wellesian inspirations are the superfast overlapping dialogue used throughout to characterize the Miller family, and the depth of focus which Bogdanovich and his cinematographer, Alberto Spagnoli, worked hard to achieve (and which is linked to the motif of voyeurism).

Wellesian deep-focus composition.

None of these devices, however, was employed as any kind of deliberate homage to Welles—as well-conceived and highly adaptable bits of technique, they simply found their place in the context of this filmed story without seeming like flourishes.

Bogdanovich intended *Daisy* to be "the simplest movie [I'd made] in terms of the way it [was] shot." Continuing the procedure he had begun with *Paper Moon* (and which would find its ultimate expression in *At Long Last Love*), Bogdanovich's visual style began to rely more and more on long takes, with a distinct de-emphasis on cutting (again, this is linked to the distancing factor)—but despite the resemblance to Welles, it was still far from baroque. In *Daisy*, as well as *Love* (though there the technique does not succeed nearly so well), Bogdanovich employs mirrors to facilitate this approach. He has said that his use of them in

Daisy "ties in with the whole voyeuristic aspect of Winterbourne: he'll look but he won't touch. He'll examine with
his eyes, but he won't make a move to really grasp it, except
perhaps obliquely."

Of course, such a reliance on long takes puts a greater
burden on the performers to sustain a scene, and can
succeed in exposing all insincerity in a performance.
Bogdanovich's best use of the technique occurs at two
important moments in the story. The first is during Daisy's
and Winterbourne's introductory meeting. He holds Shepherd and Brown in a close two-shot for nearly a full five
minutes, during which time we witness a complete delineation of the Daisy character in particular, with all of her
various traits (vanity, frivolousness, genuine sweetness,
playful abandon, deception) alternately emanating from
her ever-changing countenance. As Giacci says, it is "a bit
of masterful direction which, by its captivating rhythm
alone, makes us forget everything, even that the actors are
performing in costume, and lets us indulge again our taste
for 'pure' cinema." Of course, one cannot ignore the
contributions of Brown and Shepherd—especially the
latter—in this scene.

The other splendid sequence occurs much later in the
film. J. J. Liggera has described it in detail:

> Winterbourne comes jauntily along with a bouquet of
> flowers to Daisy's hotel. Music plays gaily but we hear no
> dialogue. We are being deliberately held back from Winter-
> bourne and forced to view him. He opens the hotel door and
> we see through lace on the window pane. He jogs up the
> stairs, at long last following his instincts and about to rescue
> Daisy. He is happy, and we who have followed him so long
> are happy, too, but then we notice there is a shadow on the
> lace curtain as door closes. Winterbourne is stopped half-
> way up the first set of stairs by the voice of the concierge,
> though we don't hear it. The flowers droop; he descends the
> stairs and passes out through the door again as the lace
> turns from brightness to gray. Daisy is dead. We know that

> Winterbourne has irrevocably lost the best and freshest part of his future. (p. 20)

For the most part, the success of the work derives more from the power of Bogdanovich's imagery than from any affection for the characters (viewed, as they are, from a necessarily distanced perspective) on the part of the audience. Bogdanovich has said that "everything you do in a movie is a pictorial effect of some kind—if you're making a good movie." This is more true of *Daisy Miller* perhaps than of any of his previous or subsequent efforts, mainly because of the use of painterly imagery throughout to flesh out the ambiguities in James' story.

Bogdanovich has credited his artist father, Borislav Bogdanovich, with the inspiration for the photographic style of the film, in particular his Byzantine background,

"Pop Goes the Weasel": Cybill Shepherd and Duilio Del Prete.

which accounted for the vividness and vibrancy of the film's colors. In fact, in describing his approach to adapting James' novella, Bogdanovich himself used artist's terms, noting that the original work was merely a "sketch," not a "finished canvas."

The process of fleshing out the tale provided Bogdanovich with a greater opportunity than ever before to allow his imagination to play. When John Simon complains that Bogdanovich's direction is "pictorial rather than psychological, preferring effect to truthfulness," he overlooks the success of such touches as the final "white-out" at the cemetery, a device which is itself the very essence of cinema—a purely visual moment conveying a wealth of possible interpretations with regard to the character of Winterbourne and his ultimate fate.

Also notable is the night scene at the Colosseum toward the end where Winterbourne searches for Daisy and Giovanelli among the corridors. Bogdanovich manages to convey viscerally the forbidding atmosphere of the place, where Roman fever was contracted by many (including Daisy). And, too, there is the final shot of the castle at Chillon from inside the carriage in which Daisy and Winterbourne are riding, a moment which Martin Rubin rightly dubs "nostalgic."

Simon characterizes the latter as simply a pictorial effect and nothing more because it is not taken from the point of view of either chraracter (unlike the scene with Sonny Crawford gazing sadly out the back window of a car at the barren Texas landscape which was cut from *Picture Show*). On the contrary, it is perfectly in keeping with Bogdanovich's remote outlook; it is not Daisy's and Winterbourne's reactions which are important here (they have already acknowledged their failed attempt at intimacy, so there is no need for them to look back), but that of the audience, which is forced by the director to put the whole scene into perspective.

Frederic Raphael, who worked on the adaptation with

Bogdanovich (Raphael alone received screen credit, though Bogdanovich fought to have his name included for deciding to throw out the initial version of the script and stick closer to James' original), rather ungenerously comments that "the lack of invention in the film is all Bogdanovich's, though the few touches of originality are mine." One suspects this criticism has much to do with his bitterness over having been denied—by his own account—his final payment on the script by Bogdanovich's lawyers after the director learned he was not to receive screen credit for his work.

Despite the fact that Raphael did invent the elaborate thermal-baths sequence with Mrs. Costello and Winterbourne (the conversation takes place in a hotel room in the novel), the success of the scene owes much to Bogdanovich's careful attendance to detail in the direction of it (and the fact that he, as director, decided it should be included in the first place). I cite in particular the moment where Mrs. Costello says to Winterbourne, "You've lived too long out of the country. You'll be sure to make some great mistake." In contrast to the rest of the scene—which, by its rather bizarre nature, was intended by Bogdanovich to create a feeling of humor and relaxation in Mrs. Costello's characterization, so that the audience would sense a definite change later in Rome—these important phrases are uttered when the two of them have stepped out of the bath ("the main reason I had them get out at all," Bogdanovich said).

But despite the success of these scenes, there *is* nevertheless about the direction a certain heavy-handedness (and Simon does have a point here) which inevitably comes from any attempt to give a "literal" interpretation to a literary work which depends solely for its effectiveness on the delicate shadings of written prose. At times Bogdanovich's film reminds one of John Huston's *Bible* (1966), roundly panned for its often tasteless pictorializations of certain events (the Garden of Eden sequence in particular) which left nothing to the imagination. Bogdanovich's source material was certainly not so sacred, but in his attempts to visualize the ambiguities in James' work, he often succeeded in, as Simon put it, "making the ambiguities obvious."

What have fared least well in the translation are the majority of the supporting characterizations (with the notable exceptions of Eileen Brennan's Mrs. Walker and Mildred Natwick's Mrs. Costello, both marvelous). Bogdanovich's use of overlapping dialogue to characterize the Miller family—Daisy's mother (Cloris Leachman) in particular—for example, seems like a good enough idea at first, given the fact that, as he said, the original story is full of lengthy speeches written as one huge paragraph, but the effect soon becomes tiresome and threatens to turn already thin parts into caricatures.

Winterbourne is informed by Daisy's mother (Cloris Leachman) that Daisy is dying.

The latter description is true also for Del Prete's Giovanelli, who comes across as rather simpleminded (though this no doubt has something to do with the actor playing him, judging from his appearance in Bogdanovich's next film, *At Long Last Love*), for little James McMurtry's Randolph, who recites all his lines by vacuous rote as though he were reading them from a scroll, and even for Brown's Winterbourne, who isn't allowed to do much except stare forlornly at the object of his unrequited love. He makes a decidedly uncomfortable surrogate for Bogdanovich, considering his inadequacy in the role and the fact that he doesn't come across as nearly so intelligent as the director—who chose him because he looked like that rare actor who had read a book—intended. Andrew Sarris's suggestion that Bogdanovich could have "beefed up" the character by "giving him interior monologues to go with his overly discreet dialogue" is particularly astute, considering that, as he says, Winterbourne as given comes across as merely "a pale shadow on the screen until the very end, when he becomes the ghost of a love lost."

Cybill Shepherd's Daisy has been cited by most critics who otherwise admire the film (and by those who do not like it at all) as its primary shortcoming. Part of the problem has been that people have viewed the idea of Shepherd—who hails from Memphis—playing this character as inappropriate. The director explains that this is really not the case at all:

> If I were telling a western with the same basic plot—an Eastern girl comes to the West, she doesn't understand the way you're supposed to behave, people don't understand her—nobody would have any difficulty at all believing the character. After all, the picture is set in the same period most westerns are set, 1875 or 1880. But the minute you take this chattering American girl, sophisticated, highbrow, artistic, pretentious—some people find it hard to believe. Still, that's essentially the *point* of Henry James' story.

One of Bogdanovich's primary motives for undertaking the project was, as he said, to provide a suitable starring vehicle for Shepherd. Both this film and his next important study of the female personality, *They All Laughed*, might be considered valentines to the women who are their centerpieces (in the case of the latter, the one in question is Dorothy Stratten, the next major love of Bogdanovich's life—though nearly all of the women in that film were intimate acquaintances of the director at some point). Significantly, until *They All Laughed*, *Daisy* was Bogdanovich's favorite among all his films.

It is interesting to note the difference in tone between the two films as they correspond to the screen projections of his two stars: *Daisy* is cold and distanced, in keeping with Shepherd's rather cool, aloof beauty (again recalling Pauline Kael's description of her as an "object"), and *They All Laughed* warm and inviting, reflecting Stratten's nature. With regard to Shepherd, it is curious to note that, of the three films in which Bogdanovich featured her, it is only *Daisy* which provided her with a characterization which could at least partly be considered likable. Sarris, comparing Bogdanovich's treatment of Shepherd in *Daisy* to Welles' treatment of the Anne Baxter and Dolores Costello characters in *The Magnificent Ambersons* (1942)—to which he thinks *Daisy* might be an homage—comments that there is "infinitely more love" in the latter.

Actually, if one looks at the film objectively, it is not hard to see what the director meant by his statement that James could have written the part with Shepherd in mind: she possesses both the icy unattainability revealed in *Picture Show* and, even more fully, in Elaine May's *Heartbreak Kid* (1972), and a newfound vulnerability which removes all traces of the spitefulness present in her role in *Picture Show*. The big problem with Shepherd—and one which would prove to be a much more seriousness detriment in her next film for Bogdanovich, *At Long Last Love*—is her incessant silliness and lack of discipline or genuine conviction. Time and time again, just when one thinks she has the character down pat, she comes up with an incredibly forced line reading that throws all her previous work straight to the winds. She never seems quite relaxed enough in the part. Also, one has great difficulty deciding whether she really understands the role or is merely projecting her own rather inane personality (this judgment is based on her appearances with Bogdanovich on daytime talk shows at the time).

As a result of these and other flaws (including the pace, which seems unnecessarily hurried, particularly in the Chillon sequence early in the film—perhaps the result of Bogdanovich's last two features having been comedies— and certain visualizations of ironic foreshadowings, like the puppet Punch slaying Death during the show at the Pincio, or Randolph's aiming his alpenstock at Winterbourne and going "Bang!" which seem merely obvious), the film often threatens to resemble a cartoon, not unlike the director's own *What's Up, Doc?*—though there, of course, that look was completely apropos—and seems to be merely another exercise in style, though this was not really what Bogdanovich had in mind. And yet—and this is the truly remarkable thing about *Daisy*—the film is not really empty in terms of content at all; in fact, as we have seen, the film is actually rife with meaning.

As I mentioned earlier, *Daisy* was Bogdanovich's first film to contain no explicit allusions to the cinema, thereby permitting more room for an exploration of his personality than ever before. This had its benefits; the funeral sequence in this film, for example, has more emotional resonance than even Sam the Lion's in *Picture Show* (because of the overdependence on the symbolic nature of the character as related to the concept of the western and the too-neat structure of the story in that film), and is the complete antithesis of that which opened *Paper Moon* (merely a device for setting up the premise).

Nevertheless, the enterprise could not help echoing the

cinephile who had made *Targets, Last Picture Show*, and *What's Up, Doc?*—in fact, critic John Baxter remarked that the whole enterprise seemed "more redolent of Henry King than Henry James." Bogdanovich in interviews compared the condition of Winterbourne at the film's conclusion, for example, to Scottie Ferguson's (James Stewart's) paralyzed state at the end of Hitchcock's *Vertigo* (1958), or Winterbourne's obsession with Daisy (crystallized in a scene invented by Bogdanovich but never filmed in which Winterbourne rummages through Daisy's room when she is out) with Scottie's for Madeline (Kim Novak) or detective Mark McPherson's (Dana Andrews) for Laura (Gene Tierney) in Preminger's *Laura* (1944).

But these are merely arbitrary—if apt—comparisons (as is Sarris's comment about *Ambersons*). Fourteen years after its release, *Daisy Miller* remains one of Bogdanovich's most original, if not wholly successful, works, and it deserves a larger audience than it has received.

7   *At Long Last Love* (1975)

At Long Last Love, Bogdanovich's infamous fiasco, the film which crippled his standing in Hollywood for years (and which still evokes scoffs and headshaking in some circles whenever it is mentioned), seems now, 14 years after its release, ready to be viewed in a somewhat different light than that which greeted its (short-lived) premiere at Radio City Music Hall in March of 1975. The solid reputation of Bogdanovich's comeback film, *Mask* (1985)—along with the decade between *Love* and that film—dispelled much of the criticism which greeted his film efforts in the 1970s. As a result, it is now possible to view his most outstanding early failure on its own (misunderstood) terms and not as the ultimate wish-fulfillment fantasy for those critics who had been out to get Bogdanovich for personal reasons from the start.

Bogdanovich has said that his main intent with the Cole Porter musical was "to try to show the very tenuousness and difficulty of a relationship that's based on what we all think is 'falling in love.' What *is* falling in love? That's what the movie was about." Therein lay his attempt to mock the conventions of the musical form, in which everything is usually taken for granted and all difficulties in relationships neatly resolved before the final fade-out. This outlook is a combination of the two opposing forces in Bogdanovich's personality—the romantic and the melancholic. While he would like everything to work out splendidly in the end, he knows it cannot, since real life is not like the movies.

Thus, he concocted a plot (actually, a series of parallel subplots, as is his wont) in which two couples meet by chance, fall instantly in love, then at midpoint stop to contemplate the nature of their feelings for each other ("Is it a fancy not worth thinking of, or is it at long last love?"). After this, the women begin to grow bored with their mates—the singer, Kitty O'Kelly (Madeline Kahn) with the playboy, Pritchard (Burt Reynolds) because he does not reciprocate her feelings, and the heiress, Brooke (Cybill Shepherd) with her Italian gambler, Johnny Spanish (Duilio Del Prete) because he is too silly and frivolous (his preoccupation is with the comic strip "Little Orphan Annie").

When opportunity presents itself, the couples switch partners and begin again—only to have the men call the whole thing off this time because they have decided they care more for their original mates than they had realized. It is the women who again are heartbroken. Finally the four get together at a dance, at which time the women inform their initial partners that they no longer have feelings for them ("A Picture of Me Without You"), and dance away with their second loves, the women finally having achieved some degree of happiness (though it cannot equal that of the first pairing), the men resigning themselves simply to having a good time, knowing that they have lost the women they cared about most.

Despite the fact that technically Bogdanovich was working within an established genre here, he—true to form—defied convention by *not* having a happy ending (in fact, he said he constructed the plot backward from the sad Porter song "I Loved Him," heard shortly before the climax). The director says the film is basically about "the difficulties of maintaining relationships, and how you like one person for sex and another person for something else." The former is particularly true for the men in the piece; it is the women who are capable of the deepest feelings, and it is they

Johnny Spanish (Duilio Del Prete) tells a poker-playing buddy that things will be brighter "Tomorrow." (Courtesy of Movie Star News)

(particularly the Madeline Kahn character) who suffer when their men take them for granted.

In the end, while both sexes have had their hopes for a pure, untroubled, lasting relationship with the ones they truly cared for shattered, the women at least have found a decent substitute in the other's partner, while the future for the men looks less satisfying. But all are no doubt a bit wiser for the wear, making the ending seem more bitter-sweet than sad.

The major problem with the film is that, despite the complications of the plot and the subsequent effects on the characters, the audience is never made to feel for any of it. Andrew Sarris has described the enterprise aptly:

> What *Love* lacks most of all is warmth and any trace of sexual attraction. . . . The audience is left hanging at the end with an unfinished quadrangle beset by coldness and casual cross-purposes. . . . If all of Bogdanovich's previous enterprises have been suspect on any single ground, it has been on the ground of emotional commitment. *Targets, Picture Show, Doc, Moon, Daisy, John Ford* stay in the mind more for the intelligence of their stylistic calculations than for any revelation of personal feeling. (Sarris, 1975)

This is particularly sad when one considers Bogdanovich's statement that in fact he *was* "every bit as involved emotionally in [the musical] as I was in a film like *Picture Show*. The fact that it doesn't come across that way to the critics or perhaps the public is another story. But it was, in point of fact, a more personal project than any I'd done so far." (Denby, B. J., p. 81). If Sarris's comment about the precedence of style over content in Bogdanovich's previous films is correct, then in many ways *Love* can be considered (unfortunately) the ultimate film of Bogdanovich's first period, a film in which style had become an end in itself.

That such a film would eventually be made by Bogdanovich should be no surprise, since in past interviews he had continually shown more concern for and interest in the process of making films than in the possible thematic concerns of his pictures. This time around, he set himself the biggest challenge of all, choosing a genre which was, as he himself acknowledged, the most specialized and difficult of all in terms of execution—particularly for someone with no prior experience in the form.

A further handicap was the decision to opt for a Lubitschian type of format in which all the musical numbers would have to be photographed in a single take—the ultimate expression of the distancing present in the films since *Moon*. Indeed, even such a master of the long take as Lubitsch heir Otto Preminger had stumbled badly when he made the stilted *Porgy and Bess* in 1959. His other musical, 1954's *Carmen Jones*, was similarly bogged down by an inability to compensate for horrendously theatrical settings; its better reputation rests solely on the score itself, the performances and the interesting *noir* atmosphere typical of Preminger.

The sole saving grace of such other veteran directors as Robert Wise who were also strangers to the musical form had been a reliance on editing skills to give strength to the numbers. Utilizing this technique, Wise managed to pull off no fewer than three—*West Side Story* (1961), *Sound of Music* (1965), *Star!* (1968)—with varied but appreciable degrees of success. His, however, was a rare case: consider the failures of Zinnemann's *Oklahoma!* (1955) and Wyler's *Funny Girl* (1968), for example.

Now, *Love*, of course, was an *original* musical, whereas all of the above (with the exception of *Star!*, the screen's last original before *Love*) were adaptations of Broadway shows, but the principle is basically the same, since Bogdanovich confined himself to an artificial studio setting (which he hated) for 90 percent of the film (still another bit of unfamiliar ground). He emphasized the look of the production.

Broadway star Kitty O'Kelly (Madeline Kahn) does her "Find Me a Primitive Man" number.

> We had the costumes made in black and white and all the gradations of black and white—from silver, to gray, to off-white, to cream; all the different values of black and white. But shooting it in color gave it a very nice look. We used pure black and pure white, which aren't used in movies very much because pure white tends to flare and pure black tends to soak up light. You're discouraged from using either of them by the cameramen who tell you it should be "teched down"—that is, gray it down or white it up. I insisted on using pure black and pure white because I thought it would look beautiful in color. (Denby, B. J., p. 78)

Also, as in *Daisy* but much more extensively, because of the preponderance of long takes (the songs themselves became the scenes), mirrors were employed throughout, and Laszlo Kovacs' photography had more of a slick shine to it than it ever had before. Unfortunately, because Bogdanovich and his cast were not able to create a sense of reality from these artificial settings, the players merely seemed adrift in an endlessly glacial sphere—a perfect metaphor for this, incidentally, is the music-box motif which frames the film; at the end the image of the foursome dancing against a mirror in a ballroom dissolves into that of the couples on the box, who remain permanently frozen in their positions.

One is reminded of Bogdanovich's observation about achieving believability in a period picture: "Anybody can get the right clothes and the right cars and so on; it's a question of the characters: they must exist in that period because they *have* to. Then the period becomes another character in the story." If *Picture Show* had been an outstanding example of this approach, *Love* only showed what could happen when the director failed to create that sense of atmosphere so essential to a film of this nature.

Barry Putterman has remarked that it seemed that this

time around Bogdanovich had "taken the analytical distancing present in the films since *Moon* to its logical conclusion and given the public nothing but the analysis yet still in the form of thirties entertainment, thus being judged anachronistic and incompetent at the same time." Now granted, the same amount of substance necessary for good drama is not required for the musical, a more lighthearted genre to be sure, but at the same time there must be a certain interest created in the characters to sustain one through the numbers and the duration of the film. Unfortunately, this time Bogdanovich failed to sustain interest in either his protagonists or their surroundings, and produced exactly the type of film he despises: a cold, academic exercise without any sense of audience participation.

What Bogdanovich originally had in mind was a "parody

Bogdanovich directs Duilio Del Prete, Cybill Shepherd, and Burt Reynolds in "Well, Did You Evah?" (Courtesy of Movie Star News)

and affectionate spoof of 1930s musicals—a celebration." However, because his last genre picture, *Doc*, had been an attempt to make a film which was close in execution to its models, most critics assumed that *Love* was intended to be one of two things: a renovated Astaire-Rogers opus (with Shepherd and Reynolds substituting for the two giants) or a Lubitsch *Love Parade*-type of musical. Because neither of the leads was a talented singer or dancer, Bogdanovich was as far from his alleged inspirations as one could imagine.

Unfortunately, the result, although original (though not for the better) in concept, adhered more closely to Webster's second definition of parody—"feeble or ridiculous imitation"—rather than to the first, "close imitation for comic effect or ridicule." If such critics as Pauline Kael had been incorrect in judging *Doc* to be infantile, they seemed right on target this time, as the resulting parody seemed on a level with that of the juvenile Mel Brooks (who incidentally had attempted a similar—though inexplicable—parody of 1930s Hollywood musicals in the closing minutes of his abysmal *Blazing Saddles* just the year before).

One must first keep in mind that the musical would seem to be the toughest genre to mock since, like the screwball comedy, it did not take itself very seriously to begin with. The only truly successful effort in this area to date is Gene Kelly and Stanley Donen's 1952 *Singin' in the Rain*, which, not coincidentally perhaps, is also the greatest movie musical of all time (by contrast, most critics regard *Love* as the genre's nadir). The crucial difference between *Singin'* and Bogdanovich's film in terms of intent lies in the fact that the premise and time frame of the former film function as a means for including as many targets for spoofing (MacDonald-Eddy operettas, Busby Berkeley–type numbers) as possible, even within the context of the brilliantly original, choreographed numbers.

On the other hand, Bogdanovich simply borrowed the basic plot situation (two couples meet, then switch partners) and character types (debonair playboy, spoiled heiress, her wisecracking maid, his sardonic valet) of the standard Lubitsch opus and left it at that. His attempt to poke fun at the conventions of the Art Deco–type musical lay—and herein lies the perversity of the concept and the main source of criticism of the film—apparently in his decision to make "a movie about some people who perform because they enjoy it, not because they are talented, who have to sing in order to communicate because they are too superficial and frivolous to do so any other way." Thus his casting of Shepherd and Reynolds, two people skilled in neither song nor dance.

The film thus took the shape of an inexplicable private joke between the director and his cast, since the numbers (the choreography of which was best described as "anything goes") did not come off—for the most part—as cute or charming, but rather irritating (ineptitude is ineptitude, first and last). At best, such a concept could work only sporadically, whenever one of the players happened to hit the right key. Consequently, there *are* pleasant and amusing moments (which the critics at the time, however, in their haste to bury Bogdanovich, failed to acknowledge), mostly involving Madeline Kahn's character, the debonair songstress Kitty O'Kelly ("Down in the Depths on the 90th Floor," "Find Me a Primitive Man," and her chorus of "At Long Last Love," nicely sustained in a long take with her perusing the grounds of the Pritchard mansion, stand out in the mind, as does one low-key duet with Shepherd, "I Loved Him").

But even in this regard there is a problem, since Bogdanovich said at the time he intended Kahn's "Find Me a Primitive Man"—the best and only valid number in the picture, since it comes closest in execution, despite its deliberately ludicrous trappings, to the type of number and film Bogdanovich was ostensibly mocking—to be the worst number of all. That it seems better than any of the others only proves how misguided the entire enterprise was. As was the case with *Doc* (though to a much greater

Madeline Kahn, Cybill Shepherd, and Eileen Brennan kick up their heels to the tune of "Most Gentlemen Don't Like Love" in the ladies' room of Lord & Taylor. (Courtesy of Movie Star News)

extent here), the picture also lacks a unifying style—all the players seem to be doing their own thing instead of uniting as a team.

If parody was what Bogdanovich was after, a truly funny idea would have been to choose people who *were* talented singers and dancers but who didn't *know* it (the point of the Astaire-Rogers and Lubitsch pictures—and those of all the good musicals, for that matter, was that the abilities of the players were always taken for granted). Then the audience would have been pleasantly surprised instead of angered when the characters (who would probably have spent the talking sections of the picture putting themselves down) suddenly burst into their routines.

What hurt the impact of the numbers further (and what made them seem even more distanced) was Bogdanovich's decision to abandon the playback method common to musicals and return to the direct recording system which had last been used in 1932, in the days of Lubitsch and Mamoulian (though revived disastrously for Rex Harrison's patter song numbers in another Fox film, 1967's *Doctor Dolittle*). He justified his choice this way:

> I was after spontaneity, and you don't get that when the actors are just lip-synching to something they recorded three months before. . . . It struck me as a terribly difficult thing to ask an actor to sing something two or three weeks before you shoot it and then not worry about anything when they're doing the scene except getting their lips in sync with what they did three weeks ago. What happens if they feel it differently? You're frozen into something you did in an atmosphere that is not particularly conducive to creativity. You're in a little room with a bunch of musicians sitting out there or you're in a little room with the musicians already having done their work and gone home.

Actually, such an approach was merely the logical extension of Bogdanovich's employment of source music over a musical track in his earlier films. Unfortunately the procedure (which added considerably to the film's budget) only seemed to discourage precision further: each take would produce a new variation or interpretation of the song, leaving Bogdanovich to choose the best of the bunch. But how can one do this when there is no standard by which to judge, when the whole format is completely arbitrary?

By demanding more and more takes using the live recording method, Bogdanovich was not necessarily moving toward a *better* performance but simply a different one each time, none of which was really that hot to begin with. He should have realized that the good musicals depended on the strength of the *players* to overcome the frozen feeling of the playback system and create that seeming spontaneity so essential to any successful entertainment— Sarris's remark that "the Astaire esthetic does not apply to amateurs" comes immediately to mind.

The material itself seemed to have encouraged the least favorable aspects of Bogdanovich's personality—chiefly an alarming silliness which had surfaced only briefly before in *Doc* (having been suppressed by Buck Henry's sharp dialogue) and *Daisy* and which would prove detrimental to *Nickelodeon* and *Illegally Yours* but not nearly so much to the romantic comedy *They All Laughed*—which can be considered Bogdanovich's generally successful attempt to make up for the failure of *Love*. One recalls Bogdanovich's comment that on *Picture Show* there existed "a kind of

Before the final change of partners: Madeline Kahn, Burt Reynolds, Duilio Del Prete, and Cybill Shepherd. (Courtesy of Movie Star News)

tension between me and the material that I think was very valuable—the very fact that it was sort of unknown to me."

No such tension existed this time (I am speaking of the dialogue and story, not of the musical form itself, which of course was new to Bogdanovich), as the director fashioned a plot ostensibly inspired by people and relationships he had known in his personal life (an idea which, as I say, would come off much better in *They All Laughed*). That the film was his most "committed" to date was particularly disturbing since it seemed to confirm what critic Jay Cocks had said about *Doc*: that Bogdanovich had no real sense of humor of his own, and that, as Sarris put it, he seemed to have been "reborn in the Hollywood archives."

> What I am reminded of instead of [the musicals I have seen] are evenings I have spent with Peter exchanging bits and pieces of film lore. I suppose that the downstairs relationship of Eileen Brennan's man-eating maid and John Hillerman's woman-hating chauffeur is based on the Lillian Roth–Lupino Lane mock–MacDonald-Chevalier routines in Lubitsch's *Love Parade* (1929). The gag with the unloosened bow ties is pure Leo McCarey. . . . Why do we need evocations when the originals are so readily available in revival? (Sarris, 1975)

The accusation of cannibalism (which would prove the death of *Nickelodeon*, which, like *Love*, seemed similarly enervated) had been overcome in *Doc* by Bogdanovich's abundant energy and superb sense of timing, making the admittedly borrowed gags seem almost like new creations, the point being that they worked within the context of the film and did not depend upon a film buff's knowledge to be appreciated (though such knowledge didn't hurt). In the case of *Love*, however, because of the unsuccessful execution of the concept, everything seemed to be at sea.

As a consequence, Bogdanovich's characterizations came

off as the thinnest and most caricaturish of all, a collection of types or people of another age at whom, as Sarris remarked, we "are supposed to laugh or at least smile, but [instead find ourselves] walking glumly through a grave-yard." What has got to be one of the ultimate artistic ironies of our time is that Cybill Shepherd, whose appearance in this film was roundly panned as a grand travesty, has recently, over ten years later, experienced a total reversal of fortune in her career by playing virtually the same type of character on a weekly basis in the television series *Moonlighting.* Indeed, Bogdanovich says that the producers of that program chose Shepherd because of her role in this film.

Most of her antics do still seem annoying to me, mainly because she was (and still is) an actress who needs to be restrained as much as possible by her director—and, of course, such a procedure was the antithesis of what Bogdanovich had in mind here. The pouty little smirk she had hitherto managed to suppress seemed to have finally overcome all her other resources, making her ridiculous (though she is pleasing in the rare moments when, as in *Daisy,* she manages to relax and not try so hard—the lead-in to "Let's Misbehave," with Reynolds, "I Get a Kick Out of You" and "I Loved Him," with Kahn, as I mentioned earlier). Her unbridled rendition of "You're the Top" in a car with Del Prete, however, has got to be the most embarrassing moment in terms of song in the whole film; it makes one cry out for Streisand's rendition in *Doc,* however obnoxious it may have seemed.

Burt Reynolds, too, has pleasant moments, but the choice of player (certainly neither Elliott Gould nor Bogdanovich himself, as originally planned, would have fared any better) still seems strange. When he warbles, "So control your desire to curse while I crucify the verse," or "At words poetic I'm so pathetic," it is difficult not to side with him. Duilio Del Prete's Italian gambler is *supposed* to be silly, but silliness portrayed by an actor who is himself frivolous merely comes across as laughable instead of appealing. His renditions of "Tomorrow" and "You're the Top" are total throwaways.

Hillerman and Brennan almost get by with "But in the Morning, No." Liam Dunn's brief bit as a surly newspaper-stand attendant seems overcalculated, making one long for the freshness of inspiration he had exuded in *Doc*. Certainly none of the dancing is notable for any reason, and some is downright unwatchable (particularly "Most Gentlemen Don't Like Love").

Following the (now legendary) disastrous opening of the film (the original print of which Bogdanovich himself described as "horseshit"), the director went back to the editing table and recut the film several times at his own expense. The 115-minute final version, which now circulates to television only (the 16mm runs 121 minutes and contains an introductory number with Shepherd, "Which," that Bogdanovich deleted, as well as extra choruses of "From Alpha to Omega," "You're the Top," and "It's De-Lovely"; it is missing Brennan and Shepherd's tap duet "It Ain't Etiquette," however), is considered by Bogdanovich to be "quite a nice little movie," although he says it isn't one of his favorite pictures; he would atone for it six years later with *They All Laughed*, which had a similar framework.

The TV print is somewhat more pleasurable to watch than the 16mm, and certainly on the whole, as Bogdanovich once said of *Doc*, it is pretty much impossible to hate it, considering the innocence and spirited good intentions behind its conception—but it is still a mess. Bogdanovich says that probably "the only way the picture will ever work is a hundred years from now after everybody's dead, and somebody digs it up and says, 'Hmmm. This is kind of interesting.' " Unfortunately, neither Bogdanovich nor I will see that day.

8   *Nickelodeon* (1976)

Nickelodeon, Bogdanovich's long-cherished project about the pioneer days of moviemaking which, in the wake of *Love*, faded from sight very quickly after its release, deserves now a treatment similar to that which I gave *Love*—and *Nickelodeon*, although a failure also, is also a slightly better effort than *Love*. But then, this was to be expected, since here Bogdanovich was back on familiar ground. In fact, it was highly significant that he did not get to make the film until 1976, since it became, as he himself said, a "summation" of all his early work.

As with *Love*, the film should be discussed in relation to its maker's assessment of its shortcomings, since it was also largely misunderstood at the time. When it came out, *Nickelodeon* was attacked mainly for seeming a pathetic exercise in cannibalism and in slapstick—which, by contrast to that featured in *Doc*, was viewed as poorly timed—and also for not maintaining a consistent tone, wavering among drama, comedy, history, and romance. Bogdanovich has since maintained that his original intent had been to do the piece as a straight drama with unknown actors (Jeff Bridges and John Ritter, who were supposed to have appeared together in *Picture Show*; Ritter ended up with a supporting role in *Nickelodeon*) in the lead roles, and in black and white, to preserve the authenticity of the settings and the anecdotes. All the incidents depicted were drawn from Bogdanovich's interviews with such directors as John Ford, Leo McCarey, Raoul Walsh, and Allan Dwan.

But the producers of the film, Irwin Winkler and Robert

Racing a train: Ryan O'Neal, John Ritter, Stella Stevens, and Tatum O'Neal.

Rehearsal: Ryan O'Neal, Burt Reynolds, and Jane Hitchcock.

Chartoff (after *Love*, Bogdanovich was denied the complete autonomy he had enjoyed in his last four projects), aiming for a more commercial effort, insisted he use Ryan O'Neal and Burt Reynolds and that he shoot the film in color. The result, Bogdanovich says, was "just another Hollywood picture about the silent era," though he plans to put back two or three dramatic scenes originally cut from the film for the videocassette. Also, Bogdanovich was forced to shoot much of it in a studio, which created an artificial feeling the director despised. Laszlo Kovacs says Bogdanovich and he worked out a very careful color scheme for the film, avoiding primary colors and concentrating on warm, monochromatic earth tones, in order to convey both a contemporary feeling—suddenly a town, Hollywood, appears out of nowhere—and the simplicity of the silent era films.

If one keeps these factors in mind, it becomes clear that the reason most everything in the first half of the film (which is composed primarily of slapstick involving the emerging film company) seems out of kilter is not that Bogdanovich's timing in staging the stunts and pratfalls is off (on the contrary, his mastery of camera placement and point of view is as acute as ever), but that the stunts themselves are simply out of place, and as such take the focus of the film away from its main subject—the birth of the movies—which only begins to surface in the second, more satisfying, section of the picture. Barry Putterman has remarked that the film looked like "the work of a very tired man"; Bogdanovich has said he had little fun making it. This is really only true of the first section (and unfortunately Kovacs' toned-down color scheme only adds to the impression, though it seems more apropos later), wherein Bogdanovich was forced against his will to drag out every conceivable type of visual gag, even resorting to stealing the suitcase-switching idea from one of his own films, *Doc*. The remainder of the gags were Keatonesque or Hawksian and filled time which could more profitably have been spent developing character. The structure of the film, though beginning with his customary parallel subplots, eventually resolves itself into a straightforward narrative once the film company has assembled; in this way, too, it seems a summation of Bogdanovich's early work, combining both his previous approaches to story development—one reason that the second half is not nearly so satisfying as it should have been.

However, it is the second section of the film (which comprises all the events following the completion of the company's first short) which bears discussion, since it is here that Bogdanovich's motives and concerns become clear. First, there is the *true* style of the film, composed—like *Targets*—of numerous Hawksian group shots, this time emphasizing the growing sense of camaraderie among the members of the company. One scene in which the technique (favoring long takes over cutting) is particularly evident is that in which a new ingenue (Jane Hitchcock) is accepted into the group, which means that the aging former ingenue (Stella Stevens) will now be taking a back seat not only in the movies, but in the affections of all the men on the crew. Within this group staging, Bogdanovich controls the dynamics of the action by moving characters into the foreground to isolate an individual point of view. In this case, we are led to identify with Stevens, who silently observes her inevitable loss of position within the company.

It is fitting that *Nickelodeon*, which closed the first period of Bogdanovich's career, should have exalted the physical process of making movies, since (as I have pointed out throughout this book) it is that aspect perhaps more than anything else which has aroused his greatest interest as a director. Also, there is the power of the image itself, which is what, in essence, Bogdanovich's films, being primarily visually oriented, are about. Both of these factors are exemplified by two stirring moments in the film. The first is the sequence where the characters all attend the premiere of Griffith's *Birth of a Nation*, and the second is

Aerial clowning: Burt Reynolds.

Jane Hitchcock, Ryan O'Neal, and Burt Reynolds view their film and observe how it's been altered in the cutting room.

the final shot of the film depicting night shooting in a glass-encased studio.

The opening of *Birth of a Nation*, with its use of actual footage from Griffith's movie (a special tinted archival print which Bogdanovich handpicked especially for the film), is precisely a moment of birth, a realization of great change and growth, an ascendance to a new and higher level—and it functions with this meaning for the characters in the story, for us in the audience, and as history—and Bogdanovich conveys this excitement well. This feeling is also present—as it had been briefly in *Targets*, though here the attempt seemed more apropos—when he focuses on the behind-the-scenes activities of those running the event: the projectionists, the members of the orchestra supplying the musical accompaniment for the film, and the woman

The head of Kinegraph Studios (Brian Keith) realizes nothing will be the same after viewing Griffith's *Birth of a Nation*.

moving up and down the aisles with an atomizer to counteract the foul odor of the cramped movie house.

His attitude really comes to the fore, however, when after the screening he shows the figure of Griffith himself walking briefly onto the stage and receiving thunderous applause from the audience—particularly Harrigan (Ryan O'Neal), the company's director. Earlier when Harrigan and his group were stopped on the street, spectators showed no interest in getting the director's autograph, only that of the stars of the film they had just been shown. And there is the producer Cobb's (Brian Keith's) sudden realization of the power of cinema after the screening when he remarks that people who are involved with making movies are "giving people little pieces of time that they never forget," a quote drawn from an early interview by Bogdanovich with James Stewart.

And finally there is the shot which runs under the end titles, a wonderfully complex metaphor. A movie crew is shooting a scene where a line of soldiers march off to World War I to the tune of "Pack Up Your Troubles." They march past the camera, then circle around behind the camera and march past again—a movie trick to make a small number of soldiers appear as an endless line. Bogdanovich stages this metaphor in a glass studio which glows with light in the surrounding darkness. John H. Dorr has described it as

> a testament to American ingenuity, a hand of applause for the ageless principles of showmanship and illusion. It catches us up in the exuberance and strength of joint undertakings of noble purpose, the spirit with which we face the darkness of new beginnings. It is the cosmic combination of the straight line of progress and the circular action of inexhaustible styles. (Dorr, p. 26)

Having exhausted his affection for the cinema of the past with *Nickelodeon*, Bogdanovich wisely decided to find new sources of inspiration with his next films, films which nevertheless would exude the same visual power and profound passion which had been evidenced during the best moments of this first cinephilic period in his career. As we shall see, *Saint Jack*, his next effort, was to be a step in the right direction.

9 *Saint Jack* (1979)

After the resounding critical and box-office failure of the
$8 million *Nickelodeon* in 1976, Bogdanovich made a
decision to go back to the smaller, tougher types of movies
he had started out making (*Targets* and *The Last Picture
Show*, for example, had cost only $130,000 and $1.3
million respectively). However, he was forced to scrap
plans for a gangster film about Bugsy Malone with Cybill
Shepherd—who was still living with him at the time—
playing the notorious Virginia Hill. After *Daisy Miller* and
At Long Last Love, Shepherd was considered box-office
poison (she had also been barred from participating in
Nickelodeon, but the film still turned out to be a flop). So
Bogdanovich took a year off in order to rethink his
priorities. "I'm tired, and I want a rest. I've been going
from picture to picture, and I need more time to prepare
the next one, more time to figure out who I am and what
I'm doing," he told the *New York Times* in January 1977.
"I've made eight films now, and I think I'm finally ready to
do some cinema," he said.

The answer to Bogdanovich's problems was once again
provided by his idol Orson Welles when, sometime early in
1978, he recommended that Bogdanovich read *Saint Jack*,
a novel by Paul Theroux about an American expatriate
who runs a brothel in Singapore. Bogdanovich was in-
trigued by the prospect of turning the book into a film.
The rights to the property, however, had been acquired by
Playboy, Inc.—which, coincidentally, was being sued by
Shepherd at the time for publishing nude shots of her

from *The Last Picture Show* without her permission. Part of the settlement in the lawsuit was that Shepherd would be given half rights to the book.

So ironically enough, the one person who to many had been the main source of Bogdanovich's troubles as a filmmaker proved to be the force behind his hoped-for redemption with the film version of *Saint Jack*, though Bogdanovich's decision to shoot the film entirely on location in Singapore caused a strain on their personal relationship and eventually ended it. Another irony was that Bogdanovich was consciously returning to his roots by asking his old boss Roger Corman to produce the low-budget ($2 million) effort for his New World Pictures.

The film proved to be a perfect catharsis for Bogdano-vich, as he promptly abandoned Hollywood and all its "bull" and headed for Singapore with only a few associates, among them George Morfogen, an old friend and some-time bit player in the director's earlier films who would serve as his associate producer on this new effort. "I wanted to see if we could make a film with as little money as possible, but with the most important things—talent and craft," he told *Cahiers du Cinéma* a few years later (1982). To back up his credo, Bogdanovich had recently turned down offers to direct two expensive efforts, a remake of the 1937 John Ford film, *The Hurricane* (certainly the director would not have accepted this project even if it had not been a question of the size of the budget, out of deference to one of his heroes), and *Heaven Can Wait*, which was eventually helmed by Warren Beatty and Buck Henry.

Bogdanovich had worked on the script for *Saint Jack* in Hollywood with Paul Theroux himself (who, strangely enough, would not even have been involved with the film had Bogdanovich not asked for his assistance; the rights to his novel had been purchased without his knowledge) and Howard Sackler, a novelist (*The Great White Hope*) and poet whose last credited film collaborations had been with

Stanley Kubrick on his first two features, *Fear and Desire* (1953) and *Killer's Kiss* (1955)—though he had worked on the scenarios for such recent films as Spielberg's *Jaws* (1975). Neither Theroux nor Sackler, however, made the journey to Singapore with Bogdanovich, so he ended up rewriting much of the script while there with his star, Ben Gazzara. The reason for the changes, Bogdanovich says, was that "you just can't write a script about Singapore sitting in Hollywood. There were no women in it originally, and it was a picture about prostitutes, after all! There was no love story, nothing." For his part, Theroux says that Bogdanovich

> respected the text and at all times wanted to be faithful to the book. He was not out to extrapolate a self-indulgent film from the book, or to loosely base a film on the basic plot of what I had written. And he wanted to follow the ideas and action of the novel—so much so that when I would say, "Let's try it a different way—let's leave that *but* out," he would pick up the book and say, "This is what it says in the book," in a rather magisterial way. Several times he would counter a suggestion of mine by saying, "That's not in the book."

This approach resembles that which the director had adopted in his screen translations of *Last Picture Show* and *Daisy Miller*. However, as had been the case with those films, Bogdanovich once again succeeded in adding a personal dimension to the original story which made the film version of it seem unmistakably his own, despite its origins.

Bogdanovich undoubtedly felt a strong sense of identification with the protagonist of his tale, Jack Flowers (Gazzara), an American soldier of fortune who attempts to cling to his own sense of morality and virtue—by building a little kingdom of commerce—amid the hypocrisies of the organized outside world. He has said that the character really is "Bogart telling America [and Hollywood] to go to

Jack Flowers (Ben Gazzara) makes a deal with a local prostitute for a visiting American, while his friend William Leigh (Denholm Elliott) looks on.

hell"—which, of course, is what Bogdanovich was doing by making this film independently 14,000 miles from home.

Certainly Bogdanovich's radical and daring departure from the Hollywood mainstream was testament to one personality trait which, as we shall see, he shared with Flowers: his resilience—a necessary reaction to the widespread opinion that he had spent whatever abilities he possessed on the Hollywood-oriented films of the previous decade. From the very first frames of *Saint Jack* one can immediately sense a startling change of pace and freshness of inspiration. The breathtaking 270-degree pan across the docks of Singapore which opens the film surely would have caused those familiar only with the director's early films to question at first the validity of the possessive credit "a Peter Bogdanovich Production."

In fact, Bogdanovich had made a decision after *Nickelodeon* to follow the advice of his detractors by making a film set in the present. His last (*What's Up, Doc?* really doesn't count) had been 1968's *Targets*. Correspondingly, *Saint Jack* had a new look, as photographed by German New Wave cameraman Robby Muller. Gone were the slick, flat, and artificial surfaces of Kovacs; this time there was an astonishing depth of field, recalling *Daisy Miller*—which, significantly, had not been photographed by Kovacs either. More important, however (and this is something which *Daisy Miller*, despite its technical virtuosity, decidedly lacked) for really the first time (the many excellences of *Last Picture Show* notwithstanding) a Bogdanovich film was teeming with life, with atmosphere, with naturalistic images and sounds.

This time, significantly, references to films of other directors were not to be discerned in either the structure or the content of the piece. The characters and situations in *Saint Jack* derived their inspiration only from their creator, Theroux (whose novel had been a personal endeavor), and from their interpreter, Bogdanovich, who at 39 appeared with this film to be laying bare aspects of his true personality for the first time, rather than cloaking them in remembrances of his movie past.

In terms of style, *Saint Jack* marked a distinct and deliberate departure from Bogdanovich's previous work. In fact, in light of the films to follow it (*They All Laughed* and *Mask*), which refined the new principles employed here, *Saint Jack* could be considered both an experimental (along with *They All Laughed*) as well as a transitional film in the director's canon. What Bogdanovich was aiming for here was to abandon as much as possible the reliance on dialogue and text which had been one of the hallmarks of his first efforts and to get back to purely visual expression, a technique he had put into practice most extensively in *Targets*.

Bogdanovich intended the exposition in *Saint Jack* to be

Shady CIA man Eddie Schuman (Peter Bogdanovich) propositions Jack over lunch.

deliberately nonexplicit, preferring the audience on this occasion to "sit forward in their seats and puzzle out what's happening rather than have them sit back and let everything wash over them." This freer, looser approach was in keeping with his choice of Muller for cinematographer; Muller, who had shot several of Wim Wenders' films, was accustomed to a reliance on imagery over story, on style over content—though this is not to say that *Saint Jack* lacks thematic depth; quite the contrary. As had been the case with several of the earlier Bogdanovich films, there was little of what one could describe as a traditional plot line—but this time there was no abundance of subplots either. The story was told in a completely spontaneous manner, though like *Paper Moon* it resolved itself into a series of longish episodes.

Barry Putterman is correct when he states that the

director's customary reliance on overlapping dialogue in this case "was no longer Hawksian or Wellesian but in the more contemporary style of Robert Altman." The distinct air of understatement which pervades the telling of all the episodes in *Saint Jack* is a direct—though unintentional—throwback to such Altman films as *M*A*S*H* (1970) and *McCabe and Mrs. Miller* (1971).

Despite Bogdanovich's seeming incompatibility with foreign filmmakers (as well as with Altman), one would not be incorrect to describe his approach here as reminiscent of Antonioni in *Blow-Up* (1966). I am referring to the appearance vs. reality concept which is the focus of *Blow-Up* and which provides a good basis for delineating the story of *Saint Jack* and its director's attitude toward the milieu of Singapore in the early 1970s, when the story takes place. As an interesting side note, this principle was applied by Bogdanovich during production of the film also. Because the Singapore government—puritanical by the standards of the Massachusetts Bay Colony—frowned upon Theroux's portrayal of the prosperous city-state as a hotbed of amiable vice, the director dispatched word that his company was filming an innocuous adventure-romance called *King of Hearts*. Fortunately, they were able to complete filming and depart before the real nature of their activities became known, though they were subsequently denounced in the local press and threatened with dire punishment if they ever returned.

Jack Flowers' nickname, "Saint," has an ironic double meaning. Although we initially discover that Saint Jack is actually a pimp, we soon find that the title has a reverse connotation also (and therein lies the truth of the character): Jack the pimp really has a heart of gold. He is good to his "girls," generous to his customers, and compassionate to a friend in need—one William Leigh (Denholm Elliott), an English accountant with a bad heart who comes in from Hong Kong once a year.

When we first meet Flowers, he seems to be nothing more than another American expatriate (he himself hails from Buffalo) forging a stingy living for himself in Singapore where he promotes business for a Chinese ship chandlers' firm. However, we soon see that he is different, because he has a dream, a big dream—to own and operate the best whorehouse in Singapore—and that after many years of hard work, he has finally seen it come to fruition. Flowers is superior in this respect to such Bogdanovich protagonists as young Sonny Crawford and Duane Jackson from *Last Picture Show*, who depended upon the advice of their hapless elders to realize their goals and were shown to be completely lost when their main guiding moral force, Sam the Lion, died midway through the film.

In his attempts to preserve some of the dignity of the Old World by building a kingdom of "nonexploitational" vice (again, an irony, because of the nature of the business he is running—but his intentions are what should concern us most here), Jack is as anachronistic as Orlock/Karloff in *Targets* or Moses Pray in *Paper Moon*. At a certain moment in their life, all these characters lose their paradise, but cling desperately to their remembrance as if it were their last hope of salvation. Pauline Kael has described this theme as it pertains to *Saint Jack* particularly well:

> *Saint Jack* considers the question of the false facade kept up by people who have been in exile for a long time. The leading characters pine nationalistically for a world of nationalism long dead. They dress to remind themselves of lost lives. At night, one guesses, they dream only of the past. Theirs is not a world of venture. . . . The heroes of *Saint Jack* live on regret, which is diet to kill a man. (p. 142)

This theme of lost paradise is echoed principally in the characters of Jack Flowers and William Leigh. As Jack Kroll (May 7, 1979) describes Flowers, he "is hardly a pillar of respectability, but he moves with the rhythms of honor and forlorn elegance, unsentimental but yearning for and forlorn elegance, unsentimental but yearning for some lost dream he sees in the laughter of his childlike hookers, in the macho profanity of GIs spending their youth between wars and whores."

With regard to Leigh, significantly, in adapting Theroux's novel, Bogdanovich made the same change with his character as he had with Sam the Lion in *Last Picture Show*—that is, he made him more sympathetic. As portrayed by Denholm Elliott here, Leigh is, as Kroll says, "a good man squeezed dry by grinding fate, the one nice chap among the colony of battered Britons who haunt the bars of post-imperial Singapore. . . . Leigh *is* the end of Empire, forever apologizing."

Thus we see that *Saint Jack*, although set in the present, is not so far removed—thematically, that is—from such previous works as *Picture Show* or *Daisy Miller*, which were set in the past. However, this time Bogdanovich's is not a tragic vision. We see this most clearly at the funeral of Leigh—it is not viewed as the irremediably devastating event which Sam the Lion's or Daisy's was; rather, this time there is a sense of life going on, of a necessary transcendence. This is a theme which will again surface—though to a much more significant degree—in *Mask*.

For Bogdanovich, Jack Flowers is the very embodiment of the individual caught in an upset—that of the mentality of the America of the 1970s. Like the heroes of the preceding films, Jack is out of sync with the political reality and the moral decomposition of the United States—in this case at the time of the war in Vietnam. Like Daisy Miller, Jack is an uprooted American. And as was the case with James' heroine, he finds himself unwilling—therefore unable—to escape his Americanism, despite the fact that he has deliberately situated himself in a foreign land. In the case of Jack Flowers, however, the move appears to be a permanent one.

Saint Jack gave Bogdanovich another opportunity to explore a segment of America's history. Interestingly, the

Jack is kidnapped and tortured by Chinese underground for infringing on their territory.

time frame of the film (1971-1972) is almost exactly 100 years after that of *Daisy Miller*. The two films can in a sense be considered companion pieces, in that the earlier picture was Bogdanovich's definitive study to date of the female personality, the distaff side of *Saint Jack* (which, for obvious reasons, would seem to be a more personal film for the director).

Although the characters in *Saint Jack* share with those in previous Bogdanovich films a longing for the past, in terms of the director's attitude toward his country, the film marked a nearly complete reversal of the idealized justification of America's influence in the world presented in *Daisy Miller*, for example. Gone was the affirmation of the image of original innocence (exemplified in the character of Daisy and especially her demise) which had been the hallmark of his earlier work. One could not say that this

attitude had not been foreshadowed in past films, however—recall the violent society represented in *Targets* with
its cultural sterility, a society whose beginnings were
explored in *Last Picture Show*—but this time the theme
appeared to take on added personal significance.

Bogdanovich's allowing the viewer to draw parallels
between himself and his protagonist, the decidedly amoral
(albeit engaging) Jack Flowers, was a particularly courageous move by a director seeking redemption for his
failures. "This movie was really saying in essence, 'To hell
with America; it's better to be a pimp in Singapore,' " he
told *Cahiers*. Recall that most people's impressions of him
were not particularly favorable at that point, due to his
compulsive name dropping and numerous promotional
appearances on TV talk shows with Cybill Shepherd, his
live-in protégée, over the last few years, which were still
fresh in many people's minds.

But Bogdanovich went even farther than that. He
himself chose to play the most amoral man in the film, an
American government wheeler-dealer named Eddie Schuman—this after Charles Grodin turned the part down and
following a bit of advice from Jean Renoir, who said, "I
think a director should appear in his pictures once in a
while." It is Schuman who convinces Jack to join him in
operating a "rest and recreation" hostel for American
soldiers from Vietnam—and Jack soon realizes he is really
fattening up the soldiers for the kill.

Whereas Bogdanovich's part in *Targets* had been an
obvious self-portrait, this was intended to be just the
opposite, a reflection of what the public *assumed* to be his
true self ("everybody thinks I'm a heavy, so I might as well
play one" was his reasoning). Thus, the director used his
own public persona—which at that point he had already
begun to shed—to challenge the viewer's perception of
both himself and, by extension, his views about American
society in the early 1970s.

Unfortunately, however, the trick did not come off the

way Bogdanovich had hoped, mainly because his performance lacks the sinister edge which Orson Welles, for
example, had imparted to his Harry Lime in *The Third
Man.* As a rather ingratiating (and seemingly harmless) big
shot who smokes ten-inch Cuban cigars, he appeared to be
playing himself, more or less—though not the same self
seen in *Targets* and not the egotistical monster most
assumed he was. Vincent Canby remarked about Bogdanovich's appearance that he seemed to be standing in for the
actor who was supposed to play the part—a not uncommon
reaction when a director appears in one of his own films.
However, unlike John Huston's bit part in *Treasure of the
Sierra Madre*, for example, Bogdanovich's role *was* meant to
be taken seriously.

At any rate, the discerning viewer senses that the really
significant autobiographical connections in the film exist
between Bogdanovich and his main character, Flowers.
Above all, there is Jack's admirable resilience. When the
Chinese underworld destroys the dream house he has set
up and marks him with traditional obscene tattoos, he has
an artist convert the obscenities to flowers and continues
with his next venture—much as Bogdanovich had done by
switching gears and going back to the smaller, "purer" type
of film with which he had begun his career after the failure
of *Nickelodeon* (though the director did take a respite before
launching onto this new phase).

Most important in this regard and in terms of the overall
message of the film is the ending, which Bogdanovich
altered from the novel. After the war ends (and his hostel
for GIs closes down), Jack is at loose ends, considering a
return to the homeland he had left 15 years before.
Friends are gone, the days-of-Empire sighs of the English
colonialists have turned to senile mutterings, the faces of
the Chinese are as closed as ever. Schuman makes the offer
that would pay enough to take him home in style: $25,000
for a little blackmail data to shut up a visiting senator
certain Washingtonians consider "a bit too opinionated."

In both novel and film, Jack goes through with obtaining the evidence; however, Bogdanovich has Flowers change his mind about delivering the goods (a roll of film) to Schuman after mailing the ashes of Leigh, who has died of a heart attack, to his widow. In the final moments we see him yell to a waiting Eddie across a busy street, "Fuck it," after which he throws the package into a nearby river. Thus Bogdanovich's intent that *Saint Jack* truly represent a "fuck *Hollywood*" film becomes unmistakably clear.

Although some have complained that such a sudden change of character seemed implausible by that point, Bogdanovich counters: "I think that's exactly what Jack *would* do. There's a point beyond which he won't sink." Bogdanovich, too, had reached that point by refusing finally to make pictures the way the studios wanted him to—with excessively large budgets and major names just for the sake of publicity.

By contrast to the characters in his earlier films, therefore, here we were presented with a central character who preserves his integrity by his *refusal to evolve* in the same direction as his country. Bogdanovich attempted to preserve the message he had made to Hollywood (and he did succeed in getting his film made and releasing it exactly as he wished), by forming upon his return his own production and distribution company, Moon Pictures.

Beyond these observations, I feel that to speculate further about Bogdanovich's politics with regard to the war in Vietnam and the general spirit of disillusionment in America since World War II would be going too far. Although *Saint Jack is* a more modern film than its predecessors in terms of its concerns, Bogdanovich was still concerned primarily with telling a story (about a rather raffish hero), not with making a political treatise.

Despite the fact that the film has decidedly cynical and ominous overtones (the Chinese underworld agents who kidnap and molest Jack are portrayed as particularly loathsome) and although much of it is dominated by

Flowers' cool, impassive gaze, there is a general feeling of warmth (the result of the absence of the tragic vision present in some of the earlier films) coupled with a rather outrageous sense of humor—mostly sexual, of course. One of the prostitutes asks Froggy, one of Jack's friends, his height, which he tells her is 6'4". She replies, "Tall enough to kiss an elephant's balls." After the old-fashioned discretion shown by Bogdanovich in his depiction of sexual encounters in such films as *Last Picture Show*, the very fact that he would undertake a story with such a *Playboy*-type atmosphere must certainly have come as a shock to many.

In reality, however, all of the sex is handled with a casual, offhand humor, typical of its purveyor, Jack. He tells Leigh his philosophy early on: "People make love for so many crazy reasons—why shouldn't money be one of them?" There is, however, one fairly explicit encounter between

Jack and William get drunk while Jack has the Chinese underground's obscene tattoos "flowered."

two prostitutes (played to the tune of "Goldfinger," no less), a show for the entertainment of some visiting men, which Frank Rich nevertheless described as "one of the least erotic sequences ever recorded in an R-rated film." In truth one does seem to feel a sense of embarrassment on the director's part about filming such activities (though there is a natural curiosity present also). This impression is confirmed by his describing in his book *Killing of the Unicorn* one particularly unpleasant incident at the Playboy mansion in Los Angeles where he was tricked into a compromising position involving several people. Bogdanovich the romantic still prefers a monogamous relationship in a private setting above all for himself and his characters—as we shall see in a discussion of *They All Laughed*.

Coupled with the sexual matter is the theme of voyeurism which, the reader will recall, had first been explored in *Daisy Miller* and which would receive its most extensive treatment in Bogdanovich's next film, *They All Laughed*. In the case of the latter work and *Saint Jack* it arises from the director's quest for purely visual expression—wordless reaction sequences. It also has to do with the depth of field which he and Muller were aiming for—and which had been prevalent in *Daisy* also.

In *Saint Jack*, however, unlike *Daisy* and *They All Laughed*, the spying has far less innocent overtones. We are not dealing with one man's obsession with a beautiful woman, but rather with a pimp and his comrades. I have already mentioned the feeling conveyed by the sex sequences, but there are other far more unpleasant incidents to which we are privy during the course of the film. These involve the shady Asians who frequent the area where Jack works. In one unsettling sequence, for example, we are taken inside the seedy headquarters of a group of Chinese underworld agents, who hold a knife to Jack's throat as they paint his arms with indelible tattoos. Another startling moment earlier in the film has Jack casually pointing out to Leigh the figure of a slain informant in the center of the city's commercial district—presumably a common occurrence.

And there is a lengthy episode toward the end where Jack follows the homosexual senator whom he is to blackmail to his hotel room and stealthily snaps photographs of him and a naked Chinese boy together. This is perhaps the best example of Bogdanovich's reliance on image over dialogue—the entire sequence (approximately seven minutes in length) is completely silent, and yet all the nuances of character and action are thoroughly and economically conveyed.

What is perhaps most remarkable about *Saint Jack* is the *look* of the film. Working with sophisticated Fuji film stock, Bogdanovich and Robby Muller were able to achieve a depth of field—a certain acuity—while at the same time retaining a soft focus. Bogdanovich had originally planned to shoot the picture in black and white (as he had with *Nickelodeon*) but again a piece of advice from Renoir persuaded him to change his mind. "I think if the audience goes into a picture knowing it was shot in Singapore, they would probably like to see the color of Singapore," he said.

That is precisely what Bogdanovich and Muller give the viewer: a Singapore alive with vibrant shadings and teeming with atmosphere—a *real* atmosphere this time, not a manufactured one (the rather luxurious texture of the images also admirably belies the low budget—this had not been the case with *Targets*). Bogdanovich has said that this film and his next, *They All Laughed*, are better than the preceding ones because they *breathe*—they were not packaged, labeled, or elaborately planned out ahead of time; therefore, they have a life of their own. Especially admirable is the fact that Bogdanovich's definition of a good period picture (having it become another character in the story) works better here than in any of the previous ventures—this in spite of the fact that the film did not

Jack jokes with visiting American GIs after setting up an R and R hostel.

require any elaborate recreations in terms of art or set direction.

Also, the time frame is important. It would seem, based on the evidence of *Saint Jack*, that the earlier films like *Last Picture Show* and *Paper Moon* were stifling precisely because of their settings, which had to be recreated—this despite the fact that all three, like *Saint Jack*, were shot on real locations. But then, the settings for *Picture Show* and *Moon* were unusually desolate and sterile—by contrast, the Singapore of *Saint Jack* (a sprawling jungle of vice and corruption) seemed as far away in terms of feeling as the locale itself was in actual distance.

Also crucial to the success of the film is the performance of Ben Gazzara as Flowers, through whose eyes we view the spectacle of occidental venality and Asian corruption. For Bogdanovich, getting to work with Gazzara (he already knew him through their mutual friendship with John Cassavetes, in several of whose films Gazzara had starred) brought back memories of his youth. In 1953, when he was just 14, Bogdanovich had a column in the Collegiate School paper. The first play he ever reviewed was *End as a Man*, starring Gazzara, who was then only 23 himself. Bogdanovich also, as I noted in the chapter on *Targets*, was a fan of Preminger's *Anatomy of a Murder* (1959), which had given Gazzara one of his mere handful of outstanding film roles to date. Because of Gazzara's relative obscurity in the motion picture business, none of the major studios was keen on releasing a film with him as its star. Happily, Bogdanovich got to make his film independently and thereby hire Gazzara.

Gazzara, then 49, lent an undeniable dignity to his role. He has that hard-worn look of a man who's seen it all (and seen much of it fade away) but who has not lost the capacity to smile. Interestingly, his reputation as a stud is put to excellent advantage here—Bogdanovich has even said that Gazzara was really playing himself to a great extent. When Frank Rich complains that Gazzara merely "wanders about aimlessly with a rueful grin plastered on his face," he misses the point: Gazzara is, as Bogdanovich says, the type of actor who commands attention the minute he steps into a room—he doesn't have to *do* anything; he just has to *be*. But at the same time he has a very low-key nonchalance (perfectly in keeping with the mood of the film), which can lead the unperceptive viewer to overlook the subtle changes of expression he conveys effortlessly at every turn. He is just right, as are Denholm Elliott as Leigh and all the Asian actors and extras in bit parts.

What, then, are *Saint Jack*'s flaws? It seems that despite its many good qualities, the film remains a somewhat insubstantial endeavor—due mainly to the experimental nature of the director's approach. Unlike the films of Bogdanovich's early phase (*At Long Last Love* and *Nickelodeon* not included), *Saint Jack* does not immediately grab and hold

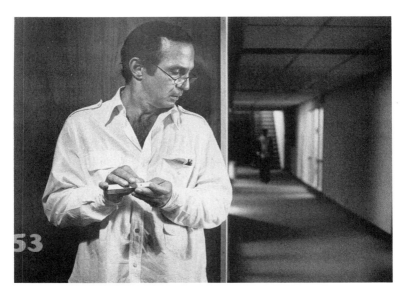

Jack surreptitiously prepares to take incriminating photos of homosexual U.S. senator.

the viewer's attention, but rather (and again, this links it to an Antonioni film also) requires him to meet it half way, due to the rather casual development of the story (the result of the inexplicit exposition Bogdanovich was aiming for) and the rather low-key behavior of its protagonist, who at times seems to be talking to himself (and this recalls the incoherent delivery in some of Altman's films).

The intent is clear—to convey the jokes and plot points as subtly as possible—but sometimes the result is too subtle, and the characters and situations do not connect with the viewer. This is not the old directorial iciness returning, however, but more accurately the result of the rather cool and aloof personality of Bogdanovich's hero. His next effort to employ a similar storytelling method, *They All Laughed*, was much warmer, due to the romantic nature of the story.

The low-key nature of *Saint Jack* seems to have kept it from becoming the popular success it probably deserves to be. The film opened to generally favorable reviews, but vanished from sight after a short run in theaters (it did, however, recoup its cost over the long run)—this despite the allure of its racy subject matter (Hugh Hefner was one of the co-producers). It remains a not terribly accessible film, though, happily, it *has* been released on videocassette. As for what it did for Bogdanovich's career, although he achieved his goal of making and releasing a film without studio interference, the picture did not bring him back into the mainstream (but then, he says he knew before he started that, as with *Daisy Miller*, the result would probably be a *succès d'estime*).

What is most important about the achievement of *Saint Jack*, however, is that Bogdanovich demonstrated a rare capacity for self-criticism by deliberately abandoning his old working methods and seeking out new sources of inspiration after his initial ones had dried up. *Saint Jack*, if nothing else (and it is considerably more), is admirable proof that directorial self-consciousness can be a virtue just as much as a shortcoming.

10   *They All Laughed* (1981)

> Making pictures is only fun when you feel that what
> you're doing is a sort of a crime, a caper. Jean Renoir
> once said that when you're making a picture you
> should gather around you not associates but conspira-
> tors.
>
> —Peter Bogdanovich

Such is the feeling generated by *They All Laughed*, the
romantic comedy which the director modeled along the
same lines as *At Long Last Love*, in a partial attempt to make
up for the failure of that film. Whereas the allegedly
personal aspects of the earlier picture's story were completely overshadowed by the stylistic aspects of its musical
framework, this time Bogdanovich devoted more attention
to the substance of his film. He was also drawing for the
first time from his private life for his story material: most of
the female characters in the film are played by women with
whom Bogdanovich had had relationships since his
breakup with Cybill Shepherd in 1979, and both of the
central male parts (but particularly that of Charles, played
by John Ritter) are autobiographical reflections of Bogdanovich himself. Even Bogdanovich's daughters, Antonia
and Alexandria, are featured as the daughters of Ben
Gazzara, the other male lead.

But despite the fact that the characters in *They All
Laughed* were to derive most of their dimension from
Bogdanovich's perceptions of their real-life counterparts,
the director recognized that in order to make the picture

John Russo (Ben Gazzara) escorts his daughters (Antonia and Alexandria Bogdanovich) to school.

appealing to a wider audience it was necessary "to cloak the personal elements in something impersonal, in order to play by the rules of the old Hollywood game." So he came up with the idea of a group of detectives falling in love with the women they're hired to tail. Bogdanovich said that with this film he "accepted the question I had asked in *Love*: What is falling in love? And I tried to define more what it was." He also molded the picture as a sort of valentine to Manhattan, where the story takes place (Bogdanovich grew up there, but said he'd never been happy there until he made this film), and to Dorothy Stratten, the blond model who is pursued in the film by the John Ritter character and with whom Bogdanovich fell in love during the shooting. Stratten was murdered shortly before the film's release, and it is dedicated to her.

Stylistically, the film is a continuation of Bogdanovich's intention in *Saint Jack* to "get back to basics." The opening five minutes or so are admirably accomplished without a word of dialogue, as we are introduced to the redheaded cabdriver Sam (Patti Hansen) and her passenger, a rather irritable sort (played by George Morfogen, Bogdanovich's oldest friend, who had earlier appeared briefly in *Doc* and *Daisy*), whom we later discover is Leondopolis, the head of the detective agency. From Sam's point of view we note a meeting at the local heliport involving Leondopolis, Jack Russo (Ben Gazzara), a middle-aged woman (Audrey Hepburn) and her husband, who waving good-bye to her, departs in the helicopter. It soon becomes clear that the husband has hired Russo, another detective, to shadow his wife (whose name is Angela).

Thus the main motif of the film—voyeurism—is introduced. What is most interesting about it is that on this occasion more than ever before (recall that it had surfaced in *Doc, Daisy*, and *Saint Jack* also—most importantly in the latter two films) it is an inherent outgrowth of the stylistic dictates of the film: the necessity to show events solely from the point of view of the detectives—who, as Putterman notes, are continually given "selected empirical evidence which usually proves to be false." Much of the picture recalls silent cinema, as whole sequences are constructed from the three male protagonists (Gazzara, Ritter, and Blaine Novak as Arthur) shadowing their quarries: Angela, Dolores (the Stratten character), and in the case of Arthur, any woman who looks available. In fact, we do not actually meet the Hepburn character for close to an hour into the film.

Many have criticized the film as a sloppy and ultimately unsatisfying and pointless narrative whose characters are never really fully developed, despite a promising opening which sets all of them up adroitly. In certain ways it begs comparison with Ophuls' 1950 classic *La Ronde*, whose flawless circular structure it does not successfully approach. Indeed it *can* give this impression upon first viewing—and it is on this occasion that the conclusion, which finds most of the principals happily paired off with their ideal mates, suggests either that the audience which is receptive to the ending has not been paying close enough attention to the (presumably) complex events depicted throughout the preceding two hours, or that Bogdanovich, as scenarist and director, has not given one sufficient reason to care about these people during that time. Therein lies the crux of the average viewer's often-puzzling first impression of the picture.

But a second viewing confirms the deceptive quality of the film; just as the evidence revealed to Bogdanovich's protagonists often doesn't turn out to be what they originally thought, so the movie in which they are featured turns out to be much more satisfying and complex than it

Arthur (Blaine Novak) and Charles (John Ritter) spy on Dolores and her husband.

Colleen Camp as country singer Christy Miller.

appeared initially. The reason for this lies in the seamless fusion of form and content which characterizes the piece; the two become synonymous and inextricably linked, and for this reason *They All Laughed* seems the ultimate Bogdanovich film. As Blake Lucas points out, Bogdanovich makes up for the lack of a clear dramatic center for the story by the use of "fluid camera movements which emphasize the persistent changes and developments within the evolving narrative, permitting it to jump lightly from one set of characters to another." This technique is perhaps best exemplified in what is surely the film's most accomplished scene: in a roller rink where the awkward Charles attempts to follow Dolores on skates. Bogdanovich's camera continually glides from dazzling subjective reverse tracking shots of Ritter stumbling about to panoramic views of the entire rink only to locate Charles' friend Arthur on the other side of the rink simultaneously searching for him and attempting to pick up two girls. The result conveys the feelings, concerns, and moods of the principal characters with a minimum of dialogue and maximum of invisible point-of-view editing while at the same time embodying the very qualities which define cinema at its purest—namely the visceral.

Also evident throughout is a quality which had been lacking in Bogdanovich's features of late: spontaneity (much of which derives from the fact that dialogue scenes were often written just before they were shot). By contrast to the characters and relationships depicted in *Love*, those in *They All Laughed* seem instantly real and fresh. This characteristic goes hand in hand with the prevalent mood, despite the consequences of the various relationships, which is embodied in the Gershwin song that gives the film its title (and that is heard briefly in a Frank Sinatra rendition)—that of a familiarity and shared consciousness about the vagaries of love that exists among the characters (particularly the women, who function as kind of an ad hoc sisterhood). This in-joke sort of tone is what puts some viewers off of the film, but in truth if one allows oneself to get caught up in the mood of it, it can be a quite rewarding experience—though it does remain a piece whose success depends to a great degree on personal taste.

Bogdanovich acknowledges that the attitudes expressed by his characters reflect the same qualities necessary to one's appreciation of the film:

> Everything in the film is based on trust. Totally. Because none of the characters *discuss*. Neither does Charles ask Dolores nor she ask him what it's really about. She in fact asks him and he lies to her and she knows he lies, and *still* likes him. So there's two people who essentially say, "Well, we love each other, and that means we just trust each other, 'cause that's *it*." On faith. In fact, Dorothy's character in the movie is totally on faith. 'Cause the audience—interesting thing is, that the audience accepts it on faith, too, because there's no idea of what she does. You don't know whether she's really having an affair with Sean Ferrer, which she doesn't seem to be. Or why she doesn't like her husband. But you take her side in it, and that's partly because Dorothy annihilates disbelief. You don't believe that there's anything wrong with her—she doesn't seem like she would be doing anything wrong.

The Charles/Dolores relationship (the one which presumably mirrors the director's own with Stratten) is handled with perhaps the most care and sensitivity by Bogdanovich, and best embodies the quality with which he and cinematographer Robby Muller set out to imbue the film, that of a vision of New York seen through lovers' eyes (Muller's gloriously lush, romantic tones here remind one of Carlo DiPalma's work on Woody Allen's 1986 *Hannah and Her Sisters*, which resembles Bogdanovich's film in other significant ways). Stratten's character is viewed as an ideal woman whose innocence, as Bogdanovich remarked, one would not question for a second. One roots for Ritter to snatch her away from her unappreciative husband, and

Bogdanovich directs Dorothy Stratten and John Ritter for palm-reading scene inside roller rink. (Courtesy of The Museum of Modern Art/Film Stills Archive)

is thrilled at the climax when, after he seems to have lost her, she returns to tell him she is seeking a divorce and accepts his offer of marriage.

The other characters seem to stand out less prominently, but are treated with equal doses of sympathy by the director. John Russo, the Gazzara character, is a stud who is introduced as showing a rather callous and indifferent attitude toward Christy Miller, the country-western singer played by Colleen Camp with whom he had been having an affair before the film began (a clever touch has Christy ending the song she is singing when we first encounter her, "Kentucky Nights," with the line "There's nothin' in this city but the heartbreak and the pain," which is directed at Russo as he enters the club where she is performing). But we soon see the more likable qualities of Russo emerge when he hooks up with Deborah Wilson (Patti Hansen), the beautiful redheaded cabdriver whom he insists on calling Sam and who is infatuated with him. She has been burned by several past lovers, and appreciates Russo's sensitivity in not forcing her to have sex with him during the first night they spend together.

Finally Russo meets and falls for Angela Niotes (Hepburn), the executive's wife whom he has been hired to follow. She has been neglected by her husband, who has been spending time with other women behind her back (as Russo tells her, people like her husband who can't be trusted have the same feelings about everyone else). Bogdanovich's casting of Hepburn here (at the suggestion of Ben Gazzara, with whom she had teamed in one of her comeback pictures, the terrible *Bloodline*, from the Sidney Sheldon novel, in 1979) was very clever, since it allowed her

Russo and Leondopolis (George Morfogen) discuss their respective love lives.

to play an older, more world-weary version of the Cinderella types she had played at the beginning of her career in such films as Wyler's *Roman Holiday* (1953) and Wilder's *Sabrina* (1954)—in fact at one point, after spending the night with Russo, she makes a subtle reference to this heritage by stating, "You'd better take me home before I turn into a pumpkin." Although she had made Russo promise they would not become romantically involved, her (and his) longing for real, lasting affection inevitably draws them to one another, despite the fact that her stay in New York is necessarily cut short. At the conclusion, Angela must bid Russo a tearful good-bye ("You break all your promises, Mr. Russo"), and Russo is left with little to console himself (though Sam intends to help him get over her). As Lucas says, for Angela it is possible that "the memory of the affair, which has reawakened her capacity for love, will sustain her after the fade-out." But the ending is more melancholy than anything else for both Angela and Russo—who is ultimately shown to be more vulnerable, despite his hard-edged veneer, than any of the other characters in the story.

For the other protagonists, however, things turn out much sweeter. Christy, after pursuing Charles (there is a delicious improvised bit in her apartment where, in an attempt to seduce him, she places her fingers on various sensitive areas of his body) to no avail, finally settles on José (Sean Ferrer), a young man whom Charles had earlier suspected of having an affair with Dolores. Christy has been comically (even obnoxiously) hell-bent on marriage all along, and finally seems, if not totally satisfied (José is the best available male, and she is most likely concerned that if she doesn't make her move now, she might never have another opportunity), at least content. The other characters are relatively minor, but are given at least one scene where they shine: Leondopolis, the owner of the detective agency who has been secretly having an affair with his secretary Amy (Linda MacEwen), informs Russo in

Angela Niotes (Audrey Hepburn) and Russo finally meet face to face.

one scene that he has reached a mid-life crisis; and Arthur (Novak), an eternal philanderer, is treated comically throughout (at one point he dreams that all his previous conquests are converging on him with sharp instruments).

What sustains the feeling of warmth which emanates from almost every frame of the film is the background score, which is almost continous and is comprised of several excellent country-western songs written by Bogdanovich himself and a musician friend, Earl Pool Ball, among them "One Day Since Yesterday," sung with great gusto by Colleen Camp (this is heard on the soundtrack, not performed), in addition to old standards of Frank Sinatra ("New York, New York," "More Than You Know"), Johnny Cash, and Louis Armstrong—all reflecting more than ever before Bogdanovich's personal tastes in music (and this use of classic tunes is another aspect which links the film to *Hannah and Her Sisters*). A brilliant stroke was the idea to use Benny Goodman's classic "Sing Sing Sing" as counterpoint to the scene in the roller rink where Ritter attempts to become comfortable on the skates; at one moment, just as he is about to reach Stratten, the music flares up and he slips and crashes to the floor. The tune provides just the right underlying pulse for the scene. Unfortunately, though, in a recut print which Bogdanovich hopes to distribute one day, he has removed the piece and inserted a very inferior Bruce Springsteen song, "Out on the Street," which all but kills the scene—though it could certainly be argued that since the film was such an intensely personal one for Bogdanovich, only he could know best which songs would provide the best accompaniment.

And the performers (all of whom are just right for their roles) themselves carry much of the film on the strength of their considerable charm alone. Standout among them is John Ritter, filling in for Bogdanovich, who decided he was too old to play the part of Charles. The director could not have picked a better surrogate; Ritter's resemblance to him is amazing, especially with the glasses he dons throughout. It seems strange, though, that Bogdanovich would fashion an image of himself as a hapless clod, when in person he gives the impression of being completely sure of himself at all times. But Ritter's achievement here goes much farther than just looks; he is an expert physical comedian. There is one hilarious improvised bit where, in an attempt to look nonchalant while spying on Stratten, he fiddles with a glass of tomato juice, ending up with a straw in his nose. He is also a gentle and touching romantic leading man. One finds comfort in knowing that in spite of the fact that he began his career in television with an inferior sitcom (*Three's Company*) of which he was the sole redeeming factor, he is finally finding a niche in the more prestigious medium of film, under the guidance of such directors as

"Feel my finger": Colleen Camp and John Ritter.

Blake Edwards. Sadly, Ritter's popularity at the time of the release of *They All Laughed* did little to help the film earn money at the box office, and as a result some of his very best work has gone unnoticed by many of his fans.

The late Dorothy Stratten, a stunning blond beauty, shines brightly here also, although her material isn't half so meaty as Ritter's; she is mainly viewed from afar, making one grateful when Ritter does on occasion catch up to her. The natural ability displayed by her makes her untimely death seem especially tragic—though at least Bogdanovich has given the world definitive proof of what she was really like, certainly enough to counteract the laughably phony portraits of her by Mariel Hemingway in Bob Fosse's absurd *Star 80* (1983) and Jamie Lee Curtis in a TV movie ostensibly based on her life. Unfortunately, however, many more people are familiar with the latter two films than Bogdanovich's.

Gazzara again displays more of his effortless skill in the role of Russo, and lends his scenes with Hepburn a special poignancy. Patti Hansen's aggressive cabdriver is drawn in the style of a Howard Hawks heroine; Bogdanovich even has her sporting the familiar Hawksian vice of smoking, for which she is admonished by Russo. Colleen Camp overdoes it a bit at times, but is generally amusing in her brashness.

The picture's weaknesses become apparent when one compares it to Allen's *Hannah*, which also explored relationships among a gallery of quirky characters in a contemporary Manhattan setting. Allen's people, though, were less sketchy and more fleshed out than Bogdanovich's, most likely the result of Allen's spending more time on his script before shooting; he is also, of course, a writer first and director second, whereas Bogdanovich is the opposite. Like *Saint Jack*, *They All Laughed* (which has become obscure because of its failure at the box office, but which, happily, is available on videocassette) has a decidedly experimental nature, being a bit too loose in all departments to make a totally satisfying whole, but with many choice moments remaining. It is, not surprisingly, Bogdanovich's favorite among his films. As Bogdanovich's next effort, *Mask*, was to prove, it is often better to start with an impersonal story and to bring one's personality to it rather than the other way around.

11 *Mask* (1985)

Mask, the film which was to mark Bogdanovich's spectacular and long-awaited comeback to mainstream filmmaking after a decade of *succès d'estime* and critical and box-office failures, has a background story reflecting that very same eerie fatalism which had in fact followed the director throughout his entire career.

The germ of the project was born back in 1977, when a woman named Anna Hamilton Phelan, a former actress and writer of several one-act plays, was working as a genetics counselor at a hospital. It was there that she met Rocky Dennis, a 16-year-old boy who suffered from a rare disease called craniodiaphyseal dysplasia, which causes calcium to deposit at an abnormal rate throughout the skull, making the victim's head grow to twice the normal size and giving his face the appearance of a bizarre mask. Every person who had ever had the disorder had died by the age of eight.

During that meeting with Rocky, Phelan said she'd experienced "that same combination of sympathy and morbid fascination that most people feel when they first see someone like that. But I couldn't get him out of my mind." She never saw him again after that, but when three years later she had quit her job to become a full-time writer, the memory of that extraordinary young man again began to occupy her thoughts. "I used to sometimes talk to my kids about Rocky and how he carried himself. He became almost a kind of folk hero to them. One day my son said to me, 'Why don't you just write about Rocky?' "

Getting information, however, wasn't easy, mainly because Rocky had died shortly after she had seen him. But eventually Phelan was able to track down the last address of Rocky's mother, Rusty, a tough-looking woman who hung around with a group of bikers. But when she called the number in Azusa, California, she found to her dismay that the phone had been disconnected. Then on a Saturday several weeks later she decided to get in her car and drive to the address to search for Rusty. She knocked on the door of the old house and said she was looking for Rusty Dennis. Though the tenant didn't know Rusty, she said a woman two doors away did.

"The next woman not only remembered Rocky and Rusty but took out a bunch of old pictures and told me about him," Phelan recalled. "Then she drove me to another woman who didn't know anything about Rusty but referred me to a guy in a boatyard who knew Rocky's father." The man in the boatyard said he thought Rusty had died from a drug overdose but told Phelan about a biker gang called "The Monks" he thought Rocky's father rode in.

"That guy told me to go to Arrow Highway to a place called House of Choppers [a motorcycle store] to see a man who knew about the gang," she said. "This new man told me he'd heard Rusty had definitely died from a drug overdose and that he didn't know anything about the father. I left my name and phone number and said that if he did hear about the father he should call me." Phelan got back in her car and drove home to Santa Monica. When she got there the phone was ringing. She answered it and a voice on the other end said, "Anna Hamilton Phelan—this is Rusty Dennis."

In an amazing coincidence, Rusty, who had moved to San Francisco after Rocky had died, was on her way to Los Angeles for the first time in three years. Just minutes after Phelan left the House of Choppers, a sprocket loosened on

Rusty (Cher), Rocky (Eric Stoltz), and their biker pals.

the back wheel of the motorcycle on which Rusty was traveling. She said to the man who was driving her that she knew of a nearby cycle repair shop where they could get it fixed. When they arrived at the House of Choppers the owner gave her Phelan's phone number. "To this day Rusty is convinced that Rocky somehow made all this happen spiritually by loosening the sprocket," says Phelan.

The two women met the next day and Rusty began to fill Phelan in on the details of her life with Rocky in her own brutally honest fashion. "Rusty sat me down and gave me a list of names of friends, relatives, schools, where Rocky went to camp—everything," the writer revealed. "Then she looked at me in the eye and said, 'You're going to hear a lot of bad things about me and . . . all of them are true.'"

Phelan spent four months researching Rocky's life and then several more months writing the story. On the wall of her office she kept three things as inspiration—a picture of Rocky, a poem he had written, and a photo of Cher, who she had decided, after seeing the film version of *Come Back to the Five and Dime, Jimmy Dean, Jimmy Dean* (1982), seemed to embody the biker image she had in mind for Rusty. Of course, at this point, she couldn't even be sure—because of her inexperience and lack of contacts—that her script would ever even be *produced*, let alone that Cher herself would eventually be cast in the role of Rusty.

Good fortune continued to stay with Phelan. After finishing the script she accidentally met a young lawyer in her neighborhood through a local mishap. He worked for an entertainment-law firm and offered to read her first draft. He liked it and got it to another client in the firm—producer Martin Starger.

Though hesitant to spend time reading a first screen-play, Starger was immediately affected by Rocky's story.

> It said all the right things, like "Don't judge someone by the way they look" and "Try to see the person inside," and it had an unusual background because his family were bikers rather than an ordinary middle-class family. But what really got to me was the raw emotion of the script. Everyone has something about themselves that they feel inferior about—whether it's not being smart enough, pretty enough, athletic enough. Rocky personifies those problems and shows us that what you really are is what's inside. He had every reason to feel sorry for himself but didn't. He just went out there, faced life and helped others to do the same thing. There's a universal message in that.

Starger showed the script to MCA president Sid Shinberg, who immediately took a liking to it and subsequently committed Universal to making the film.

Bogdanovich was Starger's first choice as director:

> I wanted a director who could handle people and could give a background to the life-style that would make it come alive.

Then I thought of *The Last Picture Show* and *Paper Moon*, both of which Peter directed. In *Paper Moon* you have an unusual father/daughter relationship where the roles are reversed. In *Last Picture Show* you have a small town that came alive. A talent that could do those pictures, I thought, could surely do this.

As we shall see later, those two early pictures of Bogdanovich were particularly important in terms of the major obstacle to be overcome in this particular story: its inherently sentimental, tearjerker quality.

Bogdanovich, however, received the script at first with only lukewarm interest. The director was just emerging from a voluntary four-year absence from pictures, during which time he had concentrated on writing a memoir about his relationship with Dorothy Stratten, one of the stars of his last effort, *They All Laughed*. The book, published in 1984 under the title *The Killing of the Unicorn*, chronicled in intimate detail Stratten's exploitation by Hugh Hefner and the Playboy empire and the events leading up to the gruesome murder of Stratten by her husband, Paul Snider.

But more important perhaps than the fact that Bogdanovich succeeded in exposing for the first time to an eager public the true sordidness of the world that Hefner had created was the incredible sense of introspection which the time alone had created in the director. Although he had decided that a comedy would end his absence from film, he soon realized, after reading the *Mask* screenplay, that the story of Rocky Dennis had close personal parallels to the life of Dorothy Stratten:

> It seemed like I was obliged to do this film. . . . I was very touched by the story. I almost felt at that point it was inevitable. For a very odd reason, which was that the first play Dorothy Stratten had ever seen was *The Elephant Man*. She was absolutely bowled over by it and talked about it all the time. Shortly after she saw it she went to a store and bought some books about John Merrick. And while I had

some difficulty looking at the photographs, she had no problem. I couldn't understand her interest until after she was killed and I had seen the play myself. I realized then that extraordinary beauty sets you apart as much as extraordinary grotesquerie does. I began to understand on a more profound level than I had before about the concept of appearances: that it is deceptive and foolish to go by them. . . . [showing Dorothy's flip side] was a key motivating factor. That whole business about appearances. "Mask" is a very important word. We all wear masks. In fact, masks are imposed on us a lot of times. You get the innocence beaten out of you until you put on a mask. Inside, though, you're saying, "Really, I don't like to be hard." . . . I believe that anything that sets you apart is something of a cross to bear. . . . This picture is aptly titled because it's about everyone's mask, not necessarily the one on this particular boy. We all hide our feelings. It's hard for people to know each other. . . . There was a remarkable contrast in my mind between the grotesqueness of John Merrick and the beauty of Dorothy Stratten. Dorothy's beauty singled her out as much as his ugliness did him. When I came to that understanding it was fascinating. Then the script of *Mask* came along and it dealt with some of these same issues—people being different and having to pay for it. I also was attracted by one issue in particular that the script dealt with: the transcendence of a certain kind of death. (Rochlin, p. 134)

As had been the case with *Saint Jack* before it, Bogdanovich's decision to undertake *Mask* arose from a knowledge of self gained from a necessary hiatus from filmmaking. With regard to the issue of appearances, perhaps another reason he felt such a strong emotional commitment to the film was that it gave him a chance to prove to a perhaps still-skeptical public that all traces of the arrogant behavior he had displayed during the 1970s (more a reaction to his failures than his successes, he said) had vanished completely, and a new Bogdanovich was now emerging: a very decent and gentle man (though certainly he had never exactly been an ogre before) who possessed a great deal of understanding and compassion for the human frailty which inevitably accompanies courage and triumph.

Despite these motivating factors, however, on the surface at least the project certainly would appear to have been an odd choice for Bogdanovich when one considers the ultraconservative outlook he had displayed in his treatment of characters and subjects (couching them in terms of traditional Hollywood genres which lent them direction and vision) in his films through *Nickelodeon* (though this was true to a certain degree of *Saint Jack* and *They All Laughed* also, despite the fact that both were set in the present and that neither contained explicit references to the cinema's past).

However, since *Saint Jack* both the director's style and his handling of characters had become much freer and more relaxed, so that by this time he would seem to have been

Rocky and Ben (Lawrence Monoson) trade baseball cards.

more ready than ever to deal with characters who were truly flesh-and-blood people (not types) with a background as far removed from the history of the movies as one could imagine (despite the fact that the type of film they inhabit, a tearjerker, has been termed a genre by some). Bogdanovich deserves much credit for stretching himself by venturing onto such unfamiliar ground; the result, happily, is his most mature and moving film to date.

The final script for *Mask* (the result of nine rewrites by Phelan, Bogdanovich, and Starger, working together) concentrates on the last year of Rocky Dennis's life. Originally it was to begin with Rocky's childhood, but according to Phelan, child labor laws in the state of California would not allow someone below the age of ten to be ensconced in such a heavy cocoon of makeup for the lengthy periods of time required for each day's shoot (23-year-old Eric Stoltz, who plays Rocky, was in fact forced to wear his "mask" approximately seven hours a day—this after a four-hour application session). Also, Bogdanovich felt much more comfortable with the shorter time frame of the story.

As the film opens we are introduced to the disfigured Rocky and his mother, the decidedly unconventional Rusty (Cher), who is a motorcycle groupie of apparently very loose morals. We first see her arriving home one morning after an all-nighter with one of her male friends, just barely in time to make her son's ninth-grade registration (they have recently moved to a new neighborhood in Azusa, California).

We soon see, however, that when it comes to Rocky, Rusty is tough, assertive, and fiercely protective. She threatens legal action (in actuality she has no attorney) against the high school principal (Ben Piazza) who has the temerity to suggest that for obvious reasons her son might be better off in a "special school more suited to his needs." Rusty: "Do you teach algebra, biology, and English here?" Principal: "Of course." Rusty: "Those are his needs."

She also berates the callous young physician who treats Rocky as though he weren't even human. Doctor: "Can we talk outside? It's about the test results . . . on him." Rusty: "Oh, *him*. Him, by the way, has a name. And if you have some information *for* him I suggest you give it *to* him." When he informs her that Rocky's life expectancy is only three to six months, she abruptly counters with, "You're not gonna really give us that 'life expectancy' number again, are you? You know, for 12 years I've been listening to you guys bullshit. First you told me he was retarded. Then you said he was gonna be blind *and* deaf. Then you told me he'd never be able to do anything that regular kids could do. You know, if I dug his grave every time one of you geniuses told me he was gonna die, I'd be in fuckin' chop suey in China by now."

We eventually meet the gang of bikers with whom Rocky and Rusty spend most of their time. Although they look like Hell's Angels, they turn out to be sweet and gentle fellows who accept Rocky for what he is, an intelligent and sensible young man whose inclinations are decent and entirely normal. We discover that Rusty is into serious drugs and that Rocky is concerned about this. Also introduced early on is Rusty's former lover, Gar (Sam Elliott); a subsequent subplot has her once again sharing a bed with him, despite her initial reluctance (Rocky's real father has disappeared without a trace). Her relationship with Gar injects some much-needed stability into her life.

Rocky faces two major obstacles at this point in the story: getting the other students at his new school to accept him and finding a girlfriend. The first is accomplished in one superbly conceived and executed scene in which Rocky volunteers to relate the story of the Trojan War to the class. He uses conventional jargon to ingratiate himself ("One of the goddesses said if Paris picked her, she'd give him this really hot wench named Helen"), and finally wins everyone over by putting them at ease when the subject of his appearance inadvertently comes up (when he comments

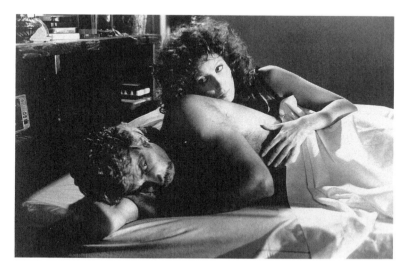

Rusty and Gar (Sam Elliott).

that "Paris went nuts when he saw Helen because she had this *face*," he immediately senses that the others are becoming uncomfortable and continues unperturbed with "a face that could launch a thousand ships").

Rocky eventually becomes known around school for his unusually high intelligence and gets an opportunity to make some money on the side, which he will put toward the trip to Europe which he and his friend Ben (Lawrence Monoson) are planning, by tutoring some of the students. One, in particular, is Eric (Craig King), whose attractive girlfriend Lisa (Alexandra Powers) Rocky secretly desires but knows he can never have, despite the fact that she is pleasant enough to him and they grow to be friends.

When Rocky expresses his sexual frustration to his mother, she responds by getting him a 19-year-old prostitute (Kelly Minter), who fortunately turns out to be sympathetic to his desire not to have sex with someone with whom he is not in love. It turns out the two of them both share a desire to see the world, and though initially shocked by his appearance, she quickly begins to sense, like everyone else, that Rocky is just as extraordinary inside as outside.

Meanwhile, Rusty's drug abuse is becoming more and more intolerable. One night she and Rocky have a particularly angry confrontation about her problem (she tells him it's none of his business) which culminates in her slapping him hard across the face—something she had made it a policy never to do. This is followed by a gripping scene wherein Rusty arrives home late with a man and finds Rocky in pain with one of his recurrent headaches. She tenderly eases his discomfort by getting him to recall a good memory and thereby "make himself well." The next morning, during an eloquent exchange with the two of them sitting on a swing set in the morning sunshine—Rusty with a bird perched on her finger—they reconcile, and she promises to cut down on the drugs.

Rusty goes back on her word, however, after a particu- larly painful encounter with her estranged parents, Abe (Richard Dysart) and Evelyn (Estelle Getty), and succeeds in finally alienating Gar and causing Rocky to leave home for summer camp, where he has been offered by the school principal a position as a counselor's aide at a camp for the blind. While there he meets Diana (Laura Dern), a beautiful blind teenager with whom he falls in love. The feeling is, to his delight, mutual—even after he describes his disfigurement to her. However, when Diana's parents meet Rocky and learn of the relationship, they are horrified and, feeling their daughter is being made a fool of, do their best to sever it.

From this point onward, Rocky becomes more and more distressed as his world seems to be crumbling around him. Although he is happy that Rusty has apparently lived up to her promise to stay away from drugs altogether, he finds himself unable to contact Diana by phone, and finds he must face estrangement from his peers once again as he enters high school. There is one strong moment where he responds to one student's cry of "If that's a mask he's wearing, I sure wish he'd take it off" by shoving him up against a locker and declaring, "I'll take my mask off if you take your mask off, you son of a bitch."

Rocky's final blow comes when Ben informs him that he will not be able to make the trek to Europe with him. One morning Rocky abruptly leaves for San Marino to see Diana. It turns out she is being sent to a school for the blind in Santa Barbara, so it is uncertain when they will be able to meet again. Rocky tells her that it doesn't matter, since she still loves him: "We'll always be together, Diana, even when we can't be together." One night soon after that Rocky dies—but not before receiving reassurance that Gar and Rusty will remain together.

Roger Ebert astutely observes that what immediately distinguishes *Mask* from the average TV disease-of-the-week movie is the fact that it "isn't the story of a disease, but the story of some people." In keeping with his intention to get the audience to see that Rocky was just a regular teenager who happened to look out of the ordinary, Bogdanovich came up with a brilliant opening scene in which we are introduced to Rocky's deformity in a very matter-of-fact manner. We catch only glimpses of the boy from outside his bedroom window, listening to rock music. A cut to the interior shows a hand arranging some baseball cards. It is not until he turns to the mirror to see how he looks in his biking jacket that we see his face clearly. The film originally was to begin at the school. Bogdanovich explains his rationale behind the scene as follows:

> I said, "We have to have a scene where the audience is alone with Rocky, absolutely alone with him before anything else happens." You don't really see him very clearly at first. You see him go by, you see him in the mirror, but you don't really

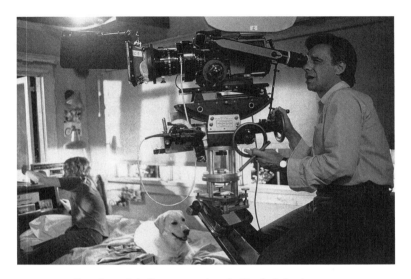

Bogdanovich lines up a shot in Rocky's bedroom.

see him boom—close-up—until the mother's there. That
way the audience is able to deal with their reaction to it, so
that by the time you get other people into it, the audience
has already gotten over the shock. In other words, "This is
it, this is what it is," and they kind of say, "Well, it's not so
bad." I thought if the audience felt like they knew him after
this, they would accept anything.

As Ebert points out, *Mask* "lands on its feet running" (as
all good movies do, after all) as Bogdanovich "doesn't waste
a lot of time wringing his hands over Rocky's fate" but
instead "moves directly to the center of his life" (though
the director jokes that throughout shooting he and the cast
kept referring to the film as a "Universal family monster
movie," in keeping with that studio's long line of horror
pictures). In the opening scenes the director concentrates

on dispelling all potential on the audience's part for feeling sorry for Rocky by swiftly winning them over to his side, where they remain for the duration of the film. He accomplishes this through a combination of unerringly precise direction and his customary propensity for overlapping dialogue.

The latter is particularly effective in the scenes at the genetics clinic delineating the nature of Rocky's illness: Rocky cheerfully recites his latest prognosis simultaneously with the doctors, shocking the cold-tempered Dr. Vinton (Andrew Robinson). There is also a nice comedic edge to Rusty's outrageous blitzing of the principal and Dr. Vinton which effectively puts the viewer at ease about the serious situation beneath the surface levity.

The film continues Bogdanovich's trademark emphasis on character over plot. However, as was not the case with

Gar tells Rocky what he was like as a child.

Saint Jack and *They All Laughed*, here the initial interest created in the protagonists by the director (and by the scenarist and performers) is strong enough to sustain the viewer through the somewhat uncertain path the script takes—this time the result of its being based upon actual events. This time one senses immediately a firm sense of direction in the telling of the story, itself a continuously fascinating and penetrating look into the inner workings of two very unusual people and their orbit (the characters are much more complex than those of either of Bogdanovich's previous films).

Bogdanovich said that "the real world doesn't usually pay attention to people like Rocky and Rusty. To the outside they're just a troubled woman and an ugly kid. But we know that they were a lot more than that." The director was fascinated by the contrast—mentioned earlier—between outer appearances and inner reality which these two characters embodied (a continuation of a theme explored earlier in *Saint Jack*):

> This story is an extreme example of that conflict dramatically because of the grotesque nature of Rocky's face and some of his mother's extreme behavior in terms of drugs and sex. She's a kind of extreme outgrowth of the sixties and he's an extreme of the personal awkwardness any of us might have. But the point to be made dramatically is how both of these people, who have trouble dealing with the world, are able to cope. Even though it's Rocky's story I was always very interested in his mother's dilemma. Because Rocky is so closely aligned with her, the story wouldn't work unless we fully understood both of them. The audience needs to see why she took drugs and behaved as she did with him and the men in her life. What we ultimately see is that it's very dangerous to judge people just by their actions because people do things for all sorts of reasons and we don't always know why. It's not enough to condemn someone for the things they do. You have to understand why they do it.

Bogdanovich handles the Rocky/Rusty relationship (the center of the film) with a disarming candor and simplicity which is always engaging (though occasionally veering toward the cornball) and which at several points in the story (mainly during the arguments between the two) recalls his treatment of the Moses/Addie pairing in *Paper Moon*. Here, however, the general tone is infinitely warmer and more satisfying, not least because the characterizations are deeper and because the people exist as completely unique entities.

We see that each depends on the other (Rocky on Rusty for tender, loving care in times of physical distress and for general encouragement to ignore the remarks of others and live for the moment; and Rusty on Rocky to take care of the affairs of the house while she gallivants with the gang members until all hours) and that it is only their combined strength which enables them to survive as a family unit. Bogdanovich does not presume to judge Rusty for her errant behavior, but instead chooses simply to present her as just another human being—though, as he says, one with extreme personal problems—and let the audience draw their own conclusions.

Bogdanovich's tough, no-nonsense direction evidenced throughout the film effectively overcomes all possibility of sweetness and sentimentality in the treatment of his characters (though he remains sympathetic to their problems at the same time) and lends most of the scenes a remarkable emotional resonance. The scene where the prostitute, Lorrie (Kelly Minter), visits Rocky, for example, could have been incredibly uncomfortable; instead, the reactions involved are handled simply and effortlessly. When she asks Rocky what happened to his face, he jokes, "I used to do a lot of drugs," which puts her—and the audience—at ease once again.

Most impressive in this regard are the scenes at the camp for the blind wherein Rocky and Diana meet and fall in love. Rocky first glimpses her briefly as she is walking

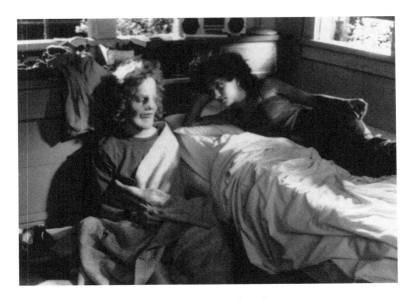

Rocky and Lorrie (Kelly Minter).

across the grounds with some of the other campers, and his
initial reaction reminds us of Charles' (John Ritter's) lonely
adoration of Dolores (Dorothy Stratten) in *They All Laughed*
("Hello, beautiful").

But as was the case with those two, Rocky and Diana
eventually meet—though, to Rocky's delight, she is unable
to see him, while he relishes her natural, childlike beauty
("You look like Alice in Wonderland," he tells her—but of
course she is unable to grasp what he's talking about,
having been blind since birth). During this first encounter
Bogdanovich frames both actors entirely in close-up,
thereby cutting directly to the heart of the situation.

There is an extraordinary and wondrously visceral,
almost palpable, quality to these all-too-brief but important
scenes (indeed, to the whole film)—hard to describe in
words but unmistakable nevertheless—it results mainly

from the director's emphasis on purely visual expression whenever possible. The moment on the hilltop where Diana touches Rocky's face and the one in the camp kitchen where he teaches her about colors by placing hot and cold rocks in her hands, in particular, manage to convey a rare power and excitement which arouses all the senses at once. The sound recording in the film is also unusually sensitive, creating a terrific sense of freshness and spontaneity which is especially felt here—Bogdanovich insisted, for example, that the crucial scene wherein Rocky reveals his condition to Diana be shot by the sea, in order to create a feeling of freedom, of escape.

Just as he allows no tears to be shed for Rocky's condition, so Bogdanovich spends no time pitying Diana for her blindness—in fact, he adds a subtle Hawksian dimension to their relationship by making her the more aggressive of the two: she asks *him* to take *her* to lunch, and during the scene in which the two of them are dancing at a "New Year's Eve in July" party, when Diana senses that Rocky is hesitant about making a move to kiss her (he has never been close to a girl before), she puts him at ease by asking him. However, we understand, of course, that like Rusty with Rocky and vice versa, she depends on him also because of her handicap.

As was the case with the relationships in *Last Picture Show*, here Bogdanovich celebrates the glory of the moment, capsulized in Rocky and Diana's sharing "that special time together that only teenagers can have: time when love doesn't mean sex so much as perfect agreement on the really important issues, like Truth and Beauty" (Ebert, 1988). Here, however, the tragic dimensions of the relationship have been softened. In the original script, during their last encounter, Rocky tells Diana not to worry about their separation, since "we'll be together . . . even though we can't be together," which indicates a fatalistic outlook brought on by the death of Red, one of Rocky's biker friends, and perhaps hinting at the fact that Rocky senses the end of his life is near. However, since Red's funeral was omitted from the release print of the film, the last line was changed to read "We'll be together even *when* we can't be together," which changes its meaning.

Some have wondered what exactly kills Rocky at the end—is it entirely physical or partly emotional? Originally Rocky had a line where he said to his dog, "I don't think I want to make myself well anymore," which could indicate that he was able to control what was happening to some extent. Bogdanovich, who eliminated that line, says that this was never the case, that "Rocky just felt like he was going to die and he did, that's all"—which is consistent with the overall light tone of the film, which will be described in more detail shortly.

Of course, much of the considerable impact of scenes like those at the camp for the blind results from the

Moment of truth: Diana (Laura Dern) touches Rocky's face.

director's stylistic expertise. The visual-narrative sense displayed by Bogdanovich in this film is surely his most acute since *Last Picture Show*. It is particularly significant that *Mask* marked a reunion with cinematographer Laszlo Kovacs, who had shot most of the films of Bogdanovich's early phase.

By contrast to the method of just "letting the story happen," so to speak, which Bogdanovich and cameraman Robby Muller had adopted on *Saint Jack* and *They All Laughed, Mask* marked a welcome return to the type of tight, explicit exposition which Bogdanovich had displayed in his pre–*Saint Jack* work with Kovacs—though, happily, the high energy level here on the part of both men was in direct contrast to their last collaboration on *Nickelodeon*, which suffered from a general feeling of enervation. One suspects it was the stylistic freedom afforded the director by his two interim efforts which enabled him to recharge his batteries.

Throughout *Mask* there are numerous assured touches which give ample evidence of Bogdanovich's thorough mastery of point of view and camera technique and which succeed in conveying emotions buried beneath the surface in a purely visual manner. Among them is a scene in which Rusty's parents return home from a baseball game with Rocky to find her lying on the couch in the living room, stoned. Neither Rusty nor the grandparents are able to express their resentment toward each other in words; suddenly, Rusty hurls a baseball at her father, who responds by tossing it back in just as hostile a fashion. This continues for about a minute. Bogdanovich conceived this ingenious little scene after hearing Phelan describe to him an unusual story conference she had been in, in which an executive, playing with a basketball, of all things, suddenly tossed it to her; she then responded by tossing it back.

Many of the best scenes in *Mask* achieve their impact solely through silent reactions—a technique which Bogdanovich was first able to explore fully in *Saint Jack* and

They All Laughed. The most affecting moment in the film for many occurs when Rocky and Rusty stare at his reflection in a fun-house mirror: they are given a glimpse of what the boy would have looked liked had he been spared his illness. The scenes at the school where Rocky is introduced to his classmates also convey ample evidence of Bogdanovich's unfailing judgment of perspective.

The final five-minute scene at the cemetery is also admirable, since it is composed entirely of reaction shots of Rusty, Gar, and Dozer. The final image of the film has Rusty standing alone in a corner staring off into the mountains, and recalling to herself a poem which Rocky had written (heard in voice-over), expressive of all the good things he represented. It is a powerful moment, reminiscent of the final image of Winterbourne at the conclusion of *Daisy Miller*—though significantly different in tone, as we shall see shortly.

Another reason *Mask* works so well has to do with the attention to realism by Bogdanovich, his collaborators, and his cast—an approach whose benefits had not shown so brightly since the early period piece *Last Picture Show*. In keeping with the semidocumentary nature of the story (based as it is on the experiences of real people) and with Bogdanovich's favored practice of filming in actual locations, much of the film was shot as close as possible to where the real Rocky lived (Azusa, California). The house where Rocky and Rusty live was an old 1920s-style bungalow in Monrovia, California, one of the few homes that had a view of the San Gabriel Mountains. Because he wanted the audience to see that Rocky was a regular teenager who just looked out of the ordinary, Bogdanovich was determined to offset Rocky's looks by making everything around him as real as possible.

> Because this subject matter is dramatic and human, I tried to place him in real surroundings. Color has a tendency to romanticize a situation on film no matter what you do. My

feeling to counter that was to be real, true. We wanted to
show this was happening in a rough, urban city so we used
real places with real lighting. I wanted people to always
know where we were so whenever possible there would be
lots of windows where we can see out. We constantly have
cars driving by. There's nowhere to get away from cars in
today's society. So by using them you get the sense that we
are in an actual place.

The film company was also able to shoot in the actual
camp Rocky attended—Camp Bloomfield, sponsored by
the Foundation for the Junior Blind—with some of the
actual camp personnel. With regard to the actors, Cher
and Eric Stoltz met and spoke with Rusty on several
occasions, and Rusty was also present during some of the
shooting. They and Lawrence Monoson spent time with
bikers near where Rocky grew up, while Laura Dern
worked with a woman at the Braille Institute and actually
walked around neighborhoods as a blind person. Dennis
Burkley (Dozer, the mute biker) talked to several speech
therapists.

Bogdanovich's dedication to realism was put to the test,
however, by his decision to shoot the film in color. A
problem arose because the type of extensive makeup job
required here (the makeup was created by veteran Michael
Westmore, who received an Oscar for his efforts) had
never before been photographed in color (the only other
film in recent memory to use a comparable makeup had
been David Lynch's black-and-white *Elephant Man*). "The
color movies with makeup always portray some kind of
monsters or animals," Bogdanovich said. It took nine or
ten makeup tests until Laszlo Kovacs was satisfied with the
way the mask looked on film. But the director admitted
that although the picture was difficult to light, and despite
the fact that certain angles didn't work, "it was worth the
challenge to find a way to do it in color since it's such a
modern story."

Rusty comforts Rocky after he makes another futile attempt to contact Diana.

In terms of the final look of the picture, however, Bogdanovich was not pleased that it is unusually bright and sunny.

> It's all wrong. Laszlo Kovacs and I worked harder than we'd ever worked trying to obtain a certain depth of focus with color. The picture was supposed to look much darker, more melancholy, like *Daisy Miller*. What happened was the producers got so angry with me over the mess I was making about the music that they went to the Technicolor lab and told them to print the picture five points brighter all the way through, which ruined everything we did. So when Vincent Canby wrote that the makeup didn't look convincing, I called him up and said, "You're damn right." That's why everything looks so out of focus in the background. People said to me, "Why did you make it so bright? It looks like TV." I said, "*I* didn't."

The name of the person responsible for giving the order to change the print was Howard Alston, Starger's assistant.

But in spite of what Bogdanovich says, I believe the picture looks fine the way it is now for two reasons. First of all, this is not an art film (as *Daisy Miller* had been) but rather a semidocumentary account of the lives of two real people. The lucid natural lighting throughout is the equivalent of that employed in the black-and-white Italian neorealist films, for example, and it always looks vibrant, never washed-out like the last Kovacs-Bogdanovich collaboration, *Nickelodeon*—the closest equivalent I can think of to the result is Robert Burks' cinematography on Hitchcock's 1959 *North by Northwest*. And contrary to what Bogdanovich says, the background elements do not appear out of focus to any significant degree. With the abundance of close-ups and reliance on cutting in the picture, who would notice or care anyway? This makes the decision to use deep focus seem particularly puzzling; *Daisy Miller*, the reader will recall, had by contrast made abundant use of long takes.

But more important, the bright look of the film is consistent with Bogdanovich's approach to his subject. Had the film been photographed in the dark tones the director wanted, the result would have resembled the look of *The Elephant Man*: Rocky would have appeared to the viewer like John Merrick, a horrific come-on, shrouded in mystery. There is nothing wrong with the way the makeup looks either. This obviously would have negated everything Bogdanovich was trying to accomplish in the opening scenes in terms of making Rocky appear as ordinary as possible, despite his deformity—and certainly the feeling of freedom he spoke of in relation to the scene between Rocky and Diana on the hill at the camp for the blind would also have been negated by the more glum look he was apparently aiming for—along with the generally upbeat, cheerful tone of the picture.

Most crucial of all with regard to this issue, however, would have been the ending, of which Bogdanovich has said, "I think people will take away hope that there can be triumph in the greatest difficulties. I like the theme of this film in the sense of what Rocky and his mother truly believed in—pressing on." The final image of Rusty standing in the cemetery, therefore, had of necessity to convey the antithesis of that profound sense of irreversible loss communicated by the camera's slowly receding from Winterbourne standing over Daisy's grave at the end of *Daisy Miller*. Significantly, there is no funeral for Rocky—the last scene takes place four years after his death. This would not have been achieved had the film turned out the way Bogdanovich intended. His reprise of key scenes from the film after the final fade-out, however, is his most eloquent since *Daisy Miller*—though in this case the effect is more bittersweet than out-and-out sad. The somewhat melancholy tone of the final half-hour of *Mask* is free from the tragic vision of that film or that of *Last Picture Show*, for example.

This leads to the central issue over which critics have

been split about *Mask*: how "truthful" the film really is to the actual people and events portrayed within it. Anna Hamilton Phelan—who should know better than anyone else—says that what the audience sees on the screen is "about 70 to 80 percent accurate"—allowing, of course, for creative license. The only aspect she says was totally fabricated was the Rocky/Diana relationship, the idea for which was sparked by a rumor at the camp that Rocky and an unidentified girl may have been interested in each other (the character Diana as written was originally supposed to be a brunet, until Bogdanovich decided that blond Laura Dern was right for the part).

Of course, one could argue about the accuracy of the scenes at the school, for example (surely not even the real Rusty would have been present at such times), but those are just things one has to take for granted—having of course accepted Anna Hamilton Phelan's judgment as generally expert, which it is. It is a tribute to her skills as a writer that the story is never maudlin or overly sentimental. Her guidelines throughout were obviously honesty and truth. Incidentally, she also has a brief cameo at the beginning as the "puppy lady."

Nevertheless, critics have complained about several aspects of the script. First, they say, the character of Rocky seems canonized. Does he have to win *all* those awards at the graduation and be unquestioningly accepted by everyone (except for Diana's parents and several other "callous" souls, that is)? These people argue that Bogdanovich and Phelan encourage the viewer to feel superior to all those who do not immediately accept Rocky for what he really is and to assume that he, too, would understand and be nice if confronted in real life by someone like Rocky. They are also irritated by the fact that Rocky does not suffer more moments of self-doubt.

In answer to the first argument, the opening scenes of the film are designed to ease one's initial discomfort with Rocky's appearance. The viewer from that point onward is presumably identifying totally with Rocky, so that when Diana's parents reject him three-quarters of the way through the picture, their reaction, as Ebert says, should "come as a shock to us, a reminder of how completely we had accepted him."

The film thus takes the form of a character test of sorts for the viewer. Those who are persuaded by the presentation of Rocky by the director, the scenarist, and Eric Stoltz will inevitably come away from the picture with a greater understanding of the human condition; those who are not, will not. The film's $40 million gross is a comforting indication that a great number of Americans are of the former variety—certainly no one goes for the first time or returns to the picture thinking it is escapist entertainment.

Furthermore, not all of those who encounter Rocky accept him (there is a moment at the carnival where Gar threatens a ticket taker with physical abuse if he does not let Rocky ride on the bumper cars), and not all those who come to know Rocky are completely comfortable around him (Eric's girlfriend Lisa is one)—but they are forced, as we are, to get used to Rocky's appearance and overlook it; they are of course aided by his ingratiating personality.

With regard to the second complaint, Rocky's whole existence was predicated on his not feeling sorry for himself, so that he could thereby maintain the high spirits which enabled him to "make himself well" over and over again. The only thing he had to feel glum about were his illness and his mother's drug addiction, and Bogdanovich and Phelan do show him becoming distraught about both of these at several key moments in the film. In fact, the entire final half-hour shows Rocky's desperation as his hopes for the future are dashed at every turn. There is one particularly touching moment where Rusty cradles his head against her as he cries after making another fruitless attempt to phone Diana.

The other objections have to do with Rusty herself and the bikers with whom she associates. It is never explained

Rusty becomes hysterical after finding Rocky dead.

in the story how Rusty became hooked on drugs, or how she and Rocky manage to subsist with him at school most of the time and her spending all her money on cocaine and other illicit substances. Phelan says that it was originally made clear in the script and in the film that Rocky was collecting disability payments and that Rusty was working part-time as a waitress. It is not known why the reference was deleted. It certainly is no major detriment to the film, though—most viewers are so caught up by the story they completely overlook it anyway.

The drug issue and the issue of the bikers seeming sentimentalized both have to do with a conscious decision on the part of the studio to soften the picture in order to appeal to a family audience (thereby making Bogdano-vich's jest about the picture being a "Universal family monster movie" seem ironically apropos). The picture is rated PG-13, not R, the viewer should note. As originally written, the picture was "much darker," Phelan says, and perhaps the look Bogdanovich was aiming for would have been more appropriate for *that* film.

For example, originally there was a rather disturbing scene (which Bogdanovich shot and which he says was "quite good, but too 'heavy' ") in which Rocky returns home late in the picture to find Rusty on the floor in her closet, having a seizure. The boy promptly sends for an ambulance, but afterward she returns home to chastise him for nearly having her arrested and to berate him for the trouble his appearance has presumably caused her all his life (in a speech which Cher refused to recite, according to the screenwriter). In the final film, Rusty tells Rocky at the camp for the blind that she is off the drugs for good, and we are given no reason afterward to doubt her sincerity.

In view of the final product, the cutting of such scenes as the one just described was justified in my view because the focus of the film is on Rocky alone; although some people might argue that both Rocky and Rusty are given equal time, in reality Rusty is only presented as important as she relates to Rocky. We see early on that a large part of the reason she takes drugs is to relieve herself of the anguish she feels for her son's condition but which she admirably hides from him. As for her motivation for taking drugs in the first place, Phelan says it was never explained in any of the drafts because it had no relevance to the story.

Also eliminated from the final cut (but against Bogdanovich's wishes) was a four-minute funeral for Red, one of the bikers. It was during this brief but important scene that one saw the more primal side of the bikers (whom Bogdanovich aptly describes as "modern cowboys")—as opposed to the goody-goody antics they displayed earlier, such as Dozer's secretly buying a puppy for Rocky or childishly fleeing from the workers at the blood bank. After the funeral the gang members were shown shooting it up and getting drunk, behavior one might normally expect from such

types. The funeral scene itself, as described by Bogdanovich, would also, incidentally, seem to have been staged in
the tradition of one of his heroes, John Ford (and, perhaps
not surprisingly, it is Ford veteran Harry Carey, Jr., who
was buried in the scene), with each biker solemnly placing
symbolic trinkets in the flowers surrounding the casket.

More important, however, the missing funeral scene
hurts the film in that it showed Rocky's attitude toward
death, which was echoed later by Rusty after he died (in a
now unclear reference). There Rusty had asked Rocky why
he was not placing something in the casket for Red, to
which he replied (in words which Bogdanovich himself
wrote, recalling something Sean Lennon said after his
father, John Lennon, was killed), "I'm not saying goodbye
to Red. He's not over there anyway. He's right here. He
went but he stayed. He's everywhere now. Nobody ever
really dies."

Bogdanovich's major complaint about *Mask* (over which
he unsuccessfully tried to sue Universal Studios) was that
the four Bruce Springsteen songs (totaling fifteen minutes)
featured on the original soundtrack of the film were
omitted by the studio in favor of less expensive ones by Bob
Seger. Producer Martin Starger and his associate, Frank
Price, have gone on record as saying that the main reason
a deal could not be reached with Springsteen was that the
singer wanted a 25 percent share of videocassette sales of
the film containing his music, in addition to his $1
million-plus fee for the songs alone. No precedent had as
yet been established for allowing a recording artist to share
in video profits, and Universal was not about to set one.

All I can say on that count is that for the studio which
produced *E.T.: The Extra-terrestrial* (1982), the top-grossing
film of all time (to date it has reaped a sum in excess of
$600 million), as well as innumerable other megahits in
recent years, this was petty squabbling indeed—especially
considering that, as Bogdanovich points out, the publicity
which would have been generated from Springsteen's

participation in the project could have earned the film *at least* another $60 million (at the time of *Mask*'s release—March 1985—Springsteen was on his triumphant "Born in the USA" tour).

On an aesthetic level, Bogdanovich feels that the picture was significantly harmed by the removal of the Springsteen music. In terms of the film's veracity, the real Rocky Dennis had been a great admirer of "The Boss," and one will note that hanging on his bedroom wall in the film, prominently displayed, is a poster of Springsteen. But more important, the director argues, the impact of some scenes was compromised by the omission of the songs. One such example involved the final sequence at the cemetery:

> After the dissolve to the truck coming toward the cemetery at the end, you were supposed to be hearing "Born in the USA" on the radio, to signal to the audience that it was not 1980 any longer but *now*, four years later. Without that transitional device, a lot of people thought it was Rocky's funeral and wondered why there weren't more people there. So the emotional impact of the picture was damaged as a result. Also, in the previews that we had, the audience responded more enthusiastically to Cher because Bruce's music was playing behind her in the background. Of course, they didn't *know* that that's why they were responding in that way. That's because the music was having an abstract, visceral effect on them that they weren't aware of.

Bogdanovich also says that the inclusion of Springsteen's music was more in keeping with his original cut (two hours and eight minutes), which, he says, was "much more of a working-class picture." Certainly a large part of the audience that made *Mask* a hit came from just that background.

As for myself, while I would not agree with Bogdanovich that the difference between Bruce Springsteen and Bob Seger is like "comparing Puccini to good chamber music," perhaps my own opinion is irrelevant here because (as was the case with *They All Laughed* and Bogdanovich's personal tastes) the choice of composer was dictated by the subject of the film—Rocky Dennis himself—and as his mother pointed out in one interview, he had never heard of Bob Seger.

Notwithstanding this conflict, Bogdanovich's employment of source music in general is without question his most impressive since *Last Picture Show*. After a consultation with Springsteen, he selected a variety of pop tunes by such artists as the Beatles, Gary U.S. Bonds, Steppenwolf, Steely Dan, and Little Richard. Particularly noteworthy are Seger's "Katmandu," used throughout to express Rocky's desire to escape from his oppressive environment and see the world; and Paul McCartney and John Lennon's "Girl" and "I Wanna Hold Your Hand," which comment on both the character of Diana and the feelings she and Rocky share for each other.

What perhaps mark *Mask*'s greatest achievement are the performances Bogdanovich elicited from his cast (again, his best work since *Picture Show*)—and under extremely difficult conditions, not the least of which was the 106-degree heat in Monrovia, where much of the picture was shot. First of all, of course, there is Cher's Rusty Dennis, an admirable mixture of bourbon-whiskey toughness and honey-smooth love. This was her first major film role, after supporting performances in Robert Altman's *Come Back to the Five and Dime, Jimmy Dean, Jimmy Dean* (1982), in which she repeated her stage success, and Mike Nichols' *Silkwood* (1983), for which she was nominated for an Oscar.

Bogdanovich says the burden of such a demanding part, coupled with Cher's unfamiliarity with his shooting technique (in contrast to Altman's and Nichols' methods, he does not shoot masters unless the entire scene will be played in the master), were the causes of the much-publicized arguments between the two of them. Also, she did not trust him because she thought he originally did not want her for the role, which was totally false. Although he

The final scene: Cher, Sam Elliott, and Dennis Burkley as Dozer.

says he had to break scenes down a lot more than he normally would with her because she "couldn't sustain them," there is no evidence of superfluous cutting in the final film—a tribute to Bogdanovich's visual skill. Bogdanovich employed an unusual number of close-ups of the actress because, he says, "that was the secret of the performance—to get close, so you could see her eyes and read what was going on in her mind beneath her surface reactions."

Ironically, her quarrels with the director may even have helped her performance by increasing her determination to do a good job in spite of the "bad advice" she felt she was receiving from him at times. In truth, she owes a lot more of the success of her performance here to her director than she has been willing to acknowledge, since, as Bogdanovich says—and Laszlo Kovacs attests to this also—she was unable to sustain scenes for more than two or three lines, the result of her unfamiliarity with the demands of a lead role, and also since none of her previous or subsequent work—all for lesser directors—can touch it. Bogdanovich, however, says he had absolute confidence in her from the start, as did Phelan, who had written the part with her in mind. Bogdanovich:

> I felt Cher's persona, or at least the persona people think is Cher, fit the character exactly. The woman had to be free, outspoken, tough, and someone you'd believe runs around with bikers. She also had to be a lot more vulnerable than she lets on, which I think is also true of the real Cher.

One other scene (also four minutes in length) that Bogdanovich regrets was cut from the release print involved Rusty's singing a number song called "Little Egypt" with Rocky around a campfire. According to Phelan, Starger and Price decided to remove the scene because they were worried that once people had gotten over the obstacle of accepting Cher the superstar recording artist as Rusty Dennis in the opening scenes, the illusion would have been destroyed if she suddenly began singing; however, the omission of the number makes a reference to it late in the film unintelligible. This would not necessarily have been the case, since, as Bogdanovich mentioned, the audience would already have been able to discern much of Cher's off-screen persona in the character by that point. The director also feels the scene was important in terms of "the sense of fun of the movie and the sense of the characters' really getting along and the fact that she was in fact talented as a performer. It was very moving, touching, funny."

Although Cher's performance may give the impression at times of having been pieced together on the cutting room floor, to her credit she brought much of her own natural talent—a rare quality among actors these days—to the part, and even improved on some of Phelan's original dialogue. Rusty's most characteristic line was in fact written by Cher herself: "You must be confusing me with someone who gives a shit," she tells Gar after he berates her for abusing drugs. If the performance seems overall to be something short of what it might have been, it is only because, as Cher herself has said, some of her best scenes (such as the one in which she has a seizure) were omitted from the final print—but for good reason, as I mentioned before. Nevertheless, she was given the Best Actress award at Cannes for her work—certainly a prestigious honor for someone to whom acting was a relatively new field.

Sharing the spotlight with Cher (he actually has more scenes than she) is 23-year-old Eric Stoltz, who is no less than miraculous as the resilient Rocky. Communicating the emotions of this complex character to the audience was no simple task, considering that all one could see of Stoltz's real face under his makeup were his eyes, but the young actor managed to pull it off brilliantly. His Rocky is one of the most endearing screen characters to come along in years (this despite his grotesque appearance), and unlike John Hurt's portrayal of John Merrick in *The Elephant Man*, Stoltz never allows us to pity Rocky; he does not trivialize the character, but rather allows him to keep his dignity.

Another remarkable "find" is 17-year-old Laura Dern (the daughter of actors Bruce Dern and Diane Ladd), who plays Diana, Rocky's love interest. What could have been an embarrassingly icky-sweet and clichéd role (the gimmick being that she was blind and therefore could only see the hero's beautiful soul) was magically transformed by this gifted young talent into a thing of exquisite beauty and sensitivity, the quintessence of that dream girl described in McCartney's lyric. When she tells Rocky that she loves him during their final encounter, there is possibly not a male alive who would not kill at that moment to be in Rocky's shoes, despite his condition. She makes us so completely overlook her character's handicap that we believe she actually *can* see. Among her many resources is an effective method of cramping her mouth slightly when she smiles, which curbs any excess of sweetness in her expression. A few critics complained that Bogdanovich seemed to be molding her too much in the image of Dorothy Stratten; if that is true, it is only a compliment.

Sam Elliott is also very good as the macho but gentle-hearted Gar. He has a monologue at one point which rivals Ben Johnson's in *Last Picture Show* for warmth and sheer depth of feeling. All the supporting performances are exceptional also, with particular praise going to Kelly Minter's prostitute (again, a triumph over a possibly clichéd characterization) and Ben Piazza's principal.

In sum, *Mask* could not have been a more worthy comeback picture for a director whom too many had written off as washed up. The critical and commercial success of this film reestablished Bogdanovich as one of the primary talents in American film today—and indeed, it is one of the major directorial achievements in recent years. But perhaps more important than what it did for Bogdanovich's career is his triumph over the inherent pitfalls of the material itself. The result is not a medicine which viewers feel they have to take, but instead a thoroughly positive, irresistible affair which in fact demands multiple viewings. What better reward for a man who had proven himself once again to be just as resilient as the hero of his picture.

12 *Illegally Yours* (1988)

After *Mask*, Bogdanovich worked on a number of aborted projects, one of which was a film version of the play *To Gillian on Her 37th Birthday*, which was to star Molly Ringwald, one of the new generation of actors with whom the director had become familiar since his last film. One of these young people, 23-year-old Rob Lowe, had auditioned for the part of Rocky in *Mask* and had also in the interim befriended Bogdanovich, who decided he would be right for a comedy, should one happen to come along. Late in 1986, Bogdanovich read a script which he thought had an amusing premise and would provide a part for Lowe similar to the bumbling fools for love whom Ryan O'Neal and John Ritter had played in *Doc* and *They All Laughed*: that of a juror who falls for his former grade-school obsession, a woman who is on trial for murder. His affection for her naturally prejudices him, and he sets out against the law to prove her innocence. In fact, as Bogdanovich points out, everything the protagonist, Richard Dice, does is against the law.

Unfortunately, however, the result was to prove the low point in Bogdanovich's career—although it is on a much lower aesthetic plane than any of his earlier efforts, so therefore simply negligible, it is a most embarrassing comedown after the superb *Mask*. At least the releasing company was wise enough to spare Bogdanovich's reputation by not giving it a theatrical run in any of the major cities in the U.S.—shelving it after several disastrous previews and consigning it to cable television and home video, where the advertisements played down Bogdanovich's name and emphasized instead star Lowe—so it is doubtful that it will have any really significant impact on Bogdanovich's standing. Certainly the era of *At Long Last Love* has long passed; no one is out to get the director any longer.

Bogdanovich says making this film was the most unpleasant experience of his entire career (evidence of his lack of interest was his decision to use a second unit for the chase sequences, something which he had deliberately avoided in *Doc*). The screenplay is what caused most of the problems Bogdanovich and company encountered, reminding one again of a bit of advice by one of the director's mentors, Howard Hawks: If it isn't on the printed page, it only gets worse when you try to shoot it. The original script was

Bogdanovich and costars Rob Lowe and Colleen Camp attempt to rewrite the script on the set.

written by two novices, Michael Kaplan and John Levenstein—although through a most reprehensible Hollywood
practice of protecting no-talents from the derision and
harm they deserve they have been allowed to use pseudo-
nyms ("M. A. Stewart and Max Dickens"). Bogdanovich
and cast were actually forced to rewrite most of the script
hastily on the set because of the pitiful incompetence of
those two; needless to say, their efforts proved futile, since
the material was unsalvageable to begin with; if anything,
trying to fix it only magnified its already major shortcomings (nevertheless, one sees the potential in the premise
and admires Bogdanovich's determination to redeem the
material, despite the staggering odds against him). Quite
simply, there isn't a single funny line or situation throughout the incredible 102-minute running time. Actually,
Bogdanovich seemed aware of this when he walked out on

Juvenile slapstick.

a preview after half an hour, then went back to the cutting room and for months attempted to repair the damage, but to no avail.

The entirety of the scenario consists of a seemingly endless parade of cartoonlike characters scrambling about spying on and chasing after one another while trying to discern the motives of their respective quarries. The story begins with a narration by Richard Dice (Lowe) which introduces far more people and situations than any viewer could possibly hope to digest—and this before the credits have even ended. Everything becomes more and more convoluted and pointless from that moment on, since everyone involved is introduced far too hastily and ambiguously for anyone to develop real interest in their situations. The story is literally all plot, with no attention given to the necessity of coming up with a good punch line every so often. The typical line has one character telling another he should be committed to an insane asylum—the mark of utter desperation in a screwball comedy, reminding one of Hawks' dim *Man's Favorite Sport?* (1964), for example. Everything finally resolves itself into several confusing car chases which are simply that and nothing more. And the comic situations are exceedingly juvenile (Richard or one of the other characters falling down or disguising themselves as a member of the opposite sex—and rather poorly at that). Bogdanovich claims he made the film with young viewers in mind, but even a child of five would be put off by the endlessly repetitive goings-on.

Now, all of this would seem pretty embarrassing in itself, but it becomes even more so when one compares the film to *Doc*, which had all the qualities it lacks and then some. And the problems continue with the central casting. Lowe has been almost universally classified by critics as the least-promising working actor of his generation; by giving him such a major part (his earlier credits are smaller and totally negligible), Bogdanovich only succeeded in making more painfully obvious than ever Lowe's shortcomings. The director says Lowe had a very difficult time of it trying to adapt to broad physical comedy and fast-paced delivery of lines, and the result bears this out. Although a game player, he is embarrassingly affected, and though Bogdanovich has done the same thing with him that he had earlier with O'Neal and Ritter (suppressing his good looks by putting horn-rimmed glasses on him), Lowe lacks the sureness, the ability to play it straight without seeming self-conscious, that the two older actors possessed. He spends most of the film sporting a puppy-dog look of adoration for his beloved, which can most kindly be described as cute. Now granted, Lowe's material here cannot even begin to compare with that which was given O'Neal and Ritter, but one suspects Lowe would have done much the same thing anyway. Lowe might have been all right for the part in *Mask* (though it is almost impossible to imagine anyone but the very gifted Eric Stoltz in it), but as has been said a million times, comedy is much tougher to do than drama, as Lowe's work here certainly proves. Curiously enough, Eric Stoltz also would seem to be inadequate—too intense—for comedy, the reason he was fired by Robert Zemeckis and Steven Spielberg from *Back to the Future*. Bogdanovich has dreams of resurrecting the spirit of the golden age of screwball comedy, but he is doing himself a grave disservice by picking material as worthless as this and actors as unsuited (in ability, if not looks) as Lowe to the demands of an ostensibly Cary Grant–type role. Colleen Camp and Kenneth Mars are wasted in smaller parts, buried beneath a surfeit of plot convolutions.

If my review thus far has seemed a bit harsh, it is only because one expects something excellent from a talent like Bogdanovich each time out. But certainly his choosing a poor piece of material is a far-from-uncommon feat among directors of his generation, and everyone is entitled to a mistake once in awhile. True to form, he is as tough on himself as ever when discussing the film, admitting that had he and his cast not been rushed into production

Voyeurism rampant: Kim Myers and L. B. Straten.

Richard (Rob Lowe) and Molly (Colleen Camp).

without a chance to have a full read-through of the revised script, they never would have proceeded.

It seems sad to end this study on a down note, but one can at least feel comfort in knowing that this film has already been mercifully forgotten—happily, people remember only one's successes—and that Bogdanovich's fans are eagerly awaiting his next, the long-anticipated sequel to *The Last Picture Show—Texasville*—which is scheduled to be released in 1990 featuring members of the original cast.

Reviews of Books by Peter Bogdanovich

The Cinema of Orson Welles; *The Cinema of Howard Hawks*; *The Cinema of Alfred Hitchcock* (monographs published by the Museum of Modern Art, New York, in 1961, 1962, 1963 respectively).

These relatively brief monographs (each is approximately 50 pages) were printed in conjunction with retrospectives of the respective directors' films which Bogdanovich, then in his early 20s, organized for the Museum of Modern Art. All three (the Hawks in particular) were pioneering surveys, among the first works to examine the oeuvre of these men as art. All three contain a studious, completely nonpretentious overview of general themes and visual techniques to be found in the work of these men (Welles through 1958's *Touch of Evil*, Hawks through *Hatari!*, 1962, and Hitchcock through 1963's *The Birds*), followed by (with the exception of the Welles piece) lengthy and (particularly in the case of the Hitchcock one) probing interviews inquiring into the directors' working methods and their treatment of recurring characters and themes. All three are still considered important basic references for those interested in analysis (though not of the shot-by-shot or scene-by-scene variety) of the films of these great American directors. Good selection of illustrations.

Fritz Lang in America (Praeger, New York, 1967); *John Ford* (University of California Press, 1968, rev. ed. 1978); *Allan Dwan: The Last Pioneer* (Praeger, New York, 1971, rev. ed. 1981).

All three of these volumes are sustained in the same scholarly bent as the monographs, though a bit more probing perhaps, particularly in the case of the Ford. The majority of each volume is comprised of an interview with the director, during which time (most importantly in the case of Dwan, whose work had never before been taken seriously in America) Bogdanovich asks every type of question one would expect. Many of the responses are anecdotal, though there is good self-analysis from Lang. The fact that Ford even consented to such a session is in itself remarkable—and most of the comments he does make about the artistic aspects of his pictures are to be found nowhere else. What one comes away with is a true feel for the directors' personalities and how they approached their craft.

Pieces of Time: Peter Bogdanovich on the Movies (also published under title *Picture Shows: Bogdanovich on the Movies*) (Arbor House, New York, 1973, rev. ed. 1985; 332 pp.).

Invaluable and now-classic collection of Bogdanovich's *Esquire* pieces published between 1962 and 1972. The revised edition, which, strangely enough, is harder to find than the earlier one, contains three new entries in the "Later Impressions" section published between 1972 and 1983—"An Afternoon at the New Yorker," "Sinatra and Company," "The Murder of Sal Mineo," "Over the Hill," "The America of John Ford"—plus a revised foreword and new afterword by Bogdanovich. Of special interest is the "First Impressions" section, culled from anecdotes Bogdanovich gathered when he made his first trip to Hollywood in January of 1961 at the age of 20. There are glimpses into the personalities of such luminaries as Hitchcock (whose then-secretary, Peggy Robertson, would 20 years later become Bogdanovich's secretary), Billy Wilder, Humphrey Bogart (as told by Richard Brooks), Jerry Lewis (clowning on the set of *The Ladies' Man*), Jack Lemmon (racing Bogdanovich down Sunset Boulevard in his sports car), Clifford Odets, Walt Disney, and others. Bogdanovich's portrait of Jimmy Stewart ("Speaking of Jimmy"), and his piece about his visit to the Monument Valley location of Ford's *Cheyenne Autumn* ("The Autumn of John Ford") are also irresistible.

The Killing of the Unicorn: Dorothy Stratten, 1960-1980 (Morrow, New York, 1984, 186 pp.).

Normally a work dealing with a highly private event in Bogdanovich's life would not be discussed in a book relating to the director's professional career. But, as I mentioned in the preface, in the case of Bogdanovich, personal matters have played a large part in dictating the course of his work as a filmmaker, so anything pertaining to them deserves mention—especially considering that Bogdanovich abandoned filmmaking for four years in order to write this book. The work, a necessary emotional catharsis of sorts for the director, chronicles in intimate detail the events leading up to (and following) the brutal murder of Dorothy Stratten, the *Playboy*-playmate-turned-actress whom Bogdanovich had hoped to turn into a star with *They All Laughed* and whom he planned to marry. Bogdanovich describes Stratten as "the noblest person I ever met, the gentlest and the bravest," and considers his relationship with her to be a momentous turning point in his life in that it humbled him for good by teaching him "a selfless kind of love, something unique in my experience." The memoir was written as a testament to his feelings for her: "How better could I serve her memory, or keep her love and spirit alive, than to honor her with the whole truth and nothing but, until death do us join?"

And indeed Bogdanovich has made every effort to be truthful, having painstakingly and obsessively researched, recounted and, most importantly, interpreted, the events preceding and following his initial meeting with Stratten at the Playboy Mansion in 1978. The book is also largely an indictment of the Playboy philosophy (which Bogdanovich describes with brutal candor as taking "masturbation out of the bathroom and [putting] it on the newsstands") and of its founder, Hugh Hefner, who for a time was a buddy of Bogdanovich's (the two having become acquainted following the settlement of a lawsuit against Hefner's publication by Cybill Shepherd).

Before I can go any further, an issue raised by several reviewers of the book must be settled. These critics have noted a questionable discrepancy in Bogdanovich's condemning an institution in which he himself participated for a time. But they have apparently missed something: as Bogdanovich notes, there is a public mansion and a private one, and the latter is something he (with one exception, a repugnant—for him—experience where he was tricked into participating in one of the frequent upstairs orgies) had nothing to do with, his main motivating factor for visiting the place having been boredom—"There's not much to do in this town; it goes to sleep early."

Curiosity for information, and a certain undeniable fascination with its popular and expensive bad taste. Hefner, *Playboy*, the mansion, the Bunnies, the Clubs, the whole setup, were grotesque fifties kitsch. This cultural phenomenon was part of a world I knew I could never belong to or be comfortable in, but one I wanted to understand more than superficially.

Unfortunately, Bogdanovich would have to suffer a sacrifice in order to be able to come to that understanding. "Mainly I didn't *do* anything up at the mansion [except] play some pinball, have a little dinner, play some Monopoly."

Now granted, Bogdanovich's decision to go to the mansion at all could be objected to on moral grounds, but such considerations are irrelevant here. Whether Bogdanovich should have become involved with Hefner is not the point; rather, it is the fact that he *did* do so and did experience certain things as a result which should be the focus for discussion, since without such knowledge he would not have been able to write such an exposé. Moreover, had the tragedy—his motivating factor—not occurred, Bogdanovich would never, he says, have been interested in undertaking such a venture: "I had certain privileged information about things Hefner had done and said which involved Dorothy, but I would have dealt with them on a private level."

It is difficult to accuse Bogdanovich of concealing the truth or of not taking responsibility for his own less-than-respectable behavior at the time, particularly when he admits to having used cocaine and marijuana on a number of occasions, and especially when he makes such statements as "I found myself on the kind of sexual merry-go-round that very much caught the beat of the time: the commitmentless, shallow gratification of profound needs and desires." The general tone of the work is unusually confessional for a man heretofore reluctant to reveal details about his personal life—indeed Bogdanovich said his intention was "to tell the story in a way that was so revealing no one would ever tell it unless it was the truth." The style and tone are simple and straightforward, with nothing written for sensational or shock value. The growing sense of introspection which is evident is admirable also.

But strangely enough, despite these merits, questions arise, mainly the result of a curious tendency of the author's to undermine the very purpose for his embarking on a deliberate suspension from work in order to write: his profound love for Stratten. The following passage concerns his worry that at one point Stratten's face might have been permanently damaged by possibly cancerous growths:

> Would disfigurement honestly, or would it not, affect my love for her? Was love irretrievably bound to outward appearances? Or did it finally have to do with feelings and spirits, both invisible and indefinable? I never asked myself this question then but I think I knew that my passion for Dorothy and my empathy with her was far too strong to be lessened by a change in her physical appearance.

The very fact that Bogdanovich could have asked himself such a question leaves one to ponder to a degree the exact nature of his attraction to Stratten. And indeed, if it was purely physical (the growths turned out to be benign and she was not scarred, so we will never know for sure whether it would have altered his feelings for her), the whole enterprise would seem rather silly and embarrassing (especially considering the book's title, *The Killing of the Unicorn*). But one must also consider the weight and significance of the endeavor. After all, Stratten's death caused Bogdanovich to want to give up, for a time, his one great talent. Also, it became an obsession which lasted some four years. Certainly the project was not undertaken as any sort of monument to ego: Bogdanovich certainly had nothing to prove to anyone. His tone throughout is completely selfless—the book clearly was written *for* Stratten, and one senses that she would have thoroughly approved of its content and arguments. So it would seem that in the final analysis his feelings for her were genuine.

With regard to the reader's perception of Stratten herself, however, the extreme subjectivity of the book presents a problem. Although Bogdanovich draws all sorts of analogies between Stratten's situation and that of certain mythological figures and provides samples of poetry she wrote for him during the time they spent together, along with surprisingly intimate accounts of their lovemaking sessions, one cannot help but feel that Bogdanovich's feelings for her have biased him to a high degree. The fact that (with a few exceptions) the other persons depicted in the book (most of them close friends of the director) agreed with his perceptions of her does not help matters any either—though it can certainly be argued that since Bogdanovich knew her better than anyone else, he is most qualified to judge her.

Although Bogdanovich is perceptive in stressing that what happened to Stratten was inevitable, one strongly suspects it was simply due to the type of environment and characters (particularly her grisly pimp husband Paul Snider, who, angered over her leaving him to live with Bogdanovich, blasted her face away with a shotgun and then turned the weapon on himself) with whom she had become involved, and not the result of anything in the stars, as Bogdanovich would argue. Incidentally, although several of his enemies have argued otherwise, Bogdanovich himself can certainly not be blamed for what happened.

Also, the book is less an exposé of *Playboy* than a chronological diary of Bogdanovich and Stratten's time together. As such, it would seem to be of very limited interest to those outside of Bogdanovich's circle of friends—those who knew Stratten in particular. Many would most likely be put off by the extensive depiction of the privileged, la-de-da life-style of the director.

All in all, whatever the book's faults, we can be grateful for one thing: The knowledge of the human condition which Bogdanovich gained from writing it enabled him to create his most mature film to date, the wonderful *Mask*. That alone is justification enough.

Filmography

Targets

A Saticoy Production, released by Paramount, 1968. Director-Producer: Peter Bogdanovich. Associate Producer: Daniel Selznick. Executive Producer (uncredited): Roger Corman. Screenplay: Peter Bogdanovich, based on a story by Polly Platt and Peter Bogdanovich. Director of Photography: Laszlo Kovacs. Production Designer: Polly Platt. Production Manager: Paul Lewis. Assistant to the Director: Frank Marshall. Editor (uncredited): Peter Bogdanovich. Sound: Sam Kopetzky. Sound Editor: Verna Fields. Assistant Cameraman: Peter Sorel. Editorial Assistant: Mae Woods. Assistant Director: Gilles de Jurenne. Makeup: Scott Hamilton. Continuity: Joyce King. Assistant Art Director: Scott Fitzgerald. Production Assistant: James Morris. Gaffer: Richmond Aguilar. Key Grip: Tom Ramsey. Radio Music produced by Charles Greene and Brian Stone. Color Process: Pathé. Running Time: 90 minutes.

Cast: Boris Karloff (Byron Orlock), Tim O'Kelly (Bobby Thompson), Arthur Peterson (Ed Loughlin), Monty Landis (Marshall Smith), Nancy Hsueh (Jenny), Peter Bogdanovich (Sammy Michaels), Daniel Ades (Chauffeur), Stafford Morgan (Salesman, 1st shop), James Brown (Robert Thompson, Sr.), Mary Jackson (Mrs. Thompson), Tanya Morgan (Ilene Thompson), Tim Burns (Waiter), Warren White (Grocery Boy), Mark Dennis (Salesman, 2d shop), Sandy Baron (Kip Larkin), Geraldine Baron (Larkin's Girl), Gary Kent (Gas Tank Worker), Ellie Wood Walker (Woman on Freeway), Frank Marshall (Ticket Boy), Byron Betz (Projectionist), Paul Condylis (Drive-in Manager), Mike Farrell (Man in Phone Booth), Carol Samuels (Cashier), Jay Daniel (Snack Bar Attendant), James Morris (Man with Pistol), Elaine Partnow, Pete Belcher, James Bowie, Anita

Poree, Robert Cleaves, Kay Douglas, Raymond Roy, Dana Ashley, Kirk Scott, Susan Douglas (Others at Drive-in).

Cast seen in footage from *The Terror* (1963, directed by Roger Corman): Boris Karloff (Baron von Leppe), Jack Nicholson (Lieut. André Duvalier), Sandra Knight (Hélène), Richard Miller (Stefan).

Cast seen in footage from *The Criminal Code* (1931, directed by Howard Hawks): Boris Karloff (Ned Galloway), Clark Marshall (Runch).

Directed by John Ford

A Production of the American Film Institute and the California Arts Commission, 1971. Producers: George Stevens, Jr., and James R. Silke. Written and Directed by Peter Bogdanovich. Narrator: Orson Welles. Interviewer: Peter Bogdanovich. Interviewees: John Ford, John Wayne, Henry Fonda, James Stewart. Interview Cameramen: Laszlo Kovacs, Gregory Sandor, Brick Marquand, Eric Sherman. Editor: Richard Patterson. Associate Producer: David Shepard. Re-recording: Leslie Shatz. Running Time: 95 minutes.

Features clips from the following Ford films (in chronological order): *Straight Shooting* (1917), *Iron Horse* (1924), *Three Bad Men* (1926), *Salute* (1929), *Judge Priest* (1934), *The World Moves On* (1934), *The Informer* (1935), *Steamboat Around the Bend* (1936), *The Prisoner of Shark Island* (1936), *Submarine Patrol* (1938), *Young Mr. Lincoln* (1939), *Drums Along the Mohawk* (1939), *Stagecoach* (1939), *The Grapes of Wrath* (1940), *The Battle of Midway* (1942), *They Were Expendable* (1945), *My Darling Clementine* (1946), *The Fugitive* (1947), *Fort Apache* (1948), *She Wore a Yellow Ribbon* (1949), *Wagonmaster* (1950), *Rio Grande* (1950), *The Quiet Man* (1952), *The Searchers* (1956), *The Last Hurrah* (1958), *The Horse Soldiers* (1959), *Two Rode Together* (1961), *The Man Who Shot Liberty Valance* (1962), *Cheyenne Autumn* (1964).

The Last Picture Show

A BBS Production, released by Columbia Pictures, 1971. Executive Producer: Bert Schneider. Producer: Stephen J. Friedman.

Director: Peter Bogdanovich. Screenplay: Larry McMurtry and Peter Bogdanovich, based on the novel by Larry McMurtry. Director of Photography: Robert Surtees, ASC. Editor: Donn Cambern. Production Designer: Polly Platt. Art Director: Walter Scott Herndon. Sound: Tom Overton. Sound Effects: Edit-Rite. Associate Producer: Harold Schneider. Production Manager: Don Guest. Assistant Directors: Robert Rubin, Gary Chason, and William Morrison. Design Assistant: Vincent Cresciman. Casting: Ross Brown. Production Coordinator: Marilyn LaSalandra. Script Supervisor: Marshall Schlom. Construction Supervisor: Ed Shanley. Construction Coordinator: Al Litteken. Key Grip: Carl Manoogian. Dolly Grip: Leonard Lookabaugh. Gaffer: Alan Goldenhar. Co-producer: Terry Mead. Boom Man: Dean Salmon. Painter: George Lillie. Production Secretary: Elly Mitchell. Production Assistant: Mae Woods. Wardrobe: Mickey Sherrard, Nancy McArdle. Props: Walter Starkey, Louis Donelan. Location Manager: Frank Marshall. Filmed in and around Archer City, Texas. Black and white. Running Time: 118 minutes.

Contains excerpts from: Vincente Minnelli's *Father of the Bride*, Howard Hawks' *Red River*, and also the television programs *Strike It Rich* and *Your Show of Shows*.

Cast: Timothy Bottoms (Sonny Crawford), Jeff Bridges (Duane Jackson), Cybill Shepherd (Jacy Farrow), Ben Johnson (Sam the Lion), Cloris Leachman (Ruth Popper), Ellen Burstyn (Lois Farrow), Eileen Brennan (Genevieve), Clu Gulager (Abilene), Sam Bottoms (Billy), Sharon Taggart (Charlene Duggs), Randy Quaid (Lester Marlow), Joe Heathcock (Sheriff), Bill Thurman (Coach Popper), Barc Doyle (Joe Bob Blanton), Jessie Lee Fulton (Miss Mosey), Gary Brockette (Bobby Sheen), Helena Humann (Jimmie Sue), Loyd Catlett (Leroy), Robert Glenn (Gene Farrow), John Hillerman (Teacher), Janice O'Malley (Mrs. Clarg), Floyd Mahaney (Oklahoma Patrolman), Kimberly Hyde (Annie-Annie Martin), Noble Willingham (Chester), Marjory Jay (Winnie Snips), Joye Hash (Mrs. Jackson), Pamela Kelier (Jackie Lee French), Gordon Hurst (Monroe), Mike Hosford (Johnny), Faye Jordan (Nurse), Charlie Seybert (Andy Fanner), Grover Lewis (Mr. Crawford), Rebecca Ulrick (Marlene), Merrill Shepherd (Agnes), Buddy Wood (Bud), Kenny Wood (Ken), Leon Brown (Cowboy in Café), Bobby McGriff (Truck Driver), Jack Mueller (Oil Pumper), Robert Arnold (Brother Blanton), Frank Marshall

(Tommy Logan), Otis Elmore (1st Mechanic), Charles Salmon (Roughneck Driver), George Gaulden (Cowboy), Will Morris Hannis (Gas Station Man).

Songs: "Cold, Cold Heart," "Blue Velvet," "Solitaire" (Tony Bennett); "Give Me More, More, More of Your Kisses" (Lefty Frizzell); "Wish You Were Here" (Eddie Fisher); "Slow Poke" (Pee Wee King); "Rose, Rose, I Love You" (Frankie Laine); "You Belong to Me" (Jo Stafford); "A Fool Such as I" (Hank Snow); "Please, Mr. Sun" (Johnnie Ray); "Why Don't You Love Me?" "Hey, Good Lookin'," "Kawliga," "Lovesick Blues," "Half as Much," "My Son Calls Another Man Daddy," "I Can't Help It if I'm Still in Love with You," "Faded Love," "Jambalaya" (Hank Williams). Also featuring the talents of Phil Harris, Johnny Standley, Kay Starr, Hank Thompson, Webb Pierce.

What's Up, Doc?

A Saticoy Production, released by Warner Brothers, 1972. Producer and Director: Peter Bogdanovich. Screenplay: Buck Henry, David Newman, and Robert Benton; based on a story by Peter Bogdanovich. Director of Photography: Laszlo Kovacs. Music: Artie Butler. Editor: Verna Fields. Production Designer: Polly Platt. Art Director: Herman A. Blumenthal. Set Decorator: John Austin. Special Effects: Robert MacDonald. Sound: Les Fresholtz. Costumes: Nancy McArdle and Ray Phelps. Makeup: Don Cash and Fred Williams. Hairstyles: Lynda Gurasich. Property Master: Robey Cooper. Best Boy: Aaron Pazanti. Boom Man: Rich Raguse. Script Supervisor: Hazel Hall. Assistant Editor: William Neel. Stunt Coordinator: Paul Baxley. Second Assistant Directors: Jerry Ballew, Doug Morrison. Insert Car Driver: Gil Casper. Key Grip: George Hall. Dolly Grip: Leonard Lookabaugh. Gaffer: Richmond Aguilar. Assistant Cameramen: Richard Colean, Rob Guthrie. Camera Operator: Robert Byrne. Construction Coordinator: Norman Hawkins. Transportation: Bud Dawson. Production Aide: Neil Canton. Stunt Coordinator: Paul Baxley. Location Manager: Henry Zubrinsky. Casting: Nessa Hyams. Associate Producer: Paul Lewis. Production Manager: Fred Ahern. Assistant to the Producer: Frank Marshall. Assistant Director: Ray Gosnell. Director's Secretary: Mae Woods. Titles: The Golds West, Inc.

Camera Equipment by Panavision. Filmed on location in San Francisco. Technicolor. Running Time: 90 minutes.

Cast: Barbra Streisand (Judy Maxwell), Ryan O'Neal (Howard Bannister), Madeline Kahn (Eunice Burns), Kenneth Mars (Hugh Simon), Austin Pendleton (Frederick Larrabee), Sorrell Booke (Harry), Stefan Gierasch (Fritz), Mabel Albertson (Mrs. Van Hoskins), Michael Murphy (Mr. Smith), Graham Jarvis (Bailiff), Liam Dunn (Judge Maxwell), Phil Roth (Mr. Jones), John Hillerman (Mr. Kaltenborn), George Morfogen (Rudy, the Headwaiter), Randy Quaid (Professor Hosquith), M. Emmet Walsh (Arresting Officer), Eleanor Zee (Banquet Receptionist), Kevin O'Neal (Delivery Boy), Paul Condylis (Room Service Waiter), Fred Scheiwiller, Carl Saxe, Jack Perkins (Jewel Thieves), Paul B. Kililman (Druggist), Gil Perkins (Mr. Jones' Driver), Christa Land (Mrs. Hosquith), Stan Ross, Peter Paul Eastman (Musicologists), Eric Brotherson (Larrabee's Brother), Elaine Partnow (Party Guest), George P. Burrafato (Eunice's Cab Driver), Jerry Summers (Smith's Cab Driver), Mort Thompson (Airport Cab Driver), Donald T. Bexley (Skycap), Leonard Lookabaugh (Painter on Roof), Candace Brownell (Ticket Seller), Sean Morgan (Banquet Official), Patricia O'Neal (Woman on Plane), Joe Alfasa (Waiter in Hall), Chuck Hollom (Pizza Cook).

Songs: "You're the Top," music and lyrics by Cole Porter, sung by Barbra Streisand and Ryan O'Neal; "As Time Goes By," music and lyrics by Herman Hupfeld, sung by Barbra Streisand.

Paper Moon

A Directors Company (Peter Bogdanovich–Francis Ford Coppola–William Friedkin) Presentation of a Saticoy Production, released by Paramount Pictures, 1973. Producer and Director: Peter Bogdanovich. Screenplay: Alvin Sargent; based on the novel *Addie Pray* by Joe David Brown. Director of Photography: Laszlo Kovacs. Music: Extracts from the record collection of Rudi Fehr. Editor: Verna Fields. Production Designer: Polly Platt. Set Designer: James Spencer. Set Decorations: John Austin. Optical Effects: Jack Harmon. Sound: Kay Rose, Frank Warner, Bill Carruth, and Richard Portman. Costumes: Pat Kelly and Sandra

Stewart. Hairstyles: Dorothy Byrne. Prop Master: Mark Wade. Assistant Prop Man: Tony Wade. Makeup: Rolf Kelly. Mixer: Les Fresholtz. Boom Man: Norman Webster. Script Supervisor: Karen Wookey. Assistant Editor: William Neel. Hairdresser: Dorothy Byrne. Camera Operator: Robert Byrne. Gaffer: Richmond Aguilar. Key Grip: George Hill. Dolly Grip: Leonard Lookabaugh. Best Boy: Larry Peets. Assistant Cameramen: Dick Colean, Louis Noto. Casting: Gary Chason. Construction Coordinator: Ed Shanley. Painter: George Lillie. Assistant Director Trainee: Gary Daigler. Transportation Captain: Clyde Harper. Camera Car Driver: Gil Casper. Post-production Assistant: Rich Fields. Production Secretary: Selma Brown. Production Assistants: Neil Canton, Richard Waltzer. Associate Producer: Frank Marshall. Assistant to the Producer: Mae Woods. Assistant Directors: Ray Gosnell and Jerry Ballew. Black and white. Running Time: 102 minutes.

Cast: Ryan O'Neal (Moses Pray), Tatum O'Neal (Addie Loggins), Madeline Kahn (Trixie Delight), John Hillerman (Sheriff Hardin/Jess Hardin), P. J. Johnson (Imogene), Jessie Lee Fulton (Miss Ollie), Jim Harrell (Minister), Lila Waters (Minister's Wife), Noble Willingham (Mr. Robertson), Bob Young (Gas Station Attendant), Jack Saunders (Station Master), Jody Wilbur (Café Waitress), Liz Ross (The Widow Pearl Morgan), Yvonne Harrison (The Widow Marie Bates), Ed Reed (Lawman, Bates' Home), Dorothy Price (Ribbon Saleslady), Eleanor Bogart (The Widow Elvira Stanley), Dorothy Forster (The Widow Edna Huff), Lana Daniel (Moses' Girlfriend), Herschel Morris (Barber), Dejah Moore (Salesgirl, $20 bill), Ralph Coder (Store Manager), Harriet Ketchum (Store Customer), Desmond Dhooge (Cotton Candy Man), Kenneth Hughes (Harem Tent Barker), George Lillie (Photographer), Burton Gilliam (Floyd the Desk Clerk), Floyd Mahaney (Beau, Hardin's Deputy), Gilbert Milton (Leroy's Father), Randy Quaid (Leroy), Tandy Arnold, Vernon Schwanke, Dennis Beden (Leroy's Brothers), Hugh Gillin (2d Deputy), Art Ellison (Silver Mine Gentleman), Rosemary Rumbley (Aunt Billie).

Featuring the musical talents of: Jack Benny, The Blue Sky Boys, Hoagy Carmichael and his orchestra, Bing Crosby, Ramona Darby, Jimmie Davis, Tommy Dorsey and his orchestra, Nat Gonella and his Georgians, Jimmie Grier and his orchestra, Johnny Hamp's Kentucky Serenaders, Peggy Heal, Jack Hylton and his orchestra, Jim and Marian Jordan, Frank Luther, Eric Madriguerera and his orchestra, Ozzie Nelson and his orchestra, Dick Powell, Leo Reisman and his orchestra, Larry Stewart, Paul Whiteman and his orchestra, Don Wilson, Victor Young and his orchestra.

Daisy Miller

A Directors Company–Copa de Oro Production, released by Paramount, 1974. Producer and Director: Peter Bogdanovich. Screenplay: Frederic Raphael, based on the story by Henry James. Director of Photography: Alberto Spagnoli. Associate Producer: Frank Marshall. Art Director: Ferdinando Scarfiotti. Costume Designer: John Furness. Editor: Verna Fields. Production Manager: Luciano Piperno. Assistant Director: Tony Brandt. Musical Consultant: Francesco Laragnino. Assistant to Mr. Bogdanovich: Mae Woods. Camera Operator: Emilio Loffredo. Assistant Camera Operator: Giovanni Fiori. Gaffer: Elmiro Rubeo. Key Grip: Giulio Diamanti. Mixer: Basil Fenton-Smith. Set Dresser: Gianni Silvestri. Unit Manager: Lanfranco Diotallevi. Transportation Manager: Luciano Pesciarolli. Second Assistant Director: Mario Jurisic. Script Girl: Anita Borgiotti. Location Manager: Enzo Guglielmi. Production Assistants: Maurizio Lucci, William Shepherd. Wardrobe Supervisor: Mariolina Bono. Costumes: S.A.F.A.S., Rome. Miss Shepherd's Costumes: Tirelli of Rome. Makeup: Alberto DeRossi. Hairstylist: Grazia DeRossi. Propmaster: Elio Altamura. Assistant Editor: William Undemann. Sound Editor: Kay Rose. Re-recording: Richard Portman. Technicolor. Running Time: 91 minutes.

Cast: Cybill Shepherd (Annie P. Miller), Barry Brown (Frederick Winterbourne), Cloris Leachman (Mrs. Ezra B. Miller), Mildred Natwick (Mrs. Costello), Eileen Brennan (Mrs. Walker), Duilio Del Prete (Mr. Giovanelli), James McMurtry (Randolph C. Miller), Nicholas Jones (Charles), George Morfogen (Eugenio), Jean Pascal Bongard (Hotel Receptionist, Vevey), Albert Messmer (Tutor), Jacques Guhl, Hubert Geoldlin (Polish Boys), David Bush (Man at Chillon), Henry Hubinet (Chillon Guide), Maurizio Lucci (Miniaturist), Tom Felleghy (Mrs. Walker's Butler), Luigi Gabellone (Punch and Judy), John Bartha, Salamon Amedeo (Hotel Receptionists, Rome), Renato Talvacchia (Pianist), Valerio Lonforti, Aldo Alleva, Franco Persichetti, Marino Rebiscini (String Quartet), Rodolfo Lodi, Elaine Olcott, Cesare Rotondi (Mrs. Walker's Guests), Salvatore Lisitano (Opera Singer), Jill Pratt, Corinne Dunne, Richard Dunne (Opera Patrons), Bondi Esterhazy (Doctor).

Featuring the music of: Johann Sebastian Bach, Luigi Boccherini, Franz Joseph Haydn, Wolfgang Amadeus Mozart, Franz Schubert, Johann Strauss, Sr., Giuseppi Verdi.

Song: "When You and I Were Young, Maggie," by G. W. Johnson and J. A. Butterfield.

At Long Last Love

A Peter Bogdanovich Production, released through 20th Century-Fox Film Corporation, 1975. Produced, Directed, and Written by Peter Bogdanovich. Associate Producer: Frank Marshall. Director of Photography: Laszlo Kovacs. Production Design: Gene Allen. Orchestrations: Gus Levene. Music Supervised and Conducted by Artie Butler and Lionel Newman. Set Decorator: Jerry Wunderlich. Costume Designer: Bobbie Mannix. Unit Production Manager: Mel Dillar. Art Director: John Lloyd. Music Editor: Kenneth Wannberg. Film Editor: Douglas Robertson. Assistant to Mr. Bogdanovich: Mae Woods. Propmaster: Jerry Graham. Script Supervisor: Lois Thurman. Construction Coordinator: Ed Shanley. Sound Mixer: Bobby Thomas. Key Grip: Leonard Lookabaugh. Gaffer: Richmond Aguilar. Camera Operator: Bobby Byrne. Dialogue Coach: George Morfogen. Vocal Coaches: Joan Zajac, Gary Fisher. Assistant Director: Mickey McCardle. Dance Coordinators: Albert Lantieri, Rita Abrams. Additional Orchestrations: Harry Betts. Casting: Ross Brown. Hairstyles Created by Carrie White. Hairdressers: Marlene Williams, Emma DiVittorio. Makeup: Tom Ellingwood, Ken Chase. Dolly Grip: Bill Kenney. Special Effects: Charlie Spurgeon. Boom Men: Victor Godde, Eugene O'Brien. Prop Supervisors: Bob McLing, Gary Kieldrup. Production Pianist: Dick Emmons. Sound Engineer: Noel Bartlett. Assistant Editor: Bill Lindemann. Negative Cutter: Ruth Shea. Assistant Cameramen: John Connors, Cal Roberts. Wardrobe Supervisors: Nancy McArdle, Ed Wynigear. Second Assistant Director: Jerry Ballew. Assistant Director Trainee: Jack Sanders.

Location Manager: Debby Thomas. Production Assistant: William Shepherd. Best Boy: Romeo DeSantis, Jr. Craft Service: Bill King. Sound Editors: Don Hall, William Hartman. Re-recording: Theodore Soderberg. Orchestral Recording: Ted Keep. Unit Publicist: Howard Liebling. Still Man: Bruce McBroom. Startran Direct Recording System: Sycom, Inc. Titles by Pacific Title. Panavision. De-Luxe. Running Time: 115 minutes (final, "correct" version—available to television only).

Cast: Burt Reynolds (Michael Oliver Pritchard III), Cybill Shepherd (Brooke Carter), Madeline Kahn (Kitty O'Kelly), Eileen Brennan (Elizabeth), Duilio Del Prete (Johnny Spanish), John Hillerman (Rodney James), Mildred Natwick (Mabel Pritchard), and Quinn Redeker, Leonard McKinley, John Stephenson, Peter Dane, William Paterson, Liam Dunn, Elvin Moon, M. Emmet Walsh, Burton Gilliam, Albert Lantieri, Tanis Van Kirk, Ned Wertimer, Arthur Peterson, Barbara Ann Walters, Violet Cane, Loutz Gage, Diana Wyatt, Clive Morgan, Patricia O'Neal, Nelson Welch, Morgan Farley, Robert Terry, Artie Butler, Basil Hoffman, Donald Journeaux, Jeffrey Byron, Lloyd Catlett, Kevin O'Neal, Anna Bogdanovich, Rita Loewen, Maurice Prince, Christa Lang, William Shepherd, Manny Marmon, Antonia Bogdanovich, Alexandria Bogdanovich.

Music and Lyrics by Cole Porter, except where noted otherwise: "Down in the Depths (on the 90th Floor)," "Tomorrow," "Poor Young Millionaire" (music by Peter Bogdanovich and Artie Butler), "It Ain't Etiquette," "You're the Top," "Find Me a Primitive Man," "Friendship," "But in the Morning, No," "At Long Last Love," "Well, Did You Evah?" "From Alpha to Omega," "Let's Misbehave," "It's Delovely," "Just One of Those Things," "I Get a Kick Out of You," "Most Gentlemen Don't Like Love," "I Loved Him," "A Picture of Me Without You."

Nickelodeon

A Columbia/British Lion/EMI Production, 1976. Producers: Irwin Winkler and Robert Chartoff. Director: Peter Bogdanovich. Screenplay: W. D. Richter and Peter Bogdanovich. Director of Photography: Laszlo Kovacs. Associate Producer: Frank Marshall. Set Decorator: Darrell Silvera. Art Director: Richard Berger. Costume Design: Theodora Van Runkle. Film Editor:

William Carruth. Casting: Lynn Stalmaster. Stunt Coordinator:
Hal Needham. Stunts: Hal Needham, Julie Ann Johnson, Joe
Ansler, Ron Stein, Charles Tamburro. Music Arranger and
Conductor: Richard Hazard. Music Editor: Ken Wannberg.
Sound Editors: Kay Rose, Richard Burrow, Michael Colgan,
Vickie Sampson, Mort Tubor. Re-recording Mixers: Arthur
Piantadosi, Les Fresholtz, Michael Minkler. Production Sound:
Barry Thomas. Choreography: Rita Abrams. Production Man-
ager: Mel Dillar. Camera Operator: Bobby Byrne. Property
Master: Richard Valesko. Assistant Director: Jack Sanders.
Script Supervisor: Lois Thurman. Construction Coordinator:
Ed Shanley. Gaffer: Richmond Aguilar. Key Grip: Len Look-
abaugh. Transportation Coordinator: James Brubaker. Assis-
tant to Mr. Bogdanovich: Mae Woods. Special Effects: Cliff
Wenger. Head Wrangler: Stevie Myers. Makeup: Tom Elling-
wood. Hairdressers: Marlene Williams, Ruby Ford. Wardrobe:
Norman Salling, Sandra Berke. Second Assistant Directors:
Arne Schmidt, Steve Lim. Assistant Camera Operators: Joe
Thibo, Ted Suguira. Boom Operators: Glen Lambert, Morris
Feingold. Best Boy: Paul Claven. Dolly Grip: Rick Borchardt.
Props: Dean Wilson, Max Miller. Assistant Editor: Bill Linde-
mann. Leadman: George Tours. Producer's Assistant: Neil
Canton. Painter: Bob Lawless. Craft Service: Grant Olson.
Production Secretary: Marge Rowland. Dog Trainer: Robert
Weatherwax. *The Birth of a Nation* footage: Paul Killiam. Piano
Rolls and Cylinders: Lennie Marvin Collection. Optical Effects:
Howard A. Anderson Co. Location Unit: Mobile Cinema
Service. Lenses and Panaflex Camera by Panavision. Color by
Metrocolor. Special thanks to Allan Dwan and Raoul Walsh.
Running Time: 121 minutes.

Cast: Ryan O'Neal (Leo Harrigan), Burt Reynolds (Buck
Greenway), Tatum O'Neal (Alice Forsythe), Brian Keith (H. H.
Cobb), Stella Stevens (Marty Reeves), John Ritter (Franklin
Frank), Jane Hitchcock (Kathleen Cooke), Jack Perkins (Michael
Gilhooley), Brian James (Bailiff), Sidney Armus (Judge), Joe
Warfield (Defense Attorney), Tamar Cooper (Edna Mae
Gilhooley), Alan Gibbs (Patents Hooligan), Matthew Anden
(Hecky), Lorenzo Music and Arnold Soboloff (Cobb's Writers),
Jeffrey Byron (Steve), Priscilla Pointer (Mabel), Don Calfa
(Waldo), Philip Burns (Duncan), Edward Marshall (Rialto Hotel
Clerk), John Blackwell (Louie), E. J. Andre, Christa Lang, and
Maurice Manson (Stage Performers), Louis Guss (Dinsdale),

Frank Marshall (Dinsdale's Assistant), Andrew Winner (Stage Manager), Matilda Calnan (German Bakery Lady), Gustaf and Bertil Unger (German Producers), James O'Connell and Ric Mancini (Patents Thugs), Mark Dennis (Cobb's Cutter), E. Hampton Beagle (Leo's Train Conductor), Hedgemon Lewis (Train Waiter), Bill Riddle (Sally), Dino Judd (Old-Timer), Harry Carey, Jr. (Dobey), James Best (Jim), Jack Verbois (Jack), John Chappell (John), George Gaynes (Reginald Kingsley), Carleton Rippel (Depot Man), Rita Abrams, Sara Jane Gould, and Mary Beth Bell (Dutch Damsels), M. Emmet Walsh ("Father" Logan), Miriam Bird Nethery (Aunt Lula), Rusty Blitz (Nickelodeon Barker), Les Josephson (Nickelodeon Bouncer), Tom Erhart (Nickelodeon Projectionist), Griffin O'Neal (Bicycle Boy), Patricia O'Neal, Morgan Farley, Anna Thea, Elaine Partnow, Joseph G. Medalis, Billy Beck, and Roger Hampton (Movie Fanatics), Gordon Hurst (Policeman), Charles Thomas Murphy (Hollywood Realtor), Hamilton Camp (Blacker), Ted Gehrig (Stoneman), Stanley Brock (Parker), Vincent Milana (Frank's Director), Lee Gordon Moore (Alice's Director), John Finnegan (Kathleen's Director), Christian Grey (Buck's Director), Robert E. Ball (Leo's Actor), Chief Elmer Tugsmith (Elmer), Rude Frimel (Orchestra Conductor).

Saint Jack

A Peter Bogdanovich Production, released by New World Pictures, 1979. Executive Producers: Hugh M. Hefner, Edward L. Rissien. Producer: Roger Corman. Assistant Producer: Lisa Lu. In Charge of Production: Pierre Cottrell. Associate Producer: George Morfogen. Director: Peter Bogdanovich. Screenplay: Howard Sackler, Paul Theroux, and Peter Bogdanovich, based on the novel by Paul Theroux. Director of Photography: Robby Muller. Editor: William Carruth. Art Director: David Ng Cc. Assistant Director: Denys Granier-Deferre. Sound: Jean-Pierre Ruh. Gaffer: Jacques Steyn. Key Grip: Hugo Van Baren. Assistant Cameraman: Pim Tjujerman. Best Boy: Theo Bierkens. Boom Men: Guillaome Sciama, Maryte Kavaliavskas. Wardrobe Supervisors: Lorita Ong, Louise Walker. Script Supervisor: Patricia A. Kirck. Makeup: Graham Freeborn. Casting: Agnes D. Chia, Sally Tunnicliffe. Set Decorators: Lucius Wong, Richard Chew M.F. Prop Man: Edward Young. Location Manager: Claude Doral. Transportation: Andrew Chua P.N. Unit Manager: Park Swee. Director's Secretary: Clara Pang. Production Secretary: Morna Ko. Second Assistant Directors: Tjacn Tan Leng Teck, Robin Ruse-Rinehart, Sonny Tan. Assistant Film Editors: Sophie Cornu, Janet Weinberg, Susan Styrmoe. Wardrobe Assistant: Laura Ong. Assistant to the Director: Rajkumar. Assistant Boom Man: Gregory Solosa. Assistant Unit Manager: Jennifer Kay. Production Assistant: Elizabeth Gazzara. Postproduction Secretary: Joyce Thompson. Assistant Prop Men: Flint Yip K.G., Ronald Ng. Post-production Assistants: Howard Hirdler, Allan Smith. Sound Editing Service: MAG City, Hollywood. Mixer: Ray West. Re-recording: Ryder Sound Service. Titles and Opticals: MGM. Technicolor. Running Time: 112 minutes.

Cast: Ben Gazzara (Jack Flowers), Denholm Elliott (William Leigh), James Villiers (Frogget), Joss Ackland (Vardley), Rodney Bewes (Smale), Mark Kingston (Yates), Lisa Lu (Mrs. Yates), Monika Subramaniam (Monika), Judy Lim (Judy), George Lazenby (Senator), Peter Bogdanovich (Eddie Schuman), Joseph Noel (Gopi), Ong Kian Bee (Hing), Tan Yan Meng (Little Hing), Andrew Chua (Andrew, Taxi Driver), Peter Pang, Ronald Ng, Seow Teow Keng (Triad Gang), Ken Wolinski (Australian Businessman), Peter Tay (Mike, Prince's Desk Clerk), Osman Zailani (Bob, Prince's Manager), Elizabeth Ang (Shirley), S. M. Sim (Mr. Tan), Choh Poh Ain (Wally), Charles M. Longbottom (Stanley—"George Milton"), Sonny Ng (Sonny), Bridgit Ang (Bridgit), Lily Ang (Lily), Diana Voon (Mammy), Oggi (Djamila), Ken Burke (Australian Customer), Keith Masavage (Marvin), Chris Corrigan ("Houston"), Beau John Owens ("Memphis"), Prentice Gaines ("Wichita Falls"), Sally Tunicliffe (Katie Horner), Goh Luck Kwang (Raffles Desk Clerk), Paul Ganesan (Raffles Bellboy), Juliana Loi (Rosie), Tan Tee Boon (Toh—Midget), Harry Yong (Fourth Triad), K. M. Goh (Triad Tattoist), Cheong Ah Lew (Triad Driver), H. C. Goh (Harry—Tattoo), Col. L. T. Firbank (Col. Gunstone), Elsie Quah (Esther), Nancy Koh, Doreen Kiong (Elsie's Cronies), Bill Snorgrass (Floyd), Kitty Ooi (Wong May), Yusof (Salem Sanwan), H. G. Zaccheus (Ganapathy—Gatekeeper), Teo Bee Hui (Jimmy Khoo—cook), Mary Lim Ling Ling, Mel Sophian ("Swastika" Man), Mary Livee ("Swastika" Girl), Larry Osterhaus, Barry Gaines, Kevin Stern, Gibson Del, Richard Newberry, Michael Barron, Richard Goodman, John Sakellar, Andy Nickson (GIs at Paradise Gardens), Brian Leonard (Harmonium Player), Patrick

Waterman (Minister), Nina Bacharib (Nina), Edward Tan
(Tony), Teo Mui Hwa (GPO Postal Clerk).

Songs: "I Ain't Gonna Give Nobody None of My Jelly Roll,"
"Basin St. Blues," "Someday You'll Be Sorry," sung by Louis
Armstrong; "Goldfinger," sung by Shirley Bassey; "An Okie
from Muskogee," "If We Make It Through December," sung by
Merle Haggard; "Sunday Mornin' Comin' Down," sung by
Johnny Cash.

They All Laughed

A PSO/Moon Pictures/Time-Life release, 1981. Producers:
George Morfogen and Blaine Novak. Direction and Screenplay:
Peter Bogdanovich. Director of Photography: Robby Muller.
Colleen Camp's songs arranged and conducted by Earl Pool Ball.
Song: "Kentucky Nights," words and music by Eric Kaz; song:
"One Day Since Yesterday," words and music by Eric Pool Ball,
Peter Bogdanovich, Kert Lundell. Editors: Scott Vickrey and
William Carruth. Art Director: Kert Lundell. Sound: Ray West,
Met Metcalfe, Richard Tyler, Michael Hilkeney. Music Direc-
tion: Douglas Dilge. Unit Production Manager: Martin Danzig.
First Assistant Director: Robert Girolami. Second Assistant
Director: Henry Bronchtein. Costumes: Peggy Farrell. Location
Coordinator: Amy Sayres. Camera Operator: Ed Lachman. Film
Editor: Robert Barrere. Assistant Cameraman: Tom Weston. Set
Designer: Joe (Peppy) Bird. Script Supervisor: Pat Depew.
Assistant Editors: Miriam Weeks, Catherine Peacock, Wendy
Wank, Fred Rosenberg, Sonya Jones. Sound Editing: Echo
Films, Michael Hilkene. Re-recording: Glen Glenn Sound. Music
Recording Mixing: Dale Ashby, Bell Sheniman, Stuart Tay.
Costume Coordinator: Mary Ellen Winston. Hairdresser: Verne
Caruso. Makeup: Mickey Scott. Ms. Hepburn's Hairdresser:
Grazia Rossi. Ms. Hepburn's Makeup: Nilo Iacoponi. Women's
Wardrobe: Jean Frisbie. Men's Wardrobe: Bill Christians. Assis-
tants to Mr. Bogdanovich: Sean Ferrer, Linda MacEwen. Props:
Dan Roberts, Jim Fredericks. Key Grip: Jim McGrath. Grips:
John Mazzola, Ron Mazzola, Allen Hansen, Patrick McGrath.
Best Boy: Sal Martorano. DGA Trainee: Steve Wertimer.
Production Office Coordinator: Helene Spinner. Production
Office Secretary: Sheila Flatley. Production Accountant: Ellie

Linas. Scenic Painter: Parmelee Welles. Transportation Captain: Tom O'Brien. Extra Casting: Navarro Bertoni, Jim Greenhut, Tom Hayes, Dina Laptoon. Production Assistants: Elizabeth Gazzara, Carol Hardin, Nancy Keorner. Associate Producer: Russell Schwartz. Titles: MGM. Color by Movielab. Prints by De-Luxe. Running Time: 115 minutes.

Cast: Audrey Hepburn (Angela Niotes), Ben Gazzara (John Russo), John Ritter (Charles Rutledge), Colleen Camp (Christy Miller), Patti Hansen (Deborah Wilson—"Sam"), Dorothy Stratten (Dolores Martin), Blaine Novak (Arthur Brodsky), George Morfogen (Leon Leondopolis), Linda MacEwen (Amy Lester), Sean Ferrer (José), Glenn Scarpelli (Michael Niotes), Vassily Lambrinos (Stavros Niotes), Antonia Bogdanovich (Stefania Russo), Alexandria Bogdanovich (Georgina Russo), Sheila Stodden (Barbara Jo), Lisa Dunsheath (Tulips), Joyce Hyser (Sylvia), Elizabeth Peña (Rita), Riccardo Bertoni (Mr. Martin), Shawn Casey (Laura), Brigitte Catapano, Parris Bruckner, Vivien Landau, Lillian Silverstone (Café Brigitte), Steve Cole (Rockefeller Center Guard), Steven Fromewick (Limousine Driver), Violetta Lander (Green Street Hostess), Spike Spicener, Nick Micskey, Robert Hawe (Heliport), Kennely Noble, Anthony Paige (Hotel Algonquin), William Craft, William DeNino, Kelly Donnally, Linda Ray, Andrea Weber (Rozy), Michael McGifford, Vittorio Tiburz, Alex MacArthur, George Cardini, Robert Skelling (Plaza Hotel), Noel King, Don Marino, John Murray, Sharon Spits (Foley Square), Brandy Roven, Debora Lass, Joan Lauren (City Limits), Marty Greene, Harry Matson, Bret Smrz, Brian Smrz, Victoria Van Der Kloot (Wall Street).

Songs: "New York, New York," "You and Me," "They All Laughed," "More Than You Know," performed by Frank Sinatra; "I Would Like to See You Again," "It Comes and Goes," "That's the Way It Is," performed by Johnny Cash; "Ain't Misbehavin'," "Memories of You," performed by Louis Armstrong; "Amigo," performed by Roberto Carlos; "Omaha," "We Had It All," performed by Waylon Jennings; "Sing Sing Sing," performed by Benny Goodman; "Leavin' Louisiana in the Broad Daylight," "A Fool Such as I," performed by Rodney Crowell; "My Fool Heart," "These Fool Things," performed by Scott Hamilton; "My One and Only Love," performed by Art Tatum and Ben Webster; "Back in the Country," performed by Roy Acuff; Mozart Piano Concerto No. 27 in B-flat performed by

Wilhelm Backhaus and the Vienna Philharmonic Orchestra, conducted by Karl Böhm. Christy Miller's Manhattan Cowboys: Earl Pool Ball (Piano), Jo-el Sonnier (Accordion), Eric Kaz (Acoustics), Ken Kosek (Fiddle), Larry Campbell (Pedal Steel), Lincoln Schleifer (Bass), Jon Sholler (Guitar), Michael Holliman (Drums).

Mask

A Martin Starger Production, released by Universal, 1985. Producer: Martin Starger. Director: Peter Bogdanovich. Screenplay: Anna Hamilton Phelan, based on the true story of Rocky Dennis. Director of Photography: Laszlo Kovacs, ASC. Supervising Film Editor: Eva Gardos. Art Director: Norman Newberry. Associate Producers: George Morfogen, Peggy Robertson. Coproducer: Howard Alston. Unit Production Manager: William Watkins. First Assistant Director: Katy Emde. Second Assistant Directors: Lisa Marmon, Robert Q. Engelman. Editor: Barbara Ford. Rocky Makeup: Michael Westmore. Casting: Michael Chinich, Jackie Burch. Set Decorator: Richard J. deCinces. Camera Operator: Robert Stevens. Chief Lighting Electrician: Richmond Aguilar. Key Grip: Gene Kearney. First Camera Assistant: Joseph E. Thibo. Best Boy Electrical: Paul Caven. Best Boy Grip: Steve Greaves. Property Master: Fred Chapman. Set Property Master: Tom Margozewitz. Makeup Applied by: Zoltan. Men's Costume Supervisor: Tony Scarano. Men's Costumer: Robert Chase. Women's Costume Supervisor: Marla Denise Schlom. Women's Costumer: Sandra Cutolla. Cher's Costumer: April Ferry. Cher's Makeup: Tommy Cole. Makeup Artist: John M. Elliott, Jr. Cher's Hairstylist: Renate Leuschman Pless. Hairstylist: Hazel Catmull. Construction Coordinator: Philip Read. Special Effects: Dan Lester. Lead Man: Greg Sachen. Animal Trainer: Jackie Martin. Script Supervisor: Betsy Norton. Transportation Coordinator: Robert Wilson. Location Manager: David Thomas. Production Coordinator: Rosalyn Inzerella. Supervising Sound Editors: John M. Stacy, Sam Shaw. Sound Editors: Michael H. Ford, Bruce Stambler, Lucy Coldsnow, Bruce Bell. Unit Publicist: Steve Ginsberg. Still Photographer: Gemma LaMana Wills. Production Sound Recorders: Keith Wester, CAS, Crew Chamberlain. Re-recording Mixers: Ray West, Bob Minkler, CAS, Chris Carpenter. ADR Editor: Gil Hudson. Music Editor: Dennis

Ricotta, SME. Assistant Film Editors: Richard Fields, Lisa Churgin. Second Camera Assistant: Paul Mindrup. Standby Painter: Craig Gentry. Craft Service: Willie Radcliff. Extra Casting: Karl Brindle. Casting Assistant: Nancy Nayor. Casting Coordinator: David Gonzales. Medical Technical Advisor: Marilyn Raye Bradfield. Body Makeup: Sherry Caudle. DGA Trainee: Robert Williams. Stunt Coordinator: Eddie Paul. Assistants to Mr. Starger: Ginny Durkin, Barbara Carleton. Assistant to Mr. Bogdanovich: Iris Chester. Production Assistant to Mr. Bogdanovich: Steve Foley. Assistant to Mr. Alston: Nancy Ambrose. Rocky's Vocal Coach: James Wilson. Negative Cutter: Donah Bassett. Titles by Universal Title. Panaflex Lenses and Camera by Panavision. Color by Technicolor. Sound by Glen Glenn. Running Time: 120 minutes.

Cast: Cher (Rusty Dennis), Sam Elliott (Gar), Eric Stoltz (Rocky Dennis), Estelle Getty (Evelyn), Richard Dysart (Abe), Laura Dern (Diana Adams), Micole Mercurio (Babe), Harry Carey, Jr. (Red), Dennis Burkley (Dozer), Lawrence Monoson (Ben), Ben Piazza (Mr. Simms), Craig King (Eric), Alexandra Powers (Lisa), Kelly Minter (Lorrie), Joe Unger (First Boyfriend), Todd Allen (Canuck), Howard Hirdler (Stickman), Jeannie Dimter Barton (Junior High Secretary), Steven James (Hospital Intern), Cathy Arden (Hospital Doctor), Andrew Robinson (Dr. Vinton), Ivan J. Rado (Dr. Rudinsky), Anna Hamilton Phelan (Puppy Lady), Wayne Grace (Drug Dealer), Nick Cassavetes (T.J.), Les Dudek (Bone), Jo-el Sonnier (Sunshine), Rebecca Sharkey (Angel), Paige Matthews (Stickman's Girl), Patricia Pelham (Canuck's Girl), Gale Ricketts (Sunshine's Girl), Stan Ross (Drunken Biker), Scott Willardsen (Junior High Student), Marsha Warfield (Homeroom Teacher), Allison Roth (Nancy Lawrence), David Scott Milton (History Teacher), Creed Bratton (Carnival Ticket Taker), L. Charles Taylor (Second Boyfriend), Rummel Mor (Track Runner), Barry Tubb (Dewey), Norman Kaplan (Himself), Marilyn Hamilton (Mr. Kaplan's Aide), Anna Thea (Woman Counselor), Louis Walson (Camp Cook), Tom Sawyer (Mr. Adams), Lori Felder (Mrs. Adams), Chris Rydell, Beth McKinley (Senior High Students), Jill Whitlow (Anne Marie), Eddie Paul, Mike Adams, Jeff Jensen, Jack Wright (Bikers).

Songs: "Katmandu," "Mainstreet," "Rock and Roll Never Forgets," "Roll Me Away," written and performed by Bob Seger; "Where Did That Naughty Little Girl Go?" written by F. Guida and P. Matthews; "Quarter to Three," written by F. Guida, G.

Barge, J. Royster, G. Anderson; "Not Me," written by F. Guida and G. Anderson; "Havin' So Much Fun," written by F. Guida, G. Barge, G. Anderson; "Dear Lady Twist," written by F. Guida, performed by Gary U.S. Bonds; "Stumblin' In," written by Mike Chapman and Nicky Chinn, performed by Suzi Quatro and Chris Norman; "Magic Carpet Ride," written by Ruston Moreve and John Kay, performed by Steppenwolf; "Dirty Work," "Do It Again," written by Walter Becker and Donald Fagen, performed by Steely Dan; "The Moog and Me," written by Dick Hyman, performed by Dick Hyman; "Sweet Home Alabama," written by Ronnie Van Zant, Gary Rossington, Ed King, Inc., performed by Lynyrd Skynyrd; "Good Golly Miss Molly," written by Robert Blackwell and John Marascako; "Tutti Frutti," written by Dorothy Labostric and Rich Penniman; "Can't Believe You Wanna Leave," written by Rich Penniman and Leo Price; "Slippin' 'n' Slidin'," written by Edwin J. Bocage, Albert Collins, and Rich Penniman, performed by Little Richard; "I Want to Hold Your Hand," "Girl," written by Paul McCartney and John Lennon, performed by the Beatles; "Ripple," written by Robert Hunter and Jerry Garcia, performed by the Grateful Dead.

Illegally Yours

A Crescent Moon Production for United Artists Pictures, released by MGM/UA Distribution Company, 1988. Produced and Directed by Peter Bogdanovich. Written by M. A. Stewart and Max Dickens (Michael Kaplan and John Levenstein). Co-producer: George Morfogen. Original Score Composed and Conducted by Phil Marshall. Director of Photography: Dante Spinotti. Film Editors: Richard Fields, Ronald Krehel. Production Designer: Jane Musky. Casting: Jane Jenkins, CSA, Janet Hirshenson, CSA. Associate Producer: Steve Foley. Executive Producers: Peggy Robertson, William Pfeiffer. Unit Production Managers: Kurt Neumann, Stratton Leopold. First Assistant Director: Jerry Ziesmer. Second Assistant Directors: Vicki Jackson-LeMay, Bryan Denegal. Location Manager: Mark Indig. Associate Casting: Denise Chamian. Art Director: Harold Thrasher. Set Decorator: Robert Kracik. Assistant Set Decorator: Nancy Griffith. Post-production Supervisor: James L. Honore. Assistant Editors: Dianne Ryder-Rennolds, Walton Dornisch, Irvin Paik. Post-production Assistants: Cathy Best, Mitch Rosa. Music Coordinator: Anna Thea Bogdanovich.

Music Editors: Ken Johnson, Steve Livingston. Script Supervisor: Sharon Hagen. Sound Supervision: Sync-Pop, Inc. Supervising Sound Editor: Jim Troutman. Sound Editor: Jeff Clark. ADR Editor: Craig Dellinger. Production Mixer: Art Rochester. Boom Man: Gary Holland. Cable: Sharon Smith Holley. Rerecording Mixers: Don Cahn, Artie Torgersen, James Williams. Camera Operator: Chic Anstiss. Camera Assistants: Ted Deason, Marco Mazzei, Joe D'Alessandro. Still Photographer: Richard Foreman. Makeup: Cindy Cruz. Makeup Assistant: Susan Mills. Hair Stylist: Kathy Estocin. Assistant Hair Stylist: Michelle Johnson. Costume Supervision: Nancy Fox. Associate Costumer: William T. Barton. Men's Wardrobe: Vicki Auth. Women's Wardrobe: Jai Galanti, Elizabeth Kaler. Assistant Costumer: L. B. Straten. Stunt Coordinator: Greg Walker. Special Effects: Steve Galich. Assistant Special Effects: Ray Beetz. Property Master: Douglas Fox. Property Assistants: Doug DuRose, Charlie Carnaggio. Construction Coordinator: Stephen Roll. Art Department Coordinator: Jerri Thrasher. Set Dressers: John Bankson, III, Rodger Belk. Gaffer: Alec King. Best Boy: Tom Trovato. Key Grip: Sandro Bolli. Best Boy Grip: Mandra Diamente. Assistant Location Manager: Eddie Bowen. Transportation Coordinator: Welch Lambeth. Transportation Captains: William Allison, Bill Battles. Musco Light Technician: John Denney. Location Auditor: Lyn Lucibello. Assistant Auditors: Suzanne Lore, Carol Henderson. Unit Publicist: Douglas Taylor. Executive Assistant to Mr. Bogdanovich: Iris Chester. Extra and Local Casting: Fincannon & Associates. Assistant Local Casting: E. R. Haire. Production Office Coordinator: Kathryn Colbert. Production Secretary: Linda Ammons. Production Assistant to Mr. Bogdanovich: Eric Small. Secretary to Mr. Bogdanovich: Susan Valencoure. Producer's Secretaries: Deb Brandt, Pat MacEnulty. Negative Cutter: Donah Bassett. Color Timer: Jack Garsha. Titles and Optical Effects: Cinema Research Corporation. Craft Service: Laura Brown. Second Unit Director: Greg Walker. First Assistant Director: Randall Badger. Second Assistant Director: Melanie Grefe. Directors of Photography: Daniel Hainey, Marco Mazzei. Assistant Cameraman: Bodo Halst. Storyboard Artist: Daniel Bode. Script Supervisor: Charlene Webb. Properties: Brendan Watson. Sound Mixer: Jim Hawkins. Stunt Coordinator: Rock A. Walker. Best Boy Grip: Michael Clayton. Technicolor. Running Time: 102 minutes.

Cast: Rob Lowe (Richard Dice), Colleen Camp (Molly Gilbert), Kenneth Mars (Hal. B. Keeler), Kim Myers (Suzanne Keeler),

Marshall Colt (Donald Cleary), Harry Carey, Jr. (Wally Finnegan), George Morfogen (Judge Norman Meckel), Linda MacEwen (Ruth Harrison), Rick Jason (Freddie Boneflecker), Jessica James (Mrs. Evelyn Dice), Ira Heiden (Andrew Dice), Tony Longo (Konrat), Howard Hirdler (Harry Crumrine), L. B. Straten (Sharon Woolrich), David Reeves (Arnie), Jay Glick (Mailman), Cynthia Costas (Sonja), Jim McDonald (Sonja's Boyfriend), Donald Wassler (Gas Station Attendant), Jim Shipp (Old Guard), C. T. Wakefield (Jury Selection Man), Lee Ralls (Mrs. Sobel), Laura Sullivan (Defense Counsel), Leon Rippy (Prosecutor), Tom Nowicki (Court Clerk), Nell Schapp (Mrs. Koekenbakker), Delight McCoy (Juror 3), Philadelphia Springfield (Juror 4), Thomas Henchy (Juror 5), Jan DiNicola (Juror 6), Patricia Jackson (Juror 7), Alan J. Mandell (Juror 8), Andy Fitzpatrick (Juror 9), Lori Robinson (Juror 10), William Reed (Juror 11), Herbert Huff (Juror 12), Ruth Reddinger (Alternate Juror), Theresa Hassett (Reporter #1), Richard Lavery (Reporter #2), Robert J. Wedyck (Reporter #3), Mike Wilson (Newsboy), Kathleen Cody (Cable-TV Housewife), George Clapp (Cable-TV Husband), Steve Foley (Taxi Driver), Jason Klassi (Keeler's Workman), Eric Small (Jerome), Steve Zurk (Security Guard), Thomas Fallon (Wall Hanger), Anna Thea Bogdanovich (Wall Hanger), Richard DeSpain (Record Store Manager), Earl Pool Ball (Singer/Party Pianist), Anthony Pellicano (Mr. Norris), Hilroy Distin, Antonia Bogdanovich (Reggae Singers), Victor Helou (Lamar), Irma Plummer (TV Announcer), Dominic "Nick" Nicklo (Radio Policeman), Doreen Chalmers (Mrs. Walker), Wendy Catherine Hummel (Girl with Dart Rifle), Bobby Mencner (Kid with Helmet), J. Michael Tiedeberg (Kid's Father), Kathy "Kat" Estocin, E. R. Hare, Jr. (Fountain of Youth Tourists), Phyllis Alexion (Tour Bus Woman), Ernest Goldsmith (Tour Bus Man), Tim Y. T. Chin (Ambassador Ting), Dan Foley (TV Technician).

Musical Selections: "Yesterday Only," theme by Ramon Farran. "Love Is a Gambler," "The Lady of Love," "One Wish," written by Earl Pool Ball and Peter Bogdanovich, performed by Johnny Cash; "Yesterday Only," lyrics by Robert Graves, music by Ramon Farran, performed by Tamara Champlin; "The Black-and-White Bus," written by Hilroy Distin, performed by Hilroy Distin and Antonia Bogdanovich; "Who Wins," written by Tamara Champlin and Bruce Gaitsch, performed by Tamara Champlin; "When Love Breaks," written by Steve McClintock, Tim James, and Tim Heintz, performed by Steve McClintock;

"Thinking About It," written by Steve Wood, performed by Tamara Champlin and Steve Wood.

Other credits

1966—*The Wild Angels* (Corman)—American International Pictures: uncredited second-unit director, writer, editor, post-dubber, stuntman

1967—*Voyage to the Planet of Prehistoric Women* (as Derek Thomas): reworking by Bogdanovich of a Russian science fiction picture purchased by Corman titled *Storm Clouds of Venus*; the director's main contribution was the shooting of some new footage at Leo Carrillo State Beach with a group of blond alien women led by Mamie Van Doren

1972—Chaplin Montage: Bogdanovich (assisted by Richard Patterson) compiled a 13-minute selection of clips from selected Chaplin films to be presented at that year's Academy Awards ceremony, during which Chaplin was given an honorary Oscar. Included: scenes from *A Dog's Life* (1918), *The Kid* (1921), *The Gold Rush* (1925), *The Circus* (1925), *City Lights* (1931), *Modern Times* (1936), *The Great Dictator* (1940), *Limelight* (1952)

Films of other directors in which Bogdanovich appeared as actor:

Lions Love—(as Max L. Raab)—Agnes Varda, 1969

Opening Night—John Cassavetes, 1978

The Other Side of the Wind—Orson Welles (not yet released)

Videography

	35mm	16mm	Video
Targets	P	FI	PHV
Directed by John Ford	FI	FI	NA
The Last Picture Show	C	FI/S	RCA
What's Up, Doc?	WB	S	WHV
Paper Moon	P	FI	PHV
Daisy Miller	P	FI	PHV
At Long Last Love	20th	FI	NA
Nickelodeon	C	FI/S	NA
Saint Jack	NA	NA	V
They All Laughed	NA	NA	V
Mask	U	NA	MCA
Illegally Yours	MGM/UA	NA	CBS/FOX

Key to Abbreviations

C: Columbia Pictures
CBS/FOX: CBS/FOX Home Video
FI: Films Incorporated
MCA: MCA Videocassettes
MGM/UA: MGM/United Artists
NA: Not Available
P: Paramount Pictures
PHV: Paramount Home Video

RCA: RCA/Columbia Pictures Home Video
S: Swank Motion Pictures
20th: 20th Century-Fox
U: Universal Pictures
V: Vestron Videocassettes
WB: Warner Brothers Pictures
WHV: Warner Home Video

References

In addition to the sources listed below, quotations in the text are drawn from personal communication with the director.

Assayas, O., and Krohn, B. "Entretien avec Peter Bogdanovich," *Cahiers du Cinéma*, Paris, 1982. Interview through *They All Laughed*; not available in English.

Baxter, John. "Peter Bogdanovich," in *The International Directory of Films and Filmmakers*, Vol. 2, New York: Putnam, 1984, pp. 54–55. Good short article on Bogdanovich through *They All Laughed*.

Buckley, Tom. "At the Movies: How Bogdanovich Learned to Think Small Again," *New York Times*, April 20, 1979, p. 60. Bogdanovich describes his reasons for making the low-budget *Saint Jack* and also comments about *At Long Last Love*.

Cagin, Seth. "Tracking," *Soho News*, November 24, 1981, p. 50. On *They All Laughed*.

Carroll, Jon. "What's Up, Bogdanovich?" *Village Voice*, March 17, 1975. Bogdanovich discusses the fact that *At Long Last Love* has been "misinterpreted" by the critics, and comments on his future plans.

Cocks, Jay. "Paper Moon," *Filmfacts*, Vol. 16, no. 3, 1973, pp. 58–60.

Coursodon, Jean-Pierre. "Stanley Donen," in *American Directors*, Vol. 2, New York: McGraw-Hill, 1983, pp. 99–109.

Crist, Judith. "Three Top Directors Go to Town," *50 Plus*, July 1979, p. 54.

Denby, Betty Jeffries. "An Interview with Peter Bogdanovich," *Filmmakers Newsletter*, June 1975, pp. 76–82. Through *At Long Last Love*.

Denby, David. "Bogdanovich—Will *Nickelodeon* Be His Last Picture Show?" *New York Times*, January 30, 1977, p. 1. Most perceptive critique of Bogdanovich's flaws as an artist and description of his plans to rethink his priorities.

"Dialogue on Film: Peter Bogdanovich," *American Film*, December 1977/January 1978, pp. 35–50.

"Dialogue on Film: Peter Bogdanovich," *American Film*, April 1986, pp. 13–15.

Dorr, John H. "The Birth of the Movies: A Few Kind Words for Bogdanovich's *Nickelodeon*," *Millimeter*, March 1977, pp. 25–27.

Ebert, Roger. "Paper Moon," in *Filmfacts*, Vol. 16, No. 3, 1973, pp. 58–60.

———. "Cher and Bogdanovich Tear Off the 'Mask,' " *Chicago Sun-Times*, May 15, 1985.

———. "The Last Picture Show," in *Roger Ebert's Movie Home Companion*, Kansas City, MO: Andrews, McMeel & Parker, 1988, pp. 318–319.

———. "Mask," in *Roger Ebert's Movie Home Companion*, pp. 353–354.

Gareland, A., and Grassard, G. "Bogdanovich, ou, Le Malentendu," *Image et Son*, Paris, January 1980. In the longish prelude to the interview (neither of which has been translated from the French, unfortunately), the authors compare Bogdanovich to one of his contemporaries, Coppola, and treat each one's career separately. Both the comments and interview are valuable.

Giacci, Vittorio. *Bogdanovich*. Florence, Italy: La Nuova Itàlia 1976, 109 pp. A highly perceptive if occasionally convoluted and pretentious analysis of Bogdanovich's oeuvre through *Daisy Miller*, with long and detailed chapters on each film (including the John Ford documentary), plus valuable biographical and aesthetics sections similar to the ones included in this book. Unfortunately, however, the volume is extremely obscure and has not been translated into English. For those with access to it—and the ability to read it—it should prove most rewarding. Bogdanovich himself recommends it.

Harmetz, Aljean. "Peter Still Looks Forward to His *Citizen Kane*," *New York Times*, November 14, 1971, sec. 2, p. 13. Bogdanovich's first "big" interview, conducted during production of *What's Up, Doc?*, shortly after release of *Picture Show*, in which he delineates his grandiose ambitions.

Kael, Pauline. "Saint Jack," *New Yorker*, May 1979, pp. 141–142.

Kauffmann, Stanley. "The Last Picture Show," *Filmfacts*, Vol. 14, no. 15, 1971, pp. 361–362.

Kroll, Jack. "A Saint in a Cathouse," *Newsweek*, May 7, 1979, p. 88.

Liggera, J. J. " 'She Would Have Appreciated One's Esteem': Peter Bogdanovich's *Daisy Miller*," *Literature/Film Quarterly*, Vol. 9, no. 1, 1981, pp. 15–21.

Lucas, Blake. "The Last Picture Show," in *Magill Survey of Cinema: Second Series*, Vol. 3, edited by Frank N. Magill. Englewood Cliffs, NJ: Salem Press, 1981, pp. 1314–1317.

———. "They All Laughed," in *Magill Cinema Annual, 1982*, edited by Frank N. Magill. Englewood Cliffs, NJ: Salem Press, 1982, pp. 350–355.

McCluskey, Paul, editor. *Conversations with Peter Bogdanovich.* "Making Contact" Series, New York: Harcourt Brace Jovanovich, 1974, 91 pp. A book-length interview (seamlessly synthesized from several smaller ones by Paul McCluskey) with Bogdanovich conducted during and after production of *Paper Moon.* Many important comments about Bogdanovich's background and the films through *Moon* which will not be found elsewhere. Book is out of print, but not impossible to find. Bogdanovich says he does not now agree with everything he said at the time, but on the whole it's a good read.

McMurtry, Larry. "The Last Picture Show: A Last Word," in *Film Flam: Essays on Hollywood*. New York: Simon and Schuster, 1987, pp. 120–123.

Peary, Danny. "Targets," in *Cult Movies*. New York: Dell Publishing, 1981, pp. 339–342.

Putterman, Barry. "Peter Bogdanovich," in *American Directors*, Vol. 2, New York: McGraw-Hill, 1983, pp. 49–54. Superb critique of Bogdanovich's films through *They All Laughed*, quoted extensively throughout this book.

Reed, Rex. "Born-Again Bogdanovich," *New York Daily News*, April 1979.

Rich, Frank. "Odd Man Out," *Time*, May 21, 1979, p. 86.

Roberts, Glenys. "The Rise and Fall of Peter Bogdanovich," *Los Angeles*, May 1977, pp. 127–128, 131, 214. Important study of Bogdanovich's downfall, a good companion piece to David Denby's article.

Rochlin, Margy. "Peter Bogdanovich," *Interview*, March 1985, pp. 134–136.

Rodman, Howard A. "The Last Days of Orson Welles," *American Film*, June 1987, pp. 50–53.

Rubin, Martin. "An Interview with Peter Bogdanovich," in *Daisy*

Miller, New York: special Warner Paperback Edition, 1974, pp. 7–25. Invaluable in-depth comments by Bogdanovich on *Daisy Miller* exclusively. Book (out of print but not terribly scarce) also contains the entire text of the novel, mainly the 1909 version but with footnoted excerpts from the 1878 (Bogdanovich and Frederic Raphael's script for the film was a composite of the two).

Sarris, Andrew. "Daisy & Cybill & Henry & Peter," *Village Voice*, July 11, 1974.

———. "At Long Last Lousy!" *Village Voice*, March 17, 1975.

———. "Why Has Peter Bogdanovich Lost the Midas Touch?" *Village Voice*, January 17, 1977. Excellent observations on Bogdanovich's art (or the lack thereof) and the reasons the failures may be more interesting than the successes.

Schickel, Richard. "John Ford," in *Schickel on Film*, New York: William Morrow and Company, Inc., 1989, pp. 37–56.

Sherman, Eric and Rubin, Martin. "Peter Bogdanovich," in *The Director's Event: Interviews with Five American Film-Makers*, New York: Atheneum, 1970, pp. 73–98. Very interesting early interview with Bogdanovich shortly after the release of *Targets* in which he discusses it in detail for the only time and points out parallels and comparisons between his film (and his work before it on *Wild Angels* and *Voyage to the Planet of Prehistoric Women*) and those of Hitchcock, Welles, Walsh, and others, even admitting to attempted scene duplicating (something which he was later loath to do). Also a supremely intelligent six-page analysis of *Targets*, much of which is quoted in the text.

Silverman, Stephen M. "Bogdanovich Gets into the Picture," *New York Post*, May 1, 1979.

Starr, Cecile. "Peter Bogdanovich Remembered and Assessed," *Filmmakers Newsletter*, September 1973, pp. 20–21. Bogdanovich's former Columbia film professor offers her views on his behavior during those formative years (late 1950s) and also her opinions of his films through *Paper Moon*.

Stone, Judy. "All Because of Boris Karloff," *New York Times*, September 15, 1968, p. 19. Bogdanovich and then-wife Polly Platt discuss his career through *Targets*, the origin of the film, and their life together.

Varga, Wayne. "Bogdanovich: Love, Comedy and Tragedy," *Los Angeles Times*, December 13, 1981, p. 45. Valuable interview with Bogdanovich mainly about the details of *They All*

Laughed, but with some observations about his other recent works and career progression.

Welch, James M. "Mask," in *Magill's Cinema Annual, 1986*, edited by Frank N. Magill. Englewood Cliffs, NJ: Salem Press, 1986, pp. 231–235.

"What's Up, Doc?" *Filmfacts*, Vol. 15, no. 3, 1972, pp. 46–48.

Wilson, David. "Peter Bogdanovich," in *Close-Up: The Contemporary Director*, edited by Jon Tuska. Metuchen, NJ: Scarecrow, 1981, pp. 251–290. Important survey of Bogdanovich the man and director through *Nickelodeon*. Intelligent comments about the films mixed indiscriminately with many incidental (though interesting) details about the backgrounds of the films, their stars, and creative personnel.

Zimmerman, Paul D. "What's Up, Doc?" in *Filmfacts*, Vol. 15, No. 3, 1972, p. 48.

Articles by Peter Bogdanovich not included in Pieces of Time

New Yorker Theatre Notes (issues 2, 3, and 4); "The Forgotten Film," Parts 1 and 2, "Bogey," "Henry Fonda," "Cary Grant," "Orson Welles," *New Yorker Notes*, 1965; "The Dore Schary–Stanley Kramer Syndrome," *New York Film Bulletin*, June 15, 1960; "Hitchcock's Gallery," *Daily Variety*, anniversary issue, October 26, 1965; "The Director as Target," *New York*, September 1968; "Tashlin's Cartoons," *Movie*, no. 16, winter 1968–1969; "Boris Karloff, 1887–1969," *New York Times*, Arts and Leisure section, February 16, 1969; "Josef Von Sternberg's Inner Eye Still Keeps Its Secrets," *Los Angeles Times*, January 18, 1970.

Reviews and Columns

Ivy Magazine (August, October, December 1959; February 1960); "Crusade Forgotten" (re: Frank Capra), *Frontier*, October 1959; "Come Back Africa and Pull My Daisy," *New*

York Film Bulletin, August 6, 1960; "The Man Who Knew Too Much," *New York Film Bulletin*, July 11, 1960; "Williams on the Screen," *Frontier*, July 1960; "Hatari!" *Film Culture*, no. 25, summer 1962; "Two Weeks in Another Town," *Film Culture*, no. 26, winter 1962; "The Birds," *Film Culture*, no. 28, spring 1963; "Letter from Hollywood," *Movie*, no. 9, August 1963; "Small Talk," *Movie*, no. 12, spring 1965; "Small Talk," *Movie*, no. 13, summer 1965; "Hollywood," *Movie*, no. 14, autumn 1965; "Small Talk," *Movie*, no. 16, winter 1968–1969; "Letter from Hollywood," *Movie*, no. 17, winter 1969–1970; "Marnie," *Cinema*, Vol. 1, no. 3, October–November 1964; "Point of View," *Cinema*, Vol. 2, nos. 3, 5, January, March–April 1965; "Torn Curtain," *Movies International*, Vol. 1, no. 3, July–September 1966; "The Silencers: Simon Simonized" (re: John Simon), *Washington Post Book World*, November 5, 1967.

Interviews by Peter Bogdanovich

"Sidney Lumet," *Film Quarterly*, Vol. 14, no. 2, winter 1960; "Frank Tashlin: An Interview and an Appreciation," *Film Culture*, 1960; "Encounters with Josef Von Sternberg," *Movie*, no. 13, summer 1965; "Sonny and Cher: They're What's Happening, Baby," *Saturday Evening Post*, April 1966; "Donald Siegel," *Movie*, no. 15, spring 1968; "Alfred Hitchcock," *Movies International*, Horror/Fantasy Issue, no. 7, January 1969; "Otto Preminger," *On Film*, no. 1, October 1970; "The B-Movie as Art," *Take One*, Vol. 3, no. 4, June 1972.

Name Index

Abbott, George   3
Adler, Renata   58
Adler, Stella   2
Aldrich, Robert   9, 214, 273
Allen, Woody   ix, x, 9, 30, 128, 155, 234, 241
Alston, Howard   265
Altman, Robert   ix, x, 9, 31, 273
Antonioni, Michelangelo   3, 214, 226
Archer, Eugene   4
Armstrong, Louis   238
Astaire, Fred   191, 193, 195

Ball, Earle Pool   238
Baxter, John   75, 107
Beatty, Warren   209
Bennett, Tony   98
Benton, Robert   122, 129
Bergman, Ingmar   4
Bogart, Humphrey   124, 130, 210
Bogdanovich, Borislav   1, 175, 176
Bogdanovich, Peter (as actor)   38, 63, 64, 218, 219
Boorman, John   ix, x
Bottoms, Timothy   93
Brando, Marlon   2

Brennan, Eileen   99, 178, 198
Bridges, Jeff   95, 199
Brooks, Mel   131, 191
Brooks, Richard   4, 66
Brown, Barry   168, 174
Brown, Joe David   138
Burkley, Dennis   263
Burks, Robert   265
Burstyn, Ellen   97

Camp, Colleen   235, 238, 241, 282
Canby, Vincent   131, 144, 219, 265
Capra, Frank   117, 131, 132
Carey, Harry, Jr.   271
Cash, Johnny   238
Cassavetes, John   ix, 9
Chartoff, Robert   201
Cher   245, 270, 273, 274, 275, 276
Chevalier, Maurice   196
Cimino, Michael   ix
Cocks, Jay   121, 196
Coppola, Francis Ford   ix, x, 6, 9, 18, 19, 159
Corman, Roger   6, 36, 37, 44, 56, 64, 209
Coursodon, Jean-Pierre   62

Crist, Judith   118
Cukor, George   9, 165
Curtis, Jamie Lee   240
Curtiz, Michael   2

Dean, James   16
Del Prete, Duilio 179, 197
Denby, David   105
Dennis, Rocky   242–245,
    273
Dennis, Rusty 242–245
De Palma, Brian ix, 3, 5, 12,
    30, 61, 62, 63
Dern, Laura   263, 267, 276
Dickinson, Angie   4
Dietrich, Marlene   15, 101
Di Palma, Carlo   234
Disney, Walt   4
Donen, Stanley   61, 62, 63,
    191
Dorr, John H.   206
Douglas, Gordon   4
Dunn, Liam   131, 132, 198
Dwan, Allan   199, 286

Ebert, Roger   81, 82, 83,
    148, 253, 254, 268
Edwards, Blake 136, 240
Elliott, Denholm   216, 225
Elliott, Sam   277

Fairbanks, Douglas, Jr.   2
Fellini, Federico 3
Fields, Verna   67
Fisher, Eddie   98
Flynn, Errol   2
Fonda, Henry   68, 70, 71,
    72, 77, 138
Ford, John   1, 3, 4, 6, 9, 18,
    27, 30, 32, 33, 49, 57, 65,
    66, 68–78, 87, 103, 105,
    106, 107, 112, 136, 139,
    155, 199, 209, 271, 285–
    286
Fosse, Bob   9, 240
Frankenheimer, John   ix, x
Friedkin, William   9, 18,
    159
Frizzell, Lefty 99
Fuller, Samuel   9, 15, 64

Galsworthy, John   22, 159
Gazzara, Ben   225, 226, 236,
    241
Giacci, Vittorio   2, 3, 27, 32,
    77, 78, 80, 84, 85, 86, 133,
    135, 136, 143, 160, 162,
    174
Godard, Jean-Luc   50, 79,
    80
Goodman, Benny   239
Gould, Elliott   197
Grant, Cary   4, 117, 125,
    126, 127
Graves, Robert   28
Griffith, D. W.   105, 205
Grodin, Charles   218

Hansen, Patti   241
Harrison, Rex   194
Harvey, James   79
Harvey, Laurence   4
Hawks, Howard   1, 3, 6, 7,
    9, 17, 18, 27, 32, 33, 49, 50,
    51, 57, 61, 65, 68, 79, 88,
    89, 96, 99, 100, 103, 104,
    105, 106, 107, 112, 117,
    118, 119, 120, 121, 122,
    123, 124, 125, 129, 155,
    201, 202, 241, 259, 279,
    281
Hefner, Hugh   227, 246,
    287–290
Hemingway, Mariel   240

Henry, Buck   122, 128, 129, 130, 132, 133, 195, 209
Hepburn, Audrey   236, 237
Hepburn, Katharine   117, 125, 127
Herrmann, Bernard   62
Hill, George Roy   ix
Hillerman, John   198
Hitchcock, Alfred   4, 6, 7, 13, 18, 27, 30, 32, 37, 38, 39, 40, 48, 56, 57, 58, 59, 60, 63, 65, 105, 112, 125, 126, 182, 285
Holden, William   2
Hope, Bob   128
Hopper, Dennis   8
Hurt, John   276
Huston, John   9, 177, 182, 219

James, Henry   10, 159, 170, 176, 178, 179
Johnson, Ben   64, 86, 87, 94, 277

Kael, Pauline   x, 98, 110, 136, 180, 191, 215
Kahn, Madeline   152, 192, 197
Kaplan, Michael   280
Karloff, Boris   37, 49, 50, 53, 63, 64, 65, 85, 104, 108, 111
Kauffmann, Stanley   105, 110, 111, 112, 115
Kazan, Elia   3, 112
Keaton, Buster   27, 30, 117, 133, 201
Keighley, William   2
Kelly, Gene   2, 191
Kennedy, Kathleen   35
Kovacs, Laszlo   44, 63, 150,
153, 154, 155, 189, 201, 212, 261, 263, 265, 274
Kramer, Stanley   136
Kroll, Jack   215, 216
Kubrick, Stanley   ix, 6, 9, 64, 66, 210

Laemmle, Carl, Jr.   69
Lambert, Gavin   159
Lane, Lupino   196
Lang, Fritz   12, 65, 285, 286
Leachman, Cloris   64, 96, 97
Lean, David   33
Lehman, Ernest   62
Lemmon, Jack   4, 286
Levenstein, John   280
Lewis, Jerry   4, 286
Liggera, J. J.   170, 174
Logan, Joshua   3
Lowe, Rob   170, 278, 281, 282
Lubitsch, Ernst   18, 30, 187, 191, 192, 193, 196
Lucas, Blake   85, 98, 100, 103, 110, 115, 145, 148, 233
Lucas, George   12, 15, 19, 112
Lumet, Sidney   ix
Lynch, David   263

McCarey, Leo   4, 117, 133, 199
MacDonald, Jeanette   191, 196
McMurtry, James   179
McMurtry, Larry   80, 96, 97, 103, 111, 114, 115, 142, 157
Mancini, Henry   122
Mars, Kenneth   134, 282
Martin, Dean   4

Mastroianni, Marcello   160
May, Elaine   14, 180
Mercer, Johnny   122
Minnelli, Vincente   15, 50,
   84, 85, 88
Minter, Kelly   277
Monoson, Laurence   263
Morfogen, George   209, 230
Muller, Robby   212, 213,
   223, 234
Murphy, Audie   89

Natwick, Mildred   178
Newman, Alfred   74
Newman, David   122, 129
Nichols, Mike   ix, 6, 9, 273

Odets, Clifford   4
O'Hara, John   52
O'Kelly, Tim   64, 108
O'Neal, Ryan   21, 117, 126,
   129, 132, 138, 145, 146,
   151, 152, 201, 278
O'Neal, Tatum   19, 21, 138,
   150, 151, 152
Ophuls, Max   230, 231

Peckinpah, Sam   ix
Penn, Arthur   ix, 6
Perschy, Maria   122
Phelan, Anna Hamil-
   ton   242, 243, 244, 245,
   249, 261, 267, 268, 269,
   270, 275, 276
Piazza, Ben   277
Platt, Polly   5, 13, 19, 20, 21,
   38, 42, 44, 82, 136, 138,
   139, 153, 155, 162
Polanski, Roman   ix, 60
Pollack, Sydney   ix, x, 17, 30
Porter, Cole   18, 136, 183–
   198
Powell, Michael   64

Preminger, Otto   7, 13, 18,
   42, 43, 57, 182, 187
Prentiss, Paula   122
Price, Frank   271, 275
Putterman, Barry   7, 8, 15,
   22, 57, 66, 87, 89, 98, 110,
   148, 160, 170, 172, 189–
   190, 201, 214

Rafelson, Bob   8
Raphael, Frederic   172, 176,
   177
Reed, Rex   117
Renoir, Jean   50, 218, 223,
   228
Reynolds, Burt   2, 192, 197,
   201
Rich, Frank   222, 225
Ringwald, Molly   278
Ritter, John   170, 199, 228,
   233, 239, 278
Roberts, Glenys   16
Robson, Mark   4
Rogers, Ginger   191, 193
Roth, Lillian   193
Rubin, Martin   7, 50, 58, 59,
   60, 80, 107, 176

Sackler, Howard O.   209,
   210
Sargent, Alvin   138, 139,
   145, 146, 148, 149
Sarris, Andrew   4, 179, 180,
   186, 195, 196
Schaffner, Franklin J.   ix
Schickel, Richard   71
Scorsese, Martin   ix, x, 5, 9,
   12, 15, 17, 18, 19, 30, 31,
   33, 34, 35, 98, 109, 112
Seger, Bob   272
Shepherd, Cybill   13, 14, 15,
   19, 20, 21, 97, 98, 101, 160,
   168, 174, 179, 180, 181,

192, 197, 208, 209, 218, 228
Sherman, Eric   7, 50, 58, 59, 60, 80
Shinberg, Sid   245
Silvers, Robert   4
Simon, John   x, 105, 134, 153, 154, 176, 177, 178
Sinatra, Frank   16, 233, 238
Spagnoli, Alberto   172
Spielberg, Steven   ix, x, 12, 19, 31, 32, 33, 34, 35, 210, 282
Springsteen, Bruce   25, 239, 271, 272
Starger, Martin   24, 245, 246, 249, 271, 275
Starr, Cecile   3
Sternberg, Josef von   15
Stevens, George   4, 9, 85, 105
Stewart, James   68, 70, 71, 72, 77, 138, 206, 286
Stoltz, Eric   249, 263, 268, 276, 282
Stone, Peter   63
Stratten, Dorothy   24, 25, 180, 229, 240, 246–247, 277, 286–290
Streisand, Barbra   21, 117, 124, 125, 127, 132, 136, 197
Stroheim, Erich von   50
Sturges, John   4
Surtees, Robert   84, 85, 150, 154

Tashlin, Frank   5, 42
Taylor, Elizabeth   84, 88
Temple, Shirley   144
Theroux, Paul   ix, 29, 103, 104, 208, 209, 210, 212
Toland, Gregg   155
Truffaut, François   60

Varda, Agnes   50

Walsh, Raoul   57, 199
Wayne, John   16, 68, 70, 71, 72, 77, 89, 100, 138
Welles, Orson   2, 4, 7, 9, 10, 13, 32, 57, 65, 74, 89, 112, 143, 168, 172, 173, 174, 180, 219, 285
Wenders, Wim   213
Westmore, Michael   263
Whitman, Charles   38
Widmark, Richard   2
Wilder, Billy   4, 14, 50
Williams, Hank   98
Willis, Gordon   155
Wilson, David   10, 80, 119
Winkler, Irwin   201
Wise, Robert   9, 33, 187
Witney, William   33
Wyler, William   4, 187

Yates, Peter   134
Young, Terence   60

Zemeckis, Robert   34, 282
Zimmerman, Paul D.   2, 98, 124, 125, 135
Zinnemann, Fred   187

Title Index

Addie Pray (book) 138, 142, 152
Adventures of Robin Hood, The 2
America, America 112
Anatomy of a Murder 42, 43, 225
Another Woman 30
Apple Tree, The (book) 22, 159
Appointment in Samara (book) 52
Apu Trilogy (directed by Satyajit Ray) 114
Arabesque 62
At Long Last Love 10, 14, 15, 17, 18, 20, 21, 22, 23, 27, 28, 30,
    31, 34, 63, 83, 92, 98, 103, 104, 106, 110, 136, 147, 150, 151,
    153, 156, 163, 173, 179, 180, 183–198, 199, 201, 208, 225, 228,
    233, 279

Back to the Future 34, 282
Bad and the Beautiful, The 50, 85
Beyond Therapy x
Bible: In the Beginning, The 177
Birds, The 6
Birth of a Nation 205
Blazing Saddles 191
Bloodline 236
Blow-Up 214, 226
Bogdanovich (book) 2, 3, 27, 32, 77, 78, 80, 84, 85, 86, 133, 135,
    136, 143, 162, 174
Bonheur, Le 50
Bonnie and Clyde 6
Bride Wore Black, The 60
Bringing Up Baby 18, 117, 118, 119, 120, 121, 122, 123, 124,
    125, 129
Broadway Danny Rose 9, 155
Bullitt 134

Caine Mutiny, The   130, 131
Cameraman, The   133
Carmen Jones   187
Casablanca   130, 131
Catch-22   132
Charade   62
Cheyenne Autumn   6, 74, 112
Chimes at Midnight   112
Citizen Kane   2, 10, 112, 172
Close Encounters of the Third Kind   32, 33, 34
Color Purple, The   32, 33, 34, 35
Come Back to the Five and Dime, Jimmy Dean, Jimmy
    Dean   245, 273
Contempt   50
Conversation, The   35
Cotton Club, The   18, 35
Criminal Code, The   49, 50

Daisy Miller   10, 14, 16, 18, 19, 20, 21, 22, 23, 28, 29, 33, 67, 82,
    83, 85, 86, 92, 98, 102, 104, 106, 108, 110, 143, 145, 148, 152,
    159–182, 186, 195, 208, 210, 212, 216, 217, 222, 226, 230, 262,
    265, 266
Day the Earth Stood Still, The   33
Deep Throat   101
Directed by John Ford   7, 29, 66, 68–78, 186
Directors' Event, The (book)   7, 50
Doctor Dolittle   194
Drums Along the Mohawk   1
Duel (TV)   32

Easy Rider   8
El Dorado   6, 68
Elephant Man, The   263, 266, 276
Empire of the Sun   33
E.T.: The Extra-Terrestrial   19, 32, 33, 34, 35, 271

Father of the Bride   84, 88, 111
Fear and Desire   66, 210
Finian's Rainbow   18, 19
Five Easy Pieces   8
Fort Apache   69, 74

Frankenstein   49
Funny Girl   187

Gardens of Stone   35
Giant   105
Graduate, The   6
Grapes of Wrath, The   76, 155
Great Professional: Howard Hawks (TV)   7, 68
Great Race, The   136

Hannah and Her Sisters   234, 239, 241
Hatari!   68
Heartbreak Kid, The   14, 180
Heaven Can Wait (1978)   209
High Anxiety   131
His Girl Friday   121
How Green Was My Valley   76
Hurricane, The   209

Illegally Yours   29, 35, 169, 195, 278–284
In Cold Blood   66
Informer, The   74, 112
Interiors   30
Iron Horse, The   74
It's a Mad, Mad, Mad, Mad World   136

Jaws   32, 33, 210

Kid from Texas, The   89
Killer's Kiss   66, 210
Killing, The   66
Killing of the Unicorn, The (book)   13, 24, 222, 246, 286–290
Kiss of Death   2

Last Picture Show, The   2, 7, 8, 9, 10, 11, 13, 14, 15, 16, 17, 18,
     19, 20, 21, 25, 27, 28, 29, 31, 32, 33, 35, 38, 43, 51, 54, 64, 66,
     67, 68, 78, 79–116, 132, 140, 143, 144, 145, 148, 150, 152, 153,
     154, 155, 156, 157, 161, 163, 167, 168, 176, 181, 182, 189, 195,
     196, 208, 210, 212, 215, 216, 218, 221, 224, 246, 259, 261, 262,
     266, 273, 277
Last Tango in Paris   101
Last Temptation of Christ, The   35
Last Waltz, The   35

Laura   182
Lenny   9
Little Miss Marker   144
Love and Death   128, 155
Love Parade, The   191, 196
Love Story   21, 129, 130, 131

McCabe and Mrs. Miller   214
Magnificent Ambersons, The   89, 110, 180
Manhattan   9, 155
Man's Favorite Sport?   122, 281
Man Who Shot Liberty Valance, The   7, 69, 71, 74, 112
Marnie   112
M*A*S*H   x, 214
Mask   x, 25, 26, 27, 28, 29, 31, 32, 33, 34, 35, 39, 92, 101, 102,
    108, 110, 115, 116, 149, 150, 162, 183, 212, 216, 241, 242–277,
    278
Mean Streets   9, 33, 35, 109
Midsummer Night's Sex Comedy, A   30, 155
Monkey Business (1952)   125
Monsieur Beaucaire   128
Moonlighting (TV)   197
Mother Machree   71
Mr. Deeds Goes to Town   131
My Darling Clementine   72

New York, New York   18, 35
Nickelodeon   x, 6, 10, 15, 17, 18, 20, 21, 22, 23, 29, 79, 103, 104,
    157, 195, 196, 199–207, 208, 219, 223, 225, 248, 261, 265
1941   33
North by Northwest   59, 60, 62, 125, 126, 265

Obsession   62
Oklahoma!   187
One From the Heart   18, 35
Only Angels Have Wings   1, 61, 155
Other Side of the Wind, The   10
Outsiders, The   18, 35

Paper Moon   5, 8, 10, 13, 16, 17, 19, 20, 21, 23, 28, 29, 32, 33,
    67, 82, 83, 86, 93, 102, 104, 106, 108, 110, 116, 136, 138–158,
    159, 163, 167, 169, 173, 181, 186, 190, 213, 215, 224, 246, 257

Paths of Glory   66
Picnic on the Grass   50
Pieces of Time (book)   5, 75, 286
Place in the Sun, A   85
Porgy and Bess   187
Psycho   37, 40, 47, 48, 58, 60
Purple Rose of Cairo, The   155

Queen Kelly   50

Radio Days   155
Raging Bull   9
Raiders of the Lost Ark   32, 33
Rear Window   58, 59, 60
Red Line 7000   61
Red River   1, 88, 89, 100, 104, 111
Rio Bravo   68, 112
Rio Grande   74
Roman Holiday   237
Ronde, La   230, 231
Rosemary's Baby   60
Rumble Fish   18, 35

Sabrina   237
Saint Jack   ix, 2, 23, 24, 28, 33, 64, 83, 93, 102, 104, 108, 110,
     156, 169, 208–227, 230, 241, 247, 248, 256, 261
Scarface (1932)   112
Schickel on Film (book)   71
Searchers, The   30, 76
September   30
Seven Chances   133
Seven Days in New Crete (book)   28
Shane   105
She Wore a Yellow Ribbon   1, 69, 70, 72
Silkwood   273
Sinbad the Sailor   2
Singin' in the Rain   191
Skidoo   43
Sound of Music, The   187
Stagecoach (1939)   1, 71, 76
Star!   187
Stardust Memories   9, 30
Star 80   240

Star Wars   19
Steamboat Round the Bend   139
Straight Shooting   69
Strangers on a Train   59, 60
Sugarland Express, The   32, 33
Sunset Boulevard   50

Take Me Out to the Ball Game   2
Targets   2, 7, 17, 19, 27, 28, 29, 30, 31, 32, 33, 36–67, 68, 80, 85,
     86, 89, 90, 93, 104, 105, 106, 107, 108, 110, 111, 127, 134, 140,
     145, 149, 182, 186, 205, 208, 212, 215, 218, 219, 223
Taxi Driver   30, 33, 98
Terror, The   37, 39, 54, 64
Texasville   35, 116, 284
They All Laughed   24, 25, 29, 32, 34, 92, 100, 102, 104, 108,
     112, 153, 156, 163, 169, 180, 195, 196, 198, 202, 212, 222, 223,
     226, 228–243, 248, 256, 258, 262, 273, 278, 287
Third Man, The   219
39 Steps, The (1935)   112
Three Ages, The   133
Three Bad Men   89
Three Days of the Condor   30
Three's Company (TV)   239
Tobacco Road   155
To Gillian on Her 37th Birthday   278
To Have and Have Not   61, 155
Touch of Evil   3, 168
Treasure of the Sierra Madre, The   219
Tree Grows in Brooklyn, A   112
Tucker: The Man and His Dream   35
Two Rode Together   72
Two Weeks in Another Town   50

Untouchables, The   30

Vertigo   60, 62, 182
Viaggio en Italia   50
Voyage to the Planet of Prehistoric Women   36

Wagonmaster   69, 87, 89
Wait Until Dark   60
West Side Story   187
What's Up, Doc?   2, 8, 9, 17, 18, 19, 20, 21, 22, 23, 27, 28, 29, 30,

31, 57, 63, 66, 67, 80, 103, 104, 106, 116, 117–137, 138, 140, 143, 148, 155, 158, 159, 163, 181, 182, 186, 191, 192, 193, 195, 196, 197, 199, 212, 230, 278, 279, 281
White Heat   57
Who's That Knocking at My Door?   35, 66
Wild Angels, The   6, 36
Will Success Spoil Rock Hunter?   42

You Can't Take It with You   131
Young Mr. Lincoln   1, 71, 74

Zelig   9